Golden Tongues

Golden Tongues

Adapting Hispanic Classical Theater in Los Angeles

Edited by
BARBARA FUCHS, ROBIN ALFRIEND KELLO, *and*
AINA SOLEY MATEU

methuen | drama
LONDON • NEW YORK • OXFORD • NEW DELHI • SYDNEY

METHUEN DRAMA
Bloomsbury Publishing Plc
50 Bedford Square, London, WC1B 3DP, UK
1385 Broadway, New York, NY 10018, USA
29 Earlsfort Terrace, Dublin 2, Ireland

BLOOMSBURY, METHUEN DRAMA and the Methuen Drama logo are trademarks of
Bloomsbury Publishing Plc

First published in Great Britain 2025

Copyright © Barbara Fuchs, Robin Alfriend Kello, and Aina Soley Mateu, 2025
Painting in Red © Luis Alfaro, 2025
FIXED © Boni B. Alvarez, 2025
School for Witches, or Friendship Betrayed! © Madhuri Shekar, 2025
The King of Maricopa County © Mary Lyon Kamitaki, 2025
The Woodingle Puppet Show with Host Mr. C, as Constructed by Mr. Asinine with Calculations and Articulations of the Genius Sort © Julie Taiwo Quarles, 2025
Traces of Desire © Lina Patel, 2025
Florence and Normandie © June Carryl, 2025

The authors have asserted their right under the Copyright, Designs and Patents Act, 1988, to be identified as authors of this work.

Cover design: Holly Capper
Cover illustrations: Anna Sidorova / Getty Images

All rights reserved. No part of this publication may be reproduced or transmitted in any form or by any means, electronic or mechanical, including photocopying, recording, or any information storage or retrieval system, without prior permission in writing from the publishers.

Bloomsbury Publishing Plc does not have any control over, or responsibility for, any third-party websites referred to or in this book. All internet addresses given in this book were correct at the time of going to press. The author and publisher regret any inconvenience caused if addresses have changed or sites have ceased to exist, but can accept no responsibility for any such changes.

No rights in incidental music or songs contained in the work are hereby granted and performance rights for any performance/presentation whatsoever must be obtained from the respective copyright owners.

All rights whatsoever in this play are strictly reserved. Application for performance, etc. should be made before rehearsals begin to the respective playwrights' representatives listed on page vii.
No performance may be given unless a licence has been obtained

A catalogue record for this book is available from the British Library.

A catalog record for this work is available from the Library of Congress.

ISBN: HB: 978-1-3504-3155-3
PB: 978-1-3504-3154-6
ePDF: 978-1-3504-3157-7
eBook: 978-1-3504-3156-0

Series: Methuen Drama Play Collections

Typeset by RefineCatch Limited, Bungay, Suffolk
Printed and bound in Great Britain

To find out more about our authors and books visit www.bloomsbury.com
and sign up for our newsletters.

Contents

Performance Rights vi
Preface by Jon Lawrence Rivera vii
Introduction viii
Editor Biographies xvi
Author Biographies xvii

Painting in Red by Luis Alfaro 1

FIXED by Boni B. Alvarez 47

School for Witches, or Friendship Betrayed! by Madhuri Shekar 115

The King of Maricopa County by Mary Lyon Kamitaki 151

The Woodingle Puppet Show with Host Mr. C, as Constructed by Mr. Asinine with Calculations and Articulations of the Genius Sort by Julie Taiwo Quarles 213

Traces of Desire by Lina Patel 261

Florence and Normandie by June Carryl 321

Performance Rights

For *Painting in Red*

All inquiries regarding the performance of the Play must be addressed to 41 Madison Avenue, 29th Floor, New York, NY 10010, NY Attention: Leah Hamos: (212) 634-8153, lhamos@gersh.com.

For *School for Witches, or Friendship Betrayed!*

All rights whatsoever in *School for Witches, or Friendship Betrayed*! by Madhuri Shekar are strictly reserved and application for performance, etc. should be made before rehearsals to Independent Artist Group (IAG), formerly known as APA, of 3 Columbus Circle, 23rd Floor, New York, NY 10019, USA, attn: Beth Blickers, (bblickers@independentartistgroup.com). No performance may be given unless a licence has been obtained. No rights in incidental music or songs contained in the Work are hereby granted and performance rights for any performance/presentation whatsoever must be obtained from the respective copyright owners

For *Traces of Desire*

All rights whatsoever in *Traces of Desire* are strictly reserved and application for performance, etc. should be made before rehearsal to Hansen, Jacobson, et al., L.L.P., 450 North Roxbury Drive | 8th Floor | Beverly Hills, CA 90210, USA. No reading or performance may be given unless a licence has been obtained. No rights in incidental music or songs contained in the Play are hereby granted and performance rights for any performance/presentation whatsoever must be obtained from the respective copyright owners.

For all other plays in the collection

All rights whatsoever in this play are strictly reserved and application for performance, etc. should be made before rehearsals to Permissions Department, Bloomsbury Publishing Plc, 50 Bedford Square, London, WC1B 3DP, UK. No performance may be given unless a licence has been obtained. No rights in incidental music or songs contained in the Work are hereby granted and performance rights for any performance/presentation whatsoever must be obtained from the respective copyright owners.

Preface

Jon Lawrence Rivera

It's been an adventure.

When Barbara reached out to me in early 2012 to talk about a project called "Golden Tongues," I was immediately drawn in. It was a simple idea: adapt plays from the Golden Age of Spanish theater to reach modern audiences, especially younger theatergoers.

I was thinking of all the opportunities it would provide. For playwrights – a chance to introduce (or, in some cases, reintroduce) them to the wealth of plays in the Spanish Golden Age canon. For the audience – access to those plays through modern adaptations. And for the theater – a whole new crop of imaginative retellings of long-forgotten plays.

From the very beginning, the playwrights I reached out to were all willing to participate. And the richness of their adaptations (some very loose) have entertained audiences through the years as we have presented them as staged readings. In our dozen years of Golden Tongues, we have commissioned eighteen playwrights. Of those plays, three have been fully produced on stage, and one adapted to film.

It has been thrilling to watch the dramaturgical support Barbara and her team have provided to all playwrights. Guiding them through the main points of the original source, noting where they might strengthen the storytelling or anchor their themes in the source texts as they addressed audiences unfamiliar with them.

It has been a remarkable adventure, one we hope to continue for many more years to come.

Introduction

Robin Alfriend Kello
Aina Soley Mateu

In 2013, UCLA professor Barbara Fuchs and Los Angeles theater company Playwrights' Arena, under the direction of Jon Lawrence Rivera, founded Golden Tongues, an initiative to adapt Hispanic classical theater into works that speak to modern anglophone audiences in the US and beyond. This anthology comprises seven previously unpublished plays by Los Angeles playwrights, written for various editions of Golden Tongues. The plays explore gender, sexuality, race, cultural identity, migration, and social justice, among other themes. They tell complex stories full of humor and pathos, inspired by works that moved audiences centuries ago. From the deserts of Maricopa County to a remote school for witches or the heart of the Rodney King riots in Koreatown, these stirring plays speak to readers across the world in their new guise.

The anthology offers a new way to engage with the corpus of Hispanic classical theater, long overshadowed by the works of Shakespeare. Even in parts of the United States that are predominantly bilingual and Hispanophone, the work of playwrights such as Lope de Vega, Ana Caro, Sor Juana, Maria de Zayas, and Guillén de Castro is not well known, despite how urgently it speaks to audiences today. These adaptations offer the general reader, as well as specialists in modern literature or theater, an entry point into a rich selection of underperformed works. For teachers, scholars, and practitioners already familiar with the *comedia*, we offer access to vibrant transformations of the canon.[1] While the plays in the anthology draw from *comedia* source texts, each can be read either in conjunction with that source text or entirely on its own. As successful adaptations, the Golden Tongues plays transform the source material into completely new work, while revealing their originals in a new light.[2]

Golden Tongues: Stage to Page

The Golden Tongues initiative was instrumental to the conception of Diversifying the Classics, founded in 2014 and directed since then by Fuchs to diversify the canon of classical theater as part of a larger conversation within a "multicultural, multiethnic and multilingual US."[3] Diversifying the Classics currently spearheads multiple projects to promote Hispanic classical theater in the US, including collective translations of previously untranslated or unpublished plays, audioplays, and pedagogy and materials

---

1 The Spanish-language *comedia* tradition of three-act plays is distinct from the *commedia dell'arte*, which originated in Italy as a theater based on character types and was popular across early modern Europe.
2 See Barbara Fuchs, "Engendering Golden Tongues," *Journal of Romance Studies* Vol. 23, No. 2, Summer 2023, pp. 183–204.
3 See Barbara Fuchs, "Diversifying the Classics: Adapting Hispanic Classical Theatre to Contemporary Los Angeles," *Comedia Performance* Vol. 14, No. 1, 2017, pp. 129–51.

for K-12 students, all available open-access on DTC's website. DTC also hosts LA Escena, a biennial festival of Hispanic classical theater, at which Golden Tongues adaptations have been presented since 2018 (previous editions were staged at the William A. Clark Memorial Library and the Hershey Hall Cortile at the UCLA campus). With its focus on the adaptation and subsequent performance of plays based on *comedia*, Golden Tongues provides an exciting answer to the question of how the classical corpus can embrace diversity and resonate with the present. Los Angeles company Playwrights' Arena, which has partnered with Fuchs and Diversifying the Classics from the start, was founded upon similar principles as the Golden Tongues project, and indeed served as an inspiration. Established in 1992 by Rivera and Steve Tyler in the aftermath of the Rodney King riots that convulsed Los Angeles—an event also central to *Florence and Normandie*, by June Carryl, in this collection—Playwrights' Arena "is first and foremost dedicated to diversity and inclusivity" in all processes of playmaking, and aims to be "an incubator for a re-imagined, more inclusive theatrical canon by generating and presenting new works for the stage."[4]

In most Golden Tongues plays, Los Angeles serves not only as a backdrop but as a crucial element. Language, culture, and history are addressed in this particular geography, as universal concerns are localized and grounded via the specifics of each play. As adaptations by Los Angeles authors, these works offer variations on the theme of the city's multiplicity, re-examining territories, cultural norms, and conflicts. However unfamiliar with Spanish Golden Age literature, modern audiences can readily recognize the conflicts and challenges in the adapted works. Our hope is that the adaptations—rich and delightful in their own right—can serve as a gateway to the source texts. Those plays, written in Madrid, Seville, or "New Spain" (now Mexico) some 400 years ago, tell enduring stories, as their adaptability confirms, and are still staged, translated, and adapted for their appeal.

In his 1609 *New Art of Making Plays in Our Time*, Lope de Vega proposed the novel idea that playwrights should write to engage their audiences. In hundreds of plays, Lope and his contemporaries developed highly entertaining plots that also explored complex social dynamics, for a dramatic corpus that remains engaging, suspenseful, and relevant centuries later.[5] In recent years, Red Bull Theatre, the Guthrie Theater, New York Classical Theatre, the Stratford Festival, and the Bay Area Women's Theatre Festival, as well as a multitude of universities and schools, have all performed Diversifying the Classics translations for anglophone audiences.

In dialogue with these vibrant sources, the Golden Tongues plays, despite mostly being conceived as Angeleno stories, tackle themes and issues that reach well beyond southern California. Racial injustice, inequity, and trauma rooted in institutional and police violence are still urgent concerns today, thirty years after the Rodney King verdict and riots, which deeply marked Los Angeles. While early modern theater grappled with new possibilities of social mobility and characters' ability to fashion their own personas on stage, in our own time artists confront the development of social media and celebrity culture, exploring their pull on those who must live in the public

---

4 See "About Us," Playwrights' Arena, https://playwrightsarena.org/about-us/.
5 Diversifying the Classics, "Contextualizing the Comedia," http://diversifyingtheclassics.humanities.ucla.edu/wp-content/uploads/2018/12/Contextualizing-the-Comedia.pdf.

eye. Thus in *FIXED* and *The King of Maricopa County*, respectively, Boni B. Alvarez and Mary Lyon Kamitaki explore the tragic costs of accommodating perceived expectations of what public opinion will tolerate. If gender and sexuality are central to the source texts, they are no less key for the adaptations, which challenge preconceived notions and normative pressures on characters' identities, as in Patel's *Traces of Desire* and Shekar's *School for Witches*.

Golden Tongues is rooted roughly in our contemporary Los Angeles, while preserving the playwrights' creative freedom to shape the universes in which the source texts are reborn. The precise location, historical time, language, and genre are for the writers to decide as they conjure projects aligned with their own artistic practice. Our collection foregrounds Los Angeles because we are based in the city and its flagship public university. Yet we hope our project models the possibilities for adapting the *comedia* more widely and, ideally, inspires other iterations.

Despite the fact that the term is often contested for political reasons, we use the word "Hispanic" in the broader Diversifying the Classics project and this collection in an effort to capture the broadest possible set of referents. Referring to "Spanish theater" would exclude the works written in Spain's Latin American colonies, including by such key figures as Sor Juana Inés de la Cruz or Juan Ruiz de Alarcón in what is now Mexico; "Latinx theater", while lifting up a minoritized US population in the here and now, is anachronistic for the source texts.

Adaptation, Appropriation, and Translation

Our intention is to share plays that excite us with new audiences of educators, students, theater practitioners, and other interested readers by exploring new avenues for the adaptation of classical material. Scholars such as Julie Sanders and Linda Hutcheon have made valuable theoretical advances in adaptation studies, and publications such as *Borrowers and Lenders* and the recent *Bard in the Borderlands* anthology, focused specifically on Shakespeare, address early modern dramas put to innovative adaptive use in the present.[6] We here expand on such valuable work in this field to center creative dramatic responses that draw from canonical drama in the early modern Hispanic world, reenvisioning a corpus often underperformed in the anglophone world for the aesthetic and social demands of the twenty-first century.

As works in English by playwrights who might not always have linguistic access to the original Spanish text, the dramas compiled here are also adjacent to what has been called *tradaptation*, a portmanteau term to emphasize how translation, whether intentional or otherwise, always alters meaning. In the cases of the final two plays in this volume, *Florence and Normandie* and *Traces of Desire*, authors had access to new translations by Diversifying the Classics. Other playwrights variously relied on

---

6 See Sanders, *Adaptation and Appropriation* (Routledge, 2015); Hutcheon, *A Theory of Adaptation* (Routledge, 2012); *Borrowers and Lenders*, https://borrowers-ojs-azsu.tdl.org/borrowers/index; Katherine Gillen, Adrianna M. Santos, and Kathryn Vomero Santos, *The Bard in the Borderlands: An Anthology of Shakespeare Appropriations in La Frontera, Volume 1* (University of Chicago Press, 2023).

previous translations, synopses or plot summary, and assistance from DTC dramaturgs. Notions of fidelity to the original source, then, were never part of the plan, and indeed would have hindered the creative opportunity to adapt with liberty and panache. For the purposes of this volume, the term adaptation is intended broadly, suggesting a relationship to the original that is as proximate or distant as the playwrights choose in addressing contemporary audiences.

That process involves the playwright's choice from the beginning, as the template for producing Golden Tongues has been the same since its inception in 2013. Our collaboration with Playwrights' Arena, which focuses on developing new work by Los Angeles writers, allows us to encounter playwrights interested in being commissioned to produce an original work. Once authors have committed to the project, we introduce them to *comedia* and then share Diversifying the Classics' translations, translations by other scholars, and the resources of the *Out of the Wings* database for Anglophone audiences of *comedia*. We then offer our own support and collaboration through dramaturgy in preparation for the inaugural staged readings that are now a regular feature of our biennial theater festival, LA Escena.

The resulting adaptations take the core characters and central conflict of the original work and reimagine them for an entirely different context, often contemporary Los Angeles.[7] The new plays do not depend on any audience familiarity with their originals, even though that relation to the source often gives them additional depth and bite. Their success as adaptations, though it might be of scholarly interest, is secondary to their success as theater. In our brief introductions to each play, we have provided information about the source texts, to guide any readers or theatermakers interested in the analogues between the *comedia* origin and the Golden Tongues product. Yet the new plays stand here in their own right, worthy of reading for pleasure, studying in the classroom, or putting on stage. Their creative transformations of drama from Hispanic classical theater are collected here to broaden notions of the early modern canon that are invested in authenticity and fidelity to a fetishized source, and, as is increasingly untenable in a multilingual US, relentlessly Anglo- and Shakespeare-centric. As we here aim for a readership beyond the Los Angeles area and the plays included offer a wealth of culturally and linguistically specific references, we have annotated each work in consultation with the playwright. While recognizing that there is no presumption of common knowledge among our diverse intended audiences, we intend to offer educators and theater practitioners beyond Los Angeles and even the US the necessary tools to engage with these exciting new works.

---

7 A geographical exception is *The King of Maricopa County*, which is specifically set in Arizona to examine cultural identity and migration within the context of that border zone. A temporal exception is *Florence and Normandie*, the story of which takes place during the 1992 social unrest following the LAPD beating of Rodney King and the acquittal of the officers who perpetrated the violence against him.

The Plays

1. Luis Alfaro, *Painting in Red*

Loosely adapted from Calderón de la Barca's *El pintor de su deshonra* (*The Painter of His Own Dishonor*), Luis Alfaro's *Painting in Red* focuses on a community of Los Angeles artists. The play centers on the imperiled marriage between Mano, a successful Chicano painter, and his wife Espy, who once painted but now manages his career. When Espy's former husband Cauahtémoc, long presumed drowned, shows up again, she finds herself at an impasse. While Mano explores his relationship to a Spain of the mind and an endlessly gentrifying Los Angeles, Espy confronts the need to choose between future and past selves. While both men focus on their need for her, it is only when Mano recognizes what Espy herself needs that they can move forward. Alfaro adroitly avoids Calderón's violent end, offering instead a life-giving and deeply feminist shade of red.

2. Boni B. Alvarez, *FIXED*

Also inspired by a Calderón tragedy of honor, Boni B. Alvarez's *FIXED* adapts *El médico de su honra* (*The Doctor of His Own Honor*) to a vexed present moment. Set in a world of Los Angeles massage parlors and political intrigue, the play tells the story of Filipino "ladyboy" Miracles and her lover Mariano, a closeted Chicano man who visits her at The House of Malacañang. Both Mariano's brother, Hudson, who is running for local office, and Miracles' friends in the house see the danger ahead and urge the young lovers to stop seeing each other. As Dana, Hudson's wife and campaign manager, plainly states to Mariano, the public will never accept his relationship with Miracles, and Mariano is standing in the way of Hudson's political success. Miracles seeks to resolve the "confusion" her body represents and maintain her relationship with Mariano as "a normal couple" by pursuing gender-reassignment surgery. Yet Mariano seems unable to go beyond the pressures of heteronormativity, and Miracles is unable to pass the psychological assessment required for the operation. The play concludes with the act that provides its title, as Miracles' desperation leads her to perform a violent and disturbing act of self-castration.

3. Madhuri Shekar, *School for Witches, or Friendship Betrayed!*

In her adaptation of Maria de Zayas' *La traición en la amistad* (*Friendship Betrayed*), Shekar transports the female desire and competition of the source text to the entirely female world of an insular boarding school, the titular "School for Witches." In this repressive yet hilarious set-up, Marcia, Fenisa, and Lisea try to navigate both their special powers and their burgeoning passions—and the intersection of magic and desire—in a world that keeps pushing them towards conventionality. Marcia has no real interest in men or boys, only in maintaining the appearance of being "normal," while Fenisa conjures magic to visualize a free-floating soulmate. When the rebellious, charismatic, and potentially dangerous newcomer Lisea joins the school, Fenisa and Marcia find themselves competing for her attention, perhaps at their own peril. While Lisea seeks to foment revolution in the school and carries on a relationship with Fenisa,

Marcia and Fenisa's friendship is sorely tried. Summoning all their powers, however, the two repair their bond and escape the patriarchal confines of the school.

4. Mary Lyon Kamitaki, *The King of Maricopa County*

The King of Maricopa County by Mary Lyon Kamitaki reimagines Lope de Vega's *El castigo sin venganza* (*Punishment without Revenge*) in present-day Arizona, near the border with Mexico. The King is sheriff Duke Howard, who is running for senator and facing controversy for his aggressive stance against immigration. He decides to marry Casandra, a much younger Mexican-American teacher he meets while doing crowd control at a march in Phoenix, to improve his public image and secure his position. On her way to Maricopa to get married, Casandra gets into a car accident in the middle of the desert. She immediately falls for the other driver, a young woman named Freddie, who turns out to be Duke's daughter. It is not until Casandra arrives at her new home that she and Freddie realize they are about to become step-mother and step-daughter. Kamitaki interlaces the stakes of Lope's tragedy—loyalty, public image, honor—with complex familial relations, far-right propaganda and anti-immigration rhetoric, racism, and the denial of female homosexuality.

5. Julie Taiwo Quarles, *The Woodingle Puppet Show*

Julie Taiwo Quarles's *The Woodingle Puppet Show with Host Mr. C, as Constructed by Mr. Asinine with Calculations and Articulations of the Genius Sort*, reimagines Cervantes' interlude *El retablo de las maravillas* (*The Marvelous Puppet Show*)—a story of charlatans conning a small-town audience—as a parable of identity politics and authenticity in the rapidly gentrifying Los Angeles city of Woodingle (a linguistic play on the predominantly Black municipality of Inglewood). Pupita, a pregnant Nigerian immigrant, and Marionette, a woman born to one Nigerian and one white American parent, are competing for an apartment in a majority Black area of the city where rents are skyrocketing. Mr. C., an American-born Black man, presents an invisible show, purporting to consist of Black celebrities, to determine which of the women will be considered sufficiently authentic in their Black identity to get the apartment.

Just as Mr. C. is exploited by the building owners, Pupita is initially willing to play along with the fiction, pretending to see Nat King Cole, Michael Jordan, Oprah Winfrey, and Billie Holiday in the hope of securing the much longed for apartment. Marionette, however, begins to expose the race-based manipulation and economic harm of this scenario, as Mr. C. attempts to present an updated vision of Blackness with Barack Obama and Chimamanda Ngozi Adichie replacing the previous celebrities. As the play progresses, the characters take control over representation, ultimately making the complexity of the African diaspora, old and new, into a vehicle of celebration and solidarity.

6. Lina Patel, *Traces of Desire*

Lina Patel's *Traces of Desire* takes a fresh look at the central themes of lust and agency in Lope de Vega's *La viuda valenciana* (*The Widow of Valencia*), the story of a widow's scheme to satisfy her passion while protecting her reputation. Patel's hilarious and moving adaptation begins in Bombay, where a widowed Uma Bhatt refuses a suitor. He is Muslim; she is Hindu. Unwilling to risk her reputation, Uma stifles her longing and dies shortly after. What might be the end of a tragic love story becomes the spark that lights up this choral play chronicling the struggles and pleasures of female sexuality in one Indian family. Over three generations, and through a few shenanigans and migrations, these women learn to embrace their yearnings, freeing themselves – and future generations – from long-held notions of womanhood. Taking Vega's cue, Patel explores questions of female agency and transgression and in making the play contemporary, even the idea of womanhood itself. As the self-denial of desire trickles down from daughter to daughter, the play asks, can desire be inherited?

7. June Carryl, *Florence and Normandie*

Based on Calderón's *Amar después de la muerte* (*To Love beyond Death*), which chronicles love and death in the context of a sixteenth-century Morisco uprising in Spain, June Carryl's *Florence and Normandie* dramatizes the racial tension and violence of late twentieth-century Los Angeles. At Jeong's Market, first-generation Korean American Sydney Jeong and Toony Berry, a young Black man, develop a flirtatious rapport while stocking the shelves. A few blocks away, Toony's sister, Iz, is growing impatient with the willful ignorance of her white boyfriend, Danny, on matters of race. As the unrest in the city in the wake of the Rodney King verdict engulfs Koreatown in flames, the families of Jeong, Toony, and Iz, entwined by both love and location, find themselves living the American racial nightmare. While recreating the detail and atmosphere of early 1990s Los Angeles, *Florence and Normandie* portrays the ongoing horror of cultural hierarchies backed by violence that extends from religious persecution in early modern Spain to struggles for racial justice in the American present.

Why an Anthology of Golden Tongues Now?

Golden Tongues extends across two theatrical timelines: while the plays offer an entry point into the rich tradition of Hispanic classical theater, often neglected in the United States and the anglophone world in comparison to Shakespearean drama, they are also very much of the moment, reflecting the diversity of Los Angeles in the present and the concerns of a twenty-first-century society facing intersecting social crises. Staging a radical conversation between past and present, these *Golden Tongues* speak with urgency to the now.

We hope this volume will bring scholars, educators, theater practitioners, and other interested publics to the *comedias* that inspired these plays. In line with the broad objectives of the UCLA Diversifying the Classics initiative, we hope to promote the work of authors such as Ana Caro, Juan Ruiz de Alarcón, Lope de Vega, Maria de Zayas, Sor Juana Inés de la Cruz, and others who produced dramas in Spanish on both sides of the Atlantic in the early modern period. For even in predominantly Hispanophone regions of the United States this work has been too often overlooked. Yet we also hope to expose new audiences to the vibrant dramas of Los Angeles playwrights in the now, writing in a modern English vernacular and grappling with issues such as gender and sexuality, structural racism, patriarchy, identity politics, climate change, and the long colonial legacies of overlapping Spanish and Anglo-American campaigns of domination.

The anthology is thus in line with other movements in the study of theater that seek to use early modern texts and twenty-first-century responses in concert to address present injustice and social division arising from the legacies of settler colonialism, racialized enslavement, and the global order of nation-states that restricts the movement of human beings while capital flows smoothly across borders. Though the points of connection between the original Spanish-language play and its Golden Tongues counterpart may rely on something as universal as questions of desire or identity, those psychological and affective inquiries operate against a backdrop of the workings of power within a given social structure. This anthology promotes theater as a mechanism not just to represent or comprehend the world but to imagine how we might change it.

To that end, while we certainly recommend the individual enjoyment of these powerful plays, we hope and expect that they will function best in the social arenas of education and performance. For teachers and students, we envision these plays as exciting additions to studies of early modern or modern drama, Spanish history and language, migration and mobility, adaptation studies, and other performance- or literature-based curricula. For practitioners, we offer these texts in the hope that the rich dialogue within them will find its way to the voices of actors. The space of theater as a radical site for social exploration is the ideal venue for the questions taken up by these works, and the conversations they engender will be most productive and exciting when emerging from the embodied art of performance. We hope that these Golden Tongues will start wonderful conversations in your theaters and classrooms. And so ends this prologue; now let the plays begin.

Editor Biographies

Barbara Fuchs (Distinguished Professor of Spanish and English, UCLA) is founder and director of Diversifying the Classics, its Golden Tongues adaptation initiative, and the LA Escena festival of Hispanic classical theater. Her most recent book is *Theater of Lockdown: Digital and Distanced Performance in a Time of Pandemic* (Bloomsbury/Methuen Drama 2021).

Robin Alfriend Kello is a PhD candidate in English at UCLA. His teaching and research focus on early modern drama in English and Spanish, adaptations of Shakespeare, and the theater of migration. He has been part of Diversifying the Classics since 2016, and served as a Golden Tongues dramaturg in 2020.

Aina Soley Mateu is a PhD candidate in the Department of Spanish and Portuguese at UCLA. Her dissertation considers representations of historical memory in twenty-first-century Catalan literature. She is a long-term member of Diversifying the Classics, and has worked as a dramaturg for Golden Tongues since 2020.

Author Biographies

Luis Alfaro is a Chicano playwright born and raised in downtown Los Angeles. He has received fellowships from: the John D. and Catherine T. MacArthur Foundation; American Academy of Arts & Letters, United States Artists; Ford Foundation; Joyce Foundation; Mellon Foundation, and the PEN America/Laura Pels International Foundation Theater Award. He has served as Playwright-in-Residence at the Oregon Shakespeare Festival; Chicago's Victory Gardens Theatre; Ojai Playwrights Conference, and the Los Angeles Theatre Center. His plays include *The Travelers*, *Electricidad*, *Oedipus El Rey* and *Mojada*. He is director of the MFA in Dramatic Writing program at the University of Southern California. Luis spent two decades in the Los Angeles Poetry and Performance Art communities.

Boni B. Alvarez is a Los Angeles-based actor-playwright. His plays include *America Adjacent*, *Nicky*, *Bloodletting*, *Dallas Non-Stop*, and *Ruby, Tragically Rotund*. His plays have been produced at Center Theatre Group—Kirk Douglas Theatre, Echo Theater Company, Coeurage Theatre Company, Skylight Theatre Company, and Playwrights' Arena. He is a Resident Playwright of New Dramatists.

Madhuri Shekar is an award-winning playwright based in New Jersey. Her plays include *House of Joy*, *Queen*, *A Nice Indian Boy*, and *In Love and Warcraft*. Her audio drama *Evil Eye* won a 2020 Audie Award for best original work, and she wrote the film adaptation starring Sarita Chaudhury. *A Nice Indian Boy* has also been turned into a movie, starring Jonathan Groff and Karan Soni. She has an MFA in dramatic writing from USC and is an alumnus of the Juilliard Playwriting Program.

Mary Lyon Kamitaki is a New York playwright born and raised on the Big Island of Hawaii. Her work has been produced by Playwrights' Arena and developed at Page 73, Alliance Theatre, A Noise Within, Open Fist Theatre Company, Pasadena Playhouse, Skylight Theatre, Ensemble Studio Theatre/LA, and UCLA. She is an alumna of the New West playwrights' group at EST/LA and the Page 73 writers' group. Mary's plays center mixed, queer girls, and women who reinvent themselves to survive in transforming worlds.

Julie Taiwo Quarles is a Los Angeles-based playwright, professor, and identical twin with roots in central California and Nigeria. With storytelling inspired by areas of focus in her research and teaching, she sees her dramatist and instructor identities as complementary. Her most recent playwriting looks at Africa in conversation with the West through the albinism experience and cultural ownership, her research explores August Wilson's colorblind casting and representational authenticity arguments in relation to contemporary Black performance, and her instruction includes English composition and language-learning, American pop culture, and creative writing. She teaches at Pepperdine University and resides in Los Angeles with her husband and their two sons.

Lina Patel is a multi-disciplinary artist whose work explores disability, non-traditional relationships, and power in an unstable world. Her theater work has been developed and produced across the country and in the UK. She has been an NEA grant recipient and Rising Phoenix Repertory honored Lina with the 2024 Cornelia Street American Playwriting Award, presented to a playwright of exceptional work ethic, character, and talent. Lina has had commissions from Yale Repertory Theater, Chalk Repertory Theater, and the Japanese American National Museum, among others. On television, Lina served as co-producer for Ava DuVernay's *Cherish the Day*; previously, DC's *Krypton* and CW's *Frequency*. Lina is a Lecturer of Theater at Pomona College, where she teaches playwriting.

June Carryl was raised in Denver and attended Brown University where she studied Political Science and English Literature. Her plays include *N*gga B*tch* (developed at Nancy Manocherian's the cell theatre and the Vagrancy), *The Wronged Party* (2022 IAMA Theatre's Shonda Rhimes Unsung Voices Commission), *Colossus* (2023 Ojai Playwright's Conference, semi-finalist 2021 O'Neill Playwrights Conference), *Blue* (2023 Scotsman First Fringe Award, Edinburgh Fringe Festival), *Florence and Normandie* (Playwrights Arena and UCLA Diversifying the Classics), and *Girl Blue* (developed at CTG LA Writers' Workshop). An actor as well, her theater credits include Fraulein Schneider in *Cabaret* (Celebration Theatre), Gerty Fail in *Failure: A Love Story* (Coeurage Theatre), the Nurse in *Romeo and Juliet* (A Noise Within), A.C.T.'s *Insurrection: Holding History*, Berkeley Repertory's *Civil Sex*, and Thick Description's *Venus*. Film and television credits include: *Kemba, Y: the Last Man, Helstrom*, and *Mindhunter*.

Painting in Red

Luis Alfaro

Painting in Red

Introduction by Barbara Fuchs

Of all the Golden Tongues adaptations, Luis Alfaro's "one-act whitewash" of Calderón's *El pintor de su deshonra* (*The Painter of His Own Dishonor*) is perhaps most focused on how we relate to idealized pasts, whether a Spain imagined from Los Angeles or long-ago love affairs. In his moody, mordant adaptation, Alfaro steps back from Calderón's action-packed original to explore the seemingly irreconcilable pull of past and present selves.

Calderón's *Pintor* features Juan Roca, a middle-aged artist recently married to Serafina. When her sometime lover Álvaro, long presumed dead, unexpectedly reappears, the two are devastated. Serafina chooses to remain faithful to Juan, so Álvaro decides to kidnap her instead. Given her compromised situation, Juan refuses to believe in her fidelity and shoots them both, in an abrupt and violent ending.

Alfaro, the noted Chicano writer, performer, producer, and director, sets his feminist adaptation in a perennially gentrifying downtown Los Angeles and in the anodyne coastal town of Port Hueneme, a few miles north of the city. One running thread of this "whitewash" is how much Los Angeles has changed, forcing people to leave the city for the uninspiring but cheaper locales beyond it. Alfaro explores the marriage of two painters, Mano and Espy. She no longer paints but instead manages his career, and her frustration is palpable. The marriage is further strained by the reappearance of Espy's first husband, Cuauhtémoc, long presumed drowned in a fishing accident in Mexico. Although Espy agrees to meet him, and is clearly moved by him, she will not agree to leave Mano. Meanwhile, Mano's painter friend Esteban does not hide his own longing for Mano, however unreciprocated. Off in Port Hueneme, Maribel and Raul comically explore their ambivalent commitments to each other, to domesticity, and to Los Angeles itself.

Like Calderón's original, Alfaro's adaptation features a lover miraculously—if somewhat inconveniently—restored to the world, after the woman who loved him has moved on to marry someone else. Alfaro internalizes the issue: compared to Serafina in the source, Espy has tremendous freedom to decide her own fate, but that doesn't solve the excruciating emotional dilemma of what she owes her past self and her past love. When confronted with the possibility of leaving Mano for Cuauhtémoc, Espy faces no legal or moral obligation, no male relative pushing her in any particular direction. There is no seemliness—much less honor—to consider. Faced with the immense neediness of the two men who love her, Espy is at an impasse, and neither choice will address her own frustration as an artist. Appropriately for a Los Angeles play, Espy turns to a celebrity for advice and comfort, in comical interludes of magical realism, as she remembers that Olivia Newton-John also had a boyfriend who went missing and was falsely presumed dead. While Mano gradually comes to understand the enormity of what he's made Espy give up, Cuauhtémoc's reappearance conjures her former self. Noticing Espy's immaculate hands, Cuauhtémoc offers, "let me give you your passion back" (p. 32) and begins to strip down. Beyond his cocky opportunism, he cannily invokes both her painting and their love.

After long trying to preserve his marriage by painting Espy, Mano realizes he must instead enable her to paint. Alfaro's chiasmic conclusion remediates the violent end of

Calderón's original *Pintor*, offering a richly symbolic resolution to the intractable conflict between possible lives. As Mano finally decides to give where he has always taken, Espy is restored to her former artistic and professional self. Meanwhile, Cuauhtémoc is returned to the ocean, in a gesture of both renunciation and renewal.

In a powerful metadramatic dimension, Alfaro's adaptation also reflects on the relationship between Los Angeles and Spanish or Mexican culture. The initial clue comes from the subtitle: what does Alfaro mean by "whitewash"? Aside from exculpation, the term has a strong association in urban slang with the abandonment of minority cultures for whiteness. Mano, now professionally successful, reflects often on how things used to be in Los Angeles, and the general gentrification that forces Maribel and Raul to leave it, at least for a time, for the cultural desert of Port Hueneme. Yet the play also explores the relationship of contemporary Los Angeles to the idea of Spain, in a fascination both consuming and contrived. From the imported figs Mano paints as the play opens to his memories of touristic bullfights at its close, this consumable Spain bears little relation to the characters' quotidian engagement with a Hispanic Los Angeles, even in a city increasingly whitewashed. Meanwhile, Cuauhtémoc, described as a "handsome Chinese American man," (p. 28) once but no longer blond, is named after the last Aztec emperor. He awkwardly insists on speaking Spanish after his time in Mexico, yet Espy (short for Esperanza) has no patience for it or his *boleros*. Espy's choice between the two men, and her obsession with the ever-so-blonde Newton-John, are thus subtly charged. Surely we are post-racial now, or are we merely whitewashed? Alfaro's painterly meditation on Los Angeles' many colors both acknowledges and gently ironizes them.

Painting in Red

A whitewash of *El pintor de su deshonra* (*The Painter of His Own Dishonor*), a Spanish Golden Age play written in the 1640s by Pedro Calderón de la Barca.

Painting in Red was first staged in June 2013 as part of the Golden Tongues Festival, presented by Playwrights' Arena and the Center for 17th- and 18th-Century Studies at the UCLA William Andrews Clark Memorial Library, directed by Jon Lawrence Rivera, and featuring Leandro Cano, Fran de Leon, Marlene Forte, Anthony Bryce Graham, Eric Schulman, and Carolyn Zeller.

The play was subsequently produced by Playwrights' Arena at the Greenway Court Theatre in Hollywood in October 2014, directed by Jon Lawrence Rivera, and featuring Elisa Bocanegra, Cristina Frias, Joe Hernandez-Kolski, Justin Huen, Jayme Lake, West Liang, and Rodney To, with scenic design by Christopher Scott Murillo, lighting design by Adam Blumenthal, video design by Keith Skretch, costume design by Mylette Nora, sound design by Bob Blackburn, stage management by Janette Jara, and project producer was Giselle Gilbert.

Characters

Mano, *a painter*
Espy, *his wife*
Maribel, *her best friend*
Raul, *the best friend's serious something*
Cuauhtémoc, *someone beautiful*
Esteban, *a fellow artist*

Place

Los Angeles and Ventura County in California. Transitions move quickly, as if the characters themselves are not aware of the changes they are making.

Lofty Ideals

The first harp chords of "I Honestly Love You" can be heard as we see a Boyle Heights loft with a view of the Los Angeles skyline. **Mano** *sits on a stool in front of a canvas, painting a subject,* **Espy**, *leaning across a chaise longue holding a fig in her hands. She contemplates, then impulsively bites into the fig.*

Mano   Stop eating the art.

Espy   It's not art. It's a prop. That paint you keep putting on the canvas is the art. The fig and I are in service to your vision.

Mano   You mean your vision.

Espy   I merely suggest.

Mano   Strongly towards the market.

Espy   These figs aren't cheap. Remember when I was the art?

Mano   You are still part of the art.

Espy   I used to be "the" art. Getting old sucks, you lose the best modeling jobs to . . . fruit.

Mano   You're still my art, I'm surrounding you with texture.

Espy   I doubt Diego ever said to Frida, "Don't move, I want to focus on the monkey . . ."

Mano   You shouldn't have pushed me toward the fig.

Espy   I pushed you toward change, but who knew I was pushing you away from me?

Mano   As if . . . We should do a podcast called "I tell him what to paint."

Espy   "I tell him what to paint—as dictated by the market . . ." Can I help it if everyone wants texture these days? Consumers want the new. Art is no exception.

Mano   But what do I want?

Espy   A new car.

Mano   Well, then, texture it is. I do miss splatter, though.

Espy   Splatter is worthy, but texture shows you're changing, growing. The fig is hard.

Mano   Tell me about it.

Espy   Master the fig, expand your market, there's nothing complicated about this business. Just don't texture my arms, please.

Mano   Don't worry, it's not your arms I'm focusing on . . .

Espy *giggles.* **Mano** *gets another fig and brings it to her.*

Mano   Don't eat your commission.

He kisses **Espy** *deeply. He stops and looks at her.*

Espy   What?

Mano   What's more beautiful, you or the fig?

Espy   You need to ask?

Mano   Look at the fig. Crease, color, shifts and changes into hues.

Espy   You never used to talk like that, Hue Howser.

Mano   I never used to talk.

Espy   That's true.

Mano   What did I use to do?

Espy   Nod and grunt. It was hot. I forget how little you spoke when I first met you.

Mano   We didn't do a lot of talking.

Espy   Pervert. Your brooding is a turn-on. Can we get back to that soon?

Mano   I've moved on from brooding, I express opinions. Artists can do that now.

Espy   Male artists. You have too many opinions. You should keep some to yourself.

Mano   This city forces them on you. Remember when everyone had a demonstration, a 'zine, a street festival, a neighborhood, a gang, a taco? And then the new millennium shows up and suddenly everyone is keeping everything to themselves. It's like the Great Depression of thought. Some sort of greed of success took over. Everyone decided they could be the next anything they wanted to be. How untrue is that? People running down alleys carrying cans of spray paint, convinced they were the next Keith Haring. The curse of *America's Got Talent*.

Espy   Oh, honey, please, focus on the fig, I don't want to sit here forever. I'm old.

Mano   Ugh, the fig. I keep thinking we'll drizzle them in honey or wrap them in prosciutto. I need an incentive to finish this. It's a cruel fruit, too much going on, and it goes bad so quickly. It's the Hamlet of fruit.

Espy   But this one is imported from (*making fun of the accent*) Ethspania.

Mano   Spanish figs are as beautiful as . . .

Espy   Me?

Mano   I love the way you finish my thoughts. You're the best first wife any man could ask for.

Espy   I want to be a second wife, but I arrive too early at parties.

Mano   Second wives are overrated, the money's gone by the time they show up.

Espy   Stop trying to make me happy.

Mano   Don't move.

Espy   I can't help it, I'm bored. Modeling used to be fun.

Mano   Would it help if you were naked?

Espy   Then you'd be bored.

Mano   Never. Your body changes daily, did you know that? Your cells are constantly transforming. You wake up and you look different.

Espy   That's creepy.

Mano   That's marriage. I never see you the same way twice.

Espy   You need an ophthalmologist.

Mano   I remember when you loved to pose.

Espy   The first time you are in a painting, it feels like you've reached immortality. After that, it feels like gynecology.

Mano   Ouch.

Espy   I am counting on you to make me as famous as the Mona Lisa and that woman from the Duran Duran album. Make me timeless.

Mano   What a challenge.

Espy   Do you remember the first time I posed for you?

Mano   Of course. 7th Street.

Espy   The studio in MacArthur Park, next to Langer's.

Mano   I loved that studio. Except for the shootings.

Espy   You loved the shootings.

Mano   I did. One minute you're painting, the next you're diving for the floor. I miss those days. Essential. You gave me that, the essential idea.

Espy   In a hundred years someone will discover your painting at Goodwill and buy me for a dollar.

Mano   You think so little of me. Will there still be Goodwill?

Espy   Let's face it, only a queen or a corpse can sit this still.

Mano   I sit still, you can sit still. It's an agreement of marriage.

Espy   You don't stop moving.

Mano   What are you talking about? I am so still. I meditate. It's the only way I can paint.

Espy   It's amazing what we think about ourselves. It's art, a mirage. I wish you could see yourself from here. There is so much movement when you paint, the reaching, looking, shifting. It's when you're most alive. You are channeling.

Mano You understand painting better than I do. You always did. Before we became something, I dreamed of being your assistant. Providing you your paint. The perfect color. Trying to please you by giving you the perfect palette. Now, I just try to get out of the way of my own self. Oh God, how pretentious does that sound? I used that line for a Cultural Affairs grant, and now look what it's done to me.

Espy Don't worry, you're post-pretentious.

Mano All that's left for me is making portraits of myself as historical figures. Don't you miss pretension?

Espy I don't know, I was never pretentious.

Mano Ha! Dressing like Kylie Minogue because she was the Madonna of Europe.

Espy Well, that's a truth.

Mano You told me you lived in Granada Hills to impress me.

Espy Granada, the rolling hills, it sounded like Spain. And I knew how much you loved the idea of Spain. It played right into your machismo, your conqueror aesthetic. I was the bull to your matador. How else was I going to get you to notice me?

Mano I hate Spain, except the culture, the art, and the bullfighting.

Espy What's left?

Mano The fig.

They laugh.

Espy What were we talking about?

Mano It's what we're not talking about.

A weird silence. He takes a deep breath. He puts down the brush. He looks at the canvas. Forces himself to say it.

Don't leave me . . .

Without warning, he violently throws something across the room, just not the painting. She awkwardly sits up from the pose.

You think I can't see what is going on?

Espy What a ridiculous gesture. How am I supposed to respond to that?

Mano I am painting you because I am trying to save us. I see you slipping away. Moving toward something else. Another happiness? This time here with you, I was hoping it would bring us closer, but it fills me with guilt and grief. I feel like I am doing your job. Did you stop painting because of me? You never told me why you stopped. Was it an act of pity? You just became the business of us. And look at this, none of these colors work. I don't even use these shades of red! They are not rich, they are not real, they are not right. Nothing makes sense. I'm punishing myself.

Espy What do you want me to say?

Mano You fill me with such doubt.

Espy Don't paint for me. Paint for yourself.

Mano I don't want to. You're the subject. You're the approach, You're the everything.

He goes back to the canvas. Silence.

Espy It's too much to put on me.

Mano If you're not happy, just tell me. You are entitled to your own life. To making your own art. I hope to God you don't think I took that away from you. You were supposed to be the next big thing once, but you gave up. For me? Maybe I'm your obstacle to success.

Espy Don't say that.

Mano I'm not asking you to leave me. But please, don't destroy me. I barely survived the violence of this poverty I was raised in, the projects, gentrification, even the local art movements, all two of them, to make something of myself. Will I survive you?

He stares at the canvas. A moment of thinking. A shift. We come back to something. Maybe out of necessity. He goes and picks up the brush. He stares at the canvas and begins to paint again.

Do you think America's got talent?

Cold, **Espy** *holds up the fig and poses again.*

Whining About Hueneme

A California beach house designed to look like New England because no one is happy where they are. **Espy** *and* **Maribel** *curled up on a couch in front of a big picture window with undulating waves that never stop. They casually inhale a pipe.*

Maribel Oof, that's a lot. He said all that. I thought painters lacked the words, which is why they paint in the first place.

Espy Not him.

Maribel Who was it that said, "If there is no struggle, there is no strength"?

Espy That was either Jesus or Oprah.

Maribel Jesus. Yes . . .

Espy Oprah.

Maribel Oprah. Yes . . .

Espy I don't want to hurt him.

Maribel You won't.

She hugs **Espy**.

Maribel Thanks for coming all this way, it means the world. I'm resigned to living through you now.

Espy Stop.

Maribel We've moved to Oxnard. My life is military bases, fire season, and outlet malls. There are two of them.

Espy Two outlet malls? Wow. Well, fire season must be interesting.

Maribel When a blaze breaks out, we go to Santa Barbara, have mimosas, and wait. The only heat I know are stuffed peppers. I hate my life.

Espy You have a nice life.

Maribel Why did we leave downtown LA? Sometimes I walk around littering the streets of Oxnard in resentment.

Espy Don't do that.

Maribel It's called civic engagement.

Espy Oh, I forgot! I brought you Dim Sum Express.

She pulls a little box from her purse.

Maribel You did? I thought I smelled something, but figured it was just LA.

She digs into a plump white bao.

I know I'm being ridiculous, but I feel like that woman on the Food Channel who lives on a farm and is always alone. She makes biscuits and gravy every episode.

Espy You watch the Food Channel?

Maribel Of course not.

Espy You know, if you think about it, we're only separated by Santa Monica and Malibu.

Maribel And yet, Ventura County is a world away. You're the only friend who's made the journey. All our young hipster friends in downtown, the loft people, they promised they'd come, but you know . . . always a new restaurant opening. At least you bring good gossip.

Espy Gossip? This is my life!

Maribel Don't worry. I won't tell anyone. We barely have Wi-Fi. It's 1972 here.

Suddenly, a large roar.

Espy Oh my God, what is that?

Maribel Fighter jet. I didn't know Hueneme was a military base. The only nice thing about the port is the Marines that jog by every morning. They're plump though. Without a war, the only thing they can run toward is the Homestyle Buffet.

Espy In another time, a plump Marine would have made you very happy.

Maribel Sometimes I sit here looking at all the plump Marines huffing by. I would be a terrible military wife. I'd forget when he was coming home from war, and there he would be, my plump Marine, at the port, coming off the ship, hundreds of wives and girlfriends crying, waving their little flags, confetti popping, champagne bottles broken off the side of the ship, caps thrown up into the air, and my plump Marine, waiting, while I watch that woman on the Food Channel make gravy.

Espy You do watch the Food Channel.

Maribel A little.

Espy Why did you agree to this?

Maribel One day Raul announced we were moving to the country. I thought the country was France. He's more domestic than I thought.

Espy Maybe he's having a mid-life crisis.

Maribel He hasn't even reached mid-life, but he's grown a beard.

Espy It's hard to live in the city. Maybe he's thinking of settling down with you. A sign, perhaps?

Maribel Look at that ocean. It's too big. I'd be happy with a paddleboat at Echo Park Lake.

Espy You've been common law for years.

Maribel Marriage is not in the cards.

Espy Why do you say that?

Maribel Because I showed him all my cards. Marriage is a mystery, and he knows all the secrets now.

Espy Oh, come on, he adores you.

Maribel He's comfortable. I chased him, he didn't chase me. One day, some woman, a nice one, like a sign-language interpreter, is going to sweep him off his feet. He is not going to know what hit him and he will have no other choice but to leave me. It happens all the time, especially out here in Ven-tuh-rah . . . There's no way to say that and make it sound sexy . . .

She starts on another bao.

He's so good, everything I introduce him to, he says, "Oh wow!" and falls in love with it—just not with me. He's had me. I'm a youngish old hag.

Espy You might be exaggerating.

Maribel I know men. I will have to leave him before he leaves me.

Espy You would do that?

Maribel   If I see a plump Marine, out of breath, and jogging my way, I will pursue. It's the only way I'm going to get a ring.

Silence, being high. **Maribel** *bites into the bao.*

Oh my God, I forgot!

Espy   What?

Maribel   I forgot to tell you; this is why I don't like smoking pot.

Espy   What?

Maribel   They found your dead ex-husband.

Espy   What!

Maribel   He's alive!

Bitter Fruit

Self-Help Graphics, **Mano** *and* **Esteban** *working on a silk screen.* **Esteban** *is splattered in paint, wearing it as a badge of honor.*

Esteban   Your work is awful.

Mano   You wish.

Esteban   Do you want me to lie to you?

Mano   No, but is there anything on the scale between "amazing" and "awful" for you?

Esteban   I can't help it if I'm passionate, I mean gay, I mean passionate. If you want some sort of mediocre measured response you should go to a museum, go to LACMA, it's a mausoleum, the Forest Lawn of paintings. Oh wait . . . (*He checks his phone but keeps talking.*) I hear people wear black veils strolling through their galleries. Are you supposed to climb all those light poles to get in, or do you just go around the back and risk falling into a tar pit?[1] (*Turns off his phone.*) I take it back. They own one of my paintings. I love LACMA! I meant MOCA, the IKEA of art, one large coffee table.

Mano   They own one of your collages.

Esteban   I take it back about MOCA, they have a nice café. So, what did you come here for, to point out my inconsistencies? My parents are still alive, I got that covered.

Mano *smiles for a moment.*

---

1   In front of LACMA, the Los Angeles County Museum of Art, there stands the distinctive Chris Burden sculpture "Urban Light"—a forest of lampposts. The art museum is surrounded by the La Brea Tar Pits, an Ice Age excavation site. Forest Lawn is a famous cemetery in Los Angeles. MOCA: Museum of Contemporary Art.

Mano   Good or bad, you're home for me.

Esteban   This hasn't been home for a long time. Do you even know how to do this kind of art anymore, you know, like, paint without the numbers? Oh, that was mean, I'm sorry, I meant dollar signs, paint without a dollar sign.

Mano   Yup, you're family.

Esteban   That's why your work is awful. You're too sentimental.

Mano *laughs. It's obvious he is the only person who isn't offended by* **Esteban***.*

Esteban   You would hate it here now. Everyone is young and they wear crop tops, even the women. They smile while they make their art. Why do they do that? They complain about DoorDash while making silkscreens about privilege. They say I trigger and traumatize them. How is that possible? That's ageist, right? I painted an orange the other day and someone said they couldn't process it. The orange, I mean. Anything urgent and upsetting is filtered through so many sensibilities. They want me to give my paintings pronouns. They have a list of subjects we shouldn't paint. They put me on it. I hate people.

Mano   You seem angry.

Esteban   Slightly.

Mano   Maybe you need to get laid.

Esteban   Is that an offer?

Mano   If it made you nicer.

Esteban   Buy me lunch instead. According to everyone we graduated art school with you are the one that "made" it and I did not.

Mano   Who said that?

Esteban   I do. Every day inside of my head.

Mano   You haven't even hugged me yet.

Esteban   I can't, you're an elitist pig now.

Mano   Just a pig.

Esteban   Don't touch me, I don't like people hugging me, it's meaningless. Venmo me money instead.

Mano *hugs* **Esteban**. *Surprisingly, it is sincere and heartfelt.* **Esteban** *gives in and rests his head on* **Mano***'s shoulder*

Mano   You monologue well.

Esteban   I thought we were having a dialogue. Just one last small thought . . . What is going on with this generation? Seriously. I am worried for them, and I worry about nothing. Where's the struggle? They all have galleries; a million Instagram followers. You get a Blue Ribbon just for just showing up to your opening. No one's un-talented anymore.

Mano I am sure there is someone.

Esteban Are we too old for this?

Mano I hope not. Aren't we supposed to get better with time?

Esteban Why are you here?

Mano I wanted to connect.

Esteban Liar.

Mano You're my friend.

Esteban I tolerate you. Alright, you're my friend, but I think you're smug.

Mano I am not as successful as you make me out to be.

Esteban How much do you sell your work for?

Mano I'm not going to answer that question. I know you. You'll put me in this narrow little box based on money.

Esteban Capitalist.

Mano It's not just about money.

Esteban Socialist.

Mano I believe in sharing my art.

Esteban Marxist.

Mano But I need to live too.

Esteban Back to capitalist.

Mano Seriously?

Esteban Oh my God, is Espy painting?

Mano She's not.

Esteban Thank God. I can see how she'd destroy our careers. She's better than both of us.

Mano It doesn't have to be about competition.

Esteban Ha! Two artists in one loft. If she took up painting again, your marriage would turn into Big Brother.

Mano What if she left me?

Esteban Oh . . . Is that what's going on?

Mano I can't help but feel that if the opportunity came, she would take it.

Esteban Is she having an affair?

Mano   No, but if she did, it would destroy me.

Esteban   Don't be ridiculous. This happens to me all the time. By the time my brushes have dried, I've forgotten I was in love.

Mano   She knows me better than myself. She's built my whole career. What would I do without her?

Esteban   What are you talking about, weirdo? Painting isn't a group sport! Career might be, but neither of us know anything about that. This confirms my suspicion about your mediocrity. Oh, and my work is going quite well.

Mano   I was going to ask but I didn't want to interrupt your performance.

Esteban   The Muppet people finally dropped their lawsuit. You can't threaten anybody anymore.

He stares at **Mano** *intently.*

Esteban   You are so lucky.

Mano *is surprised by the sincerity of the statement.*

Mano   I know.

Esteban   I mean it. Nobody cares about my work, which is, strangely, liberating. Failure, or whatever you call it, disinterest, gives me permission to follow my own Skittles Rainbow. I have no desire to please anyone with my art anymore.

Mano   Your work stands for itself.

Esteban   Don't do that, you're the only honest person I know.

Mano   I am being honest.

Esteban   Don't turn into Sally Field. I always push everyone away. I make art that upsets because I'm always upset. I'm not interested in the art market anymore. I like it when I get a bad review. It only proves that anyone can pick up an iPad and write a review. You don't even have to think, AI can write it for you. I feel good.

Mano   That's because you make money too.

Esteban   Maybe a little.

Mano   You're a handful.

Esteban *smiles*

Esteban   She's the right one for you, Mano.

Mano   Who else is going to love me like her?

Esteban   Me.

They laugh. **Mano** *leaves.* **Esteban** *watches him go.*

California Cottages

The beach house in Port Hueneme. **Raul**, *in boxing drag, punching paddles that* **Mano** *holds up.*

Raul It's a gentle variation on Muay Thai. You practice self-defense while building a social network for peace.

Mano It just looks like boxing.

Raul Thinking just looks like thinking too, but it's hard.

He throws a big punch.

I'm thinking of peace.

Mano That's comforting.

Raul Do you know anything about houses?

Mano Like the one you just bought.

Raul The floorboard needs to be replaced, but it's not actually floor. The whole point of buying "ready to move in" meant I would never have to know about stuff like this. What do you think of the house?

Mano It looks like New England.

Raul New California. New England, but in beige.

Mano What were you thinking?

Raul I wasn't. I bought it sight unseen.

Mano Are you insane?

Raul It was the last one on the market.

Mano Nothing is ever the last one on the market. Just toilet paper. You're not rich.

Raul Comfortable.

Mano You comfortably fell for the upsell.

Raul It's Maribel, she makes me impulsive.

He violently punches on the paddleboards.

I have no control when it comes to her. I buy her a hundred dollars' worth of See's Candy, or three cats. I want her to be happy. Like you two. It's not her issue, its mine.

Mano How could she not be happy?

Raul *punches madly. He exhausts himself.*

Mano Feel better?

Raul Anxious. Everybody wants this, right? To live at the ocean and eat Panda Express. I'm giving her the American Dream.

Mano　But what do you want?

Raul　Whatever she wants.

Mano　That's not true.

Raul　I'm going to ask her to marry me.

Mano　Oh . . . Boy . . . Okay.

Raul *pulls a ring box out of his pocket.*

Raul　I'm embarrassed to tell you I've been carrying this for three years.

Mano　Three years?

Raul　What's three years when you've been together for ten? I've been waiting for the right moment, but it never comes.

Mano　Three years?

Raul　My terror of being rejected has literally made me unable to pull the box out of my pocket.

Mano　Are you kidding?

Raul　I know what it sounds like. I gave this speech to the dog, and he pretty much responded in the same way. We are not young. We can't keep standing in line at Michelin-starred restaurants in the Art's District for a little piece of uni. That belongs to loft-living hipsters. That's for the kids. Let's face it, the only people who live in lofts are self-involved egoists who don't have anything else to fill their lives with.

Mano　Espy and I live in a loft . . .

Raul (*pretending he didn't hear that*)　I love her. This box is uncomfortable, but that's love for you. Love is pain too. I wanted to ask you a favor.

Mano　Yes.

Raul　You don't even know what the favor is.

Mano　A portrait.

Raul　I was thinking a nude.

Mano　No.

Raul　Okay, faces are good too.

Mano　It will be your wedding gift.

Raul　Oh wow, thanks, man. Come over in a couple of weeks and we can surprise Maribel. If I tell her, she'll end up dressing like Queen Elizabeth, I want to keep it real.

He starts his boxing ritual again as **Mano** *leaves.*

Manuel's El Tepeyac

The loft. **Mano** *and* **Espy** *sharing a monstrosity of a burrito served in a cardboard box.*

Espy   Why do we always get this?

Mano   Tradition.

Espy   Tradition is going to give us cardiac arrest.

Mano   Do it for the next generation.

Espy   The next generation is waiting for us to die so they can buy this loft.

They eat.

Mano   Maribel is crazy.

Espy   I know.

Mano   Her fiancé is crazier.

Espy   Wait a minute, fiancé?

Mano   He's going to ask for her hand, I would have made it her head.

Espy   They deserve each other, but Port Hueneme deserves better . . .

They dig into the burrito.

She told me some disturbing news.

Mano   I know, they're getting married.

Espy   More disturbing.

Mano   What could be more disturbing than that?

Espy   You'd be surprised.

Mano   Like what?

Espy   Like, before you, I was married.

Mano   Excuse me?

Espy   I'm sorry I didn't tell you.

Mano   Um. Me too. That's . . . big. When did we start withholding information?

Espy   I'm sorry, It's a complicated story.

Mano   Enough to withhold information?

Espy   I didn't want this whole thing to be my claim to fame.

Mano   Why would it be?

Espy   He died.

Mano   Oh. I'm sorry.

Espy   Six months after we got married, he went down to Ensenada on a fishing trip, something he always used to do, and his boat capsized.

Mano   Whoa.

Espy   They eventually found the boat, but not his body.

Mano   Oh man, I'm so sorry. I didn't expect you to say that.

Espy   It was devastating, to say the least. It tore everyone apart. We were a small but close circle. We tried everything to find him. We hired divers, sonar equipment, even a psychic.

Mano   Psychic.

Espy   I was desperate. We finally closed a chapter by having a funeral down at the beach in Baja where he was last seen. Maribel was the one who introduced us.

Mano   Six months after you got married. Wow.

Espy   I didn't want to be the bride with the drowned husband. (*She stops.*) You're not making a painting of this. I just saw your face light up.

He smiles, eats.

Maribel says they found him.

Mano   Found him? His body?

Espy   He's alive.

Mano *stops eating.*

Mano   I don't get it.

Espy   He's resurrected.

Mano   Are you kidding?

Espy   I wish. Someone he knew from his prior life was on vacation in Puerto Vallarta and saw him working, as a fisherman, on one of the little islands. He recognized him immediately.

Mano   This makes no sense.

Espy   I know. He tried to run, but they called the police, they investigated, and he confessed.

Mano   Risen from the dead.

They look at each other. So much to say, they think in silence and eat.

Espy   All I could think of was Olivia Newton-John.

Mano   Connect the dots, please.

Espy   She had a boyfriend, this Korean-American guy, very good looking, must have been a model. Always on her arm in the press. Then one day, he's down in Baja, on a rented sailboat and he falls overboard and vanishes.

Mano   What is this, an epidemic?

Espy   I read about it in the *LA Times*. I couldn't believe it. She hired private investigators, probably a psychic too, for all I know, but his body never turned up. I wrote her a letter. Sent it to her agent. I told her my story. I sent newspaper clippings. She must have thought I was insane, but . . . she wrote me back.

Mano   You need to let me paint this.

Espy   Stop. She wrote back. Then the case broke. A group of private investigators tracked down her boyfriend in Puerto Vallarta!

Mano   This isn't a mythical and magical Puerto Vallarta, right? I mean, this is the Puerto Vallarta with a Señor Frogs.

Espy   There's only one.

Mano   They found him.

Espy   They traced a bunch of IP addresses to a computer in Puerto Vallarta that was tracking what was going on with his case. He couldn't help checking in on himself. The ego! That tipped them off. They went down there and found him. I have a whole scrapbook filled with articles about Cuauhtémoc and the Olivia Newton-John case.

Mano   Cuauhtémoc is your husband.

Espy   Was. Cuauhtémoc Chang. He is . . . was . . . from the Bay Area.

Mano   San Francisco?

Espy   Fremont.

Mano   That's not San Francisco. Can I see the scrapbook?

Espy   No.

Mano   No? Why not?

Espy   Mano, I can't . . . I haven't even seen it since I put it together. It's just very painful. It's like looking at an early sketch of a painting. I'm embarrassed.

Mano   Do you want to see him?

Espy   Honestly, I have a million questions. But I don't need to see him. Maybe he was in a storm. Hit his head and lost his memory. Many things could have happened.

Mano   Maybe he staged his death.

Espy   Why would you say that?

Mano   Hundreds of people go missing every day. They fake their death. They run from taxes, abuse, Maribel. Lots of reasons to leave. What do you think he wants?

Espy   I don't know.

Mano   You?

Espy No.

Mano Did you love him?

Espy I was married to him.

An unsettling between them. They eat.

Mano He's going to come looking for you.

Espy He won't.

Mano Of course he is. That's what I would do.

Espy You would?

Mano I would prefer if you didn't see him.

Espy Don't worry.

Mano You know I will.

Espy If I wanted to see him, it would be for closure. And . . . it would be my choice. Maybe I'm the one who needs it.

Mano *gets up and walks away.*

Bromance

Esteban's *studio in the Brewery.* **Mano** *and* **Esteban** *share a bag of churros.*

Esteban God, say something, I hate this kind silence.

Mano You mean intimacy?

Esteban Whatever, it's awful. Thanks for the churros.

Mano You're welcome.

Esteban I never buy anything off the street. Which is weird because it's how I was raised. In the Philippines, everything you could want is on the street. In Davao City, in Mindanao, where my family is from, everyone eats the Bangus Fry, my favorite fish. Right there, on the street. Every year, we would climb a little of Mount Apo, my whole family, a big sacred mountain, and we would all be terrified that it would erupt, although it never has. We're very superstitious, us Filipinos. I wore hot shorts, of course. I was very hot. In case you couldn't tell. I don't know why I am telling you this. It was the happiest time of my life.

Mano How did I not know any of this?

Esteban There's lot of things you don't know about me.

Mano That's true. I don't know why, but I trust you completely. You know everything about me. I never hide anything from you. All the drugs, sex, and bad art we made up there at art school. Thank God it was just far enough away. You could experiment all you want, and no one would ever know. Except Magic Mountain employees.[2]

Esteban   Want to experiment some more?

Mano   I've done enough, but thanks for the offer.

Esteban   Then give me another churro.

Mano   Espy was married before me.

Esteban   What? I didn't know that. She never told you.

Mano   No. Six months into her first marriage, her husband's boat capsized.

Esteban   Interesting.

Mano   Everyone thought he was dead, but they just found him in Puerto Vallarta.

Esteban   He washed ashore.

Mano   He walked ashore.

Esteban   He's alive?

Mano   Yes.

Esteban   It's Olivia Newton-John all over.

Mano   Of course, you would know that.

Esteban   Are you worried?

Mano   I don't know what I am right now. I see that she is going through something. Is he the thing that she's been going through? Was she waiting for him all this time? He sounds insane. A musician performance artist.

Esteban   One of us.

Mano   I don't know what she had before. Maybe it was better than me.

Esteban   You're ridiculous. You're both so right for each other. And the reason you might have some apprehension is because you really love her. You see inside of her. Probably because you paint her so much. That's a gift of the artist. Ugh, hold on, the heart-warming quality of this conversation is making me throw up just a little bit. Has she seen him since he resurrected?

Mano   She said no.

Esteban   Well, then, you have nothing to worry about.

Mano   If it made her happy, could I let her go?

Esteban   Aren't you being a bit premature?

---

2   The noted California Institute for the Arts (CalArts) is located in suburban Santa Clarita, not far from the Six Flags Magic Mountain theme park.

Mano I don't know what to think. Change is so hard.

Esteban *looks at* **Mano** *intently, reaching over and holding his hand.*

Esteban Listen to me. I know very few things. Especially about why we are artists. But this is my territory. Remember when you first started selling your work after we graduated? You used to make those amazing, saturated posters of street vendors in all those wild colors. They looked like Mexican wrestlers. Your Superhero *Paletero* series.[3] Everyone loved them and you could have turned that into a cottage industry and stayed there forever. But you knew when to stop. And then you moved into your Chicano Aztec symbols in black and white. A necessary phase, of course. And you moved on from that too. After that, you were in your hardcore activist art period, and then your graffiti moment, and then your private murals in people's houses. Can you believe that people let you paint an entire wall in their house? And then, you finally started getting formal with your work. Not for any reason other than you were becoming a good artist. You, my friend, and imaginary lover, have changed so much. It's what you do best. Every moment in your development is a challenge you have met. And you're the better for it. But somehow, you can't do it in your marriage. Or you can't seem to let her do it. She's got to be able to do that too. Or else, what you have is a lie.

Mano I wouldn't be able to let her go.

Esteban I'm sorry, I'm not going to lie to you, especially when it comes to matters of the heart. Change, it's the only thing, otherwise we're not artists. Let her be what she wants and see if you can be that together. Let her lead. Jesus, let her be the painter. It will work itself out. It always does. Otherwise, get out of the way.

Mano *thinks.*

Mano You want another churro?

Esteban No.

He leans in and kisses **Mano** *on the lips.* **Mano**, *perhaps charmed, lets him. He doesn't return it so much as just accepts it. They pull back and smile at each other.*

Mano Did you enjoy that?

Esteban This is so boring. Get out of my face. I hate you. Really, I do. Oh, and lend me a hundred dollars.

Mano *walks away.*

Death Do Us Part

The loft. A familiar pose. **Mano** *paints,* **Espy** *with fig.*

Espy I am going to see him.

---

3 *Paleteros*: vendors who sell popsicles (lollies) from their carts along Los Angeles streets.

Mano I thought so. Did he ask, or did you?

Espy He did.

Mano The dead always return with such demands. They destroy us just by showing up.

Espy You are my husband.

Mano Currently.

Espy You have nothing to worry about.

Mano Why do you need to reassure me?

Espy Because I am your current wife.

Mano Maybe he's returned to remind you who you were.

Espy That would be a surprise. He was more self-involved than I care to admit. I doubt he really knew me.

Mano Can I be there?

Espy No. Is that okay?

Mano Does it matter?

Espy Yes.

Mano Okay, yes, it matters to me.

Quiet, tense, painting.

Espy I'm sorry you are feeling this way. I don't want it to affect you. Especially your art.

Mano What about your art?

Espy What about it?

Mano I'm not your art.

Espy Did you ever think you could be?

Mano No.

Espy That's the difference between us. Listen, he never died. This isn't some miracle. He's a fucked-up person. He cheated life. On purpose. That is who has returned.

Mano We all die in some way. Try holding up that chirimoya.

Espy Are you serious? Instead of the fig?

Mano Follow your impulse. That's what I am going to start to do. Hopefully, it includes you.

She switches out the fruit. Poses for a moment, but then gets up and walks out. He looks away.

Resurrection

Espy *and* **Maribel** *stand at the big window of the loft looking out at the city, their backs to us.* **Espy** *is gently patting* **Maribel***'s back while she finishes a good cry.*

Maribel   Raul bought the house. I hope it, and all of Hueneme, get swept away at high tide. I'll never get back to LA. I'll never get back to Philippe's or Yang Chow or Bottega Louie or Eggslut or Baco Mercat or the Urth Café. I don't want to spend a quiet evening at The Red Robin in a stupid strip mall with a Joanne's Fabrics. What am I going to do, make doilies for my tabletops?

Espy   You can visit anytime.

Maribel   I don't want to visit. I want to live! I have a Ventura County library card. Next up, gift certificates to the Olive Garden.

She takes a deep breath and remembers why she is there.

Where did Mano go?

Espy   He's out with his mistress, Esteban.

Maribel   You're not worried?

Espy   I would love it. They should be married. They can work out their aggression on each other.

Maribel *looks out the window again. She stares down for a moment.*

Maribel   He's been waiting downstairs for over an hour.

Espy   Good.

Maribel   Oh look, how cute, he's bought *chicharrones* and is feeding the pigeons.

Espy   Stop, you're nearly married.

Maribel*'s raises her ring finger.*

Maribel   He proposed at the El Torito in Oxnard. He had them roll the ring into an enchilada. I nearly broke my tooth, which is, of course, when he got down on his knees and made me spit it out so he could put it on my finger. He's not sophisticated, but at least there were refills. I will punish him before I marry him.

Espy *takes a big breath.*

Espy   Let's get this over with.

Maribel   For sure?

Espy   What am I going to do, keep him waiting forever?

Maribel He kind of did.

Espy True.

Maribel Are you mad I brought him?

Espy Yes. He hasn't entered and he's already destroying our lives.

Maribel Sorry. He insisted. And you know how intense he can be. He hasn't changed. He's still good looking. I know, I know. It doesn't forgive staging your own death and all that. Okay, I am going down. Don't let him off easy. If he offers a monetary settlement, take it. If he asks for his ring back, tell him you pawned it.

Espy I did.

Maribel You really did?

Espy Of course.

Maribel Wow, okay, let him have it.

She leaves. **Espy** *paces and looks down from the loft window. She goes over and resists looking into a mirror. She goes to the window and looks out at the city.* **Cuauhtémoc** *enters the loft. He is a handsome Chinese American man dressed in a vintage wedding tuxedo. It might be velvet, it's not black. He is not wearing socks. He's a surfer. He also wears a shell necklace.* **Espy** *knows he is there, but she can't quite turn around. He looks around the loft and waits.*

Cuauhtémoc Espy. ¿Cómo estás?

She looks out the window.

Espy Are you kidding? You speak Spanish now?

Cuauhtémoc *Pues . . . Estaba en México, qué voy a hablar?*

Espy Oh, please, Cuauhtémoc, this is ridiculous.

Cuauhtémoc *Yo no me siento ridículo. Aquí estoy, Esperanza, ¿no me quieres ver?* I can wait.

The sound of his voice, it's too much

Pues, this is more awkward than I thought it was going to be.

Espy You thought it was going to be easy?

Cuauhtémoc *En realidad, no lo pensé . . .*

Espy What did you expect?

Cuauhtémoc Us. I was hoping more than expecting, that maybe, in some strange way, you might be happy to see me.

Espy How stupid do you think I am?

Cuauhtémoc I don't. At all. There just . . . isn't a way for how this is supposed to go. Reincarnation is not a regular thing. For the reincarnated as well. It's . . . awkward.

Espy You didn't die. You ran out on me. On us. All of us. Do you realize how horrible it was?

Cuauhtémoc I do, but I can't do anything about that. I wouldn't have been able to come here if I thought I could explain it in a way that made sense. *Es lo que es.* Maybe I can make it up in some way. Are you going to look at me?

Espy I am sure at some point I will. Just not now.

Cuauhtémoc Okay . . . It's probably better this way. I lost my public-speaking skills in hiding. I don't want this to sound like some self-absorbed thing. I also don't want to kill myself over it. I mean, really kill myself. God, let me just say it and not judge it. I have a speech, but it's not rehearsed. It's more . . . considered. Are you listening?

Espy I'm waiting.

She cannot see that **Cuauhtémoc** *assumes a bit of a pose, and then suddenly begins to sing, a capella, the classic Mexican song "Júrame."*

Cuauhtémoc *Júrame! Que aunque pase mucho tiempo . . .*

Espy CUAUHTÉMOC!!

Cuauhtémoc I'm a musician, Espy. You know that. It's the way I communicate.

Espy No, it's not.

Cuauhtémoc Okay, I get your anger. *Te oigo, Espy.*

Espy Just. Talk. And in English, please.

Cuauhtémoc *Simon.* Well, first, I guess I should say that I didn't see God. I didn't reach enlightenment on this journey of self-discovery, I mean. This wasn't some *Sheltering Sky* kind of thing. I am much simpler than that, I guess.

He sits.

I left because . . . The truth is . . . I was already dead. Most of my life I have lived as a dead person.

Espy Even while you were married to me.

Cuauhtémoc Yes. I'm sorry. All my life I have hated who I am and dreaded being in this world as me. When I was fourteen, I would complain endlessly about how much I hated myself. Cute, a phase. But imagine when you're an adult and you still hate yourself. I didn't know what to do with that. I went my entire life unable to change. Maybe it was chemical, but I tried everything, and only you made me smile. You were the only one who seemed to be able to make me forget it. That's a lot to put on someone, but you did. And even then . . .

Espy My gift . . .

Cuauhtémoc If I could turn back some big giant clock with a forgiving hour hand that could rewind itself to a happier time, believe me, I would have chosen that. That hasn't been my life. It's sad when one fake dies. You think it's going to take away all your pain. Instead, it ramps up all the stomach-churning pit of awfulness that sits in your intestines. All the time. The revelation? I didn't die because I was already dead. If that makes any sense. I know it's not the most amazing revelation, but it's something.

Espy That's your explanation?

Cuauhtémoc It is. To be honest, I was relieved to be found. The minute I heard a voice shouting at me, a weight lifted from my chest. I knew what was going to happen, and I kind of knew I would end up right here, like I am now. He punched me and broke a tooth.

He opens his mouth to show her.

I deserved it. Nothing anyone could say was going to be worse than the punishment I was feeding myself on the daily in purgatory. Well, purgatory with a nice sea breeze. I didn't want to lie anymore. I owed the IRS a lot of money, but that wasn't the root of my problems. The fact that I couldn't be alone, that I couldn't be real, that I was never ever real, was a death I was already living. I am sure I'm not the only one who has ever felt this way. And I am not saying it to minimize my responsibility. Running away. Faking our own lives and deaths just to see if we can breathe on our own.

Espy You hurt us. Me. Your family.

Cuauhtémoc I know. They don't ever want to see me again. They have accepted my fake death as a real death. That's pretty fucked-up. Not a single friend will see me. Well, Maribel. But you know . . . I lost everything. Myself. You. The truth is . . . I might as well be dead "dead."

She turns to face him.

Espy You killed me too.

Cuauhtémoc Oh my God, don't be dead, Espy. It sucks.

Espy What happened to your hair?

Cuauhtémoc *Qué?*

Espy You're not blond anymore.

Cuauhtémoc And you're not a flaming redhead.

Espy You've aged.

Cuauhtémoc No shade on those islands. I slept on the beach. It affects the skin.

Espy You don't look like the lead singer of Pill Party Pill anymore.

Cuauhtémoc It's called *Pastilla de Fiesta* now.

Espy Why are you dressed that way?

Cuauhtémoc It's my wedding tux. What else would I wear to see you?

Espy Are you kidding me?

Cuauhtémoc   I came with the best wish I could bring.

Espy   For whom?

Cuauhtémoc   Both of us.

Espy   Are you insane?

Cuauhtémoc   Hold on, hold on, let's not get lost in the details here. It's just a tuxedo. A pair of pants and a matching jacket. The most important thing is, I am not dead. I am back. And I still have our marriage certificate.

Espy *can't help her exasperation.*

Espy   No! You fucking idiot. I'm married, Cuauhtémoc. A lot happened after you died. Like real life. Things went on.

Cuauhtémoc   Are you happy?

Espy   Did you hear what I just said?

Cuauhtémoc   I must make this plea because it's the only one I got.

Espy   You're ridiculous.

Cuauhtémoc   I am ridiculous, thank you! I'm an artist. I'm a singer. I'm a beach bum. I'm a free spirit. *Soy un chino mexicano.* Who else would rise from the dead and ask for their marriage back? But, Espy, this is what you have always loved in an artist. The unpredictable, the danger, the ride. This is who you are too.

Espy   I've changed. Please go, you're delusional.

Cuauhtémoc   I made a vow. Until death do us part. Real death. I can't go. And you can't bear to see me go. Just standing here, the electricity between us. It's absurd, and, tantric! I am hard as a rock.

Espy   Oh my God. GET OUT!

Cuauhtémoc *pulls off his jacket and kicks off his shoes.*

Espy   What are you doing?

Cuauhtémoc   I can see that you need me.

He begins to disrobe, piece by piece.

Espy   You can't do that here. I will have you arrested.

Cuauhtémoc   I am reconciling with my wife.

Espy   Your ex-wife.

Cuauhtémoc   That's not my problem. I have the certificate and I stake my claim.

Espy   You can't do this. You can't come in here and destroy my life.

Cuauhtémoc   Ignite. Not destroy. What life? I am about to give it back.

Espy Please. Don't do this. Let's go down to the plaza. We can get some air and talk like two civilized human beings.

Cuauhtémoc *doesn't take his eyes off her as the clothing continues to come off. Finally, he stands before her, his most naked self.*

Cuauhtémoc Sorry for my hard-on. Well, sorry not sorry.

Espy There is no place for you here anymore!

Cuauhtémoc *goes to the chaise where* **Espy** *poses, and he lays on it, ignoring what she has said. He extends a hand to her, a frozen pose.*

Cuauhtémoc I can see by your hands, you stopped painting.

Espy *hides them behind her back.*

Cuauhtémoc Don't be ashamed. I will bring them back. You haven't painted since I left. Paint me.

Espy No.

Cuauhtémoc Yes. Paint me and let me give you your passion back. I have a purpose now. A reason to live. I give myself to you. And then we'll make love.

Espy No.

Cuauhtémoc *Sí. Aquí. Ahora.*

Espy *walks to the window shaking her head. She looks out at the city. A naked* **Cuauhtémoc** *waits.*

Oxymoroxnard

Mano *and* **Raul** *sit at a table at La Gloria Market in Oxnard.*

Raul She accepted my proposal.

Mano Congratulations, buddy.

They shake, possibly hug.

Raul With stipulations . . .

Mano I figured. Leniency for time served.

Raul Do you believe in a shared email address?

Mano How much do you love her?

Raul Shared email it is.

Mano Fight for golf time.

Raul She's asking for curfew on boys' night.

Mano Real love. So, when am I doing this portrait?

Raul How long will it take?

Mano   I'm not like those guys at the beach, if that's what you were thinking?

Raul   Mind reader.

Mano   How about two weeks?

Raul   Fine. I'm waiting for her to get a glow.

Mano   Glow?

Raul   You know, some happiness about all this. I've spent a ton to make her happy. She's a tough nut to crack. I bought her a house, moved her to the beach. Maybe I should buy her a car! A Fiat, those little compressed ones from Europe. A car is so American Dream, especially a little European one. It should be black and red. A convertible to go with her hair. I am such a fool, a car, of course. You know what this means?

Mano   No, what?

Raul   I would do anything for her.

Suddenly he feels vulnerable, exposed.

Do you think I made the right choice?

Mano   A car?

Raul   Marriage.

Mano   Do you love her?

Raul   I do. But I'm scared. I'm old. But I am very immature.

Mano   Oof, that's the most honest thing you've ever said to me.

Raul   Really? I try not to be too deep.

Mano   I know. I read somewhere that you take your relationship and cut it in half, and that is how long you have either been breaking up or growing in love.

Raul   Whoa. That's so deep I don't understand it. I finally did something right.

He starts crying. **Mano***, annoyed, looks away. He bawls,* **Mano** *has no choice but to go over and hug him.*

La Plaza de los Mariachis

Espy *and* **Mano** *sitting on a bench in a big empty plaza. A Mariachi conjunto can be heard playing "Cielito Lindo." They bite churros.*

Espy   That's original. I bet the musicians are miserable. They can play this with their eyes closed. Each note a dagger to their hearts.

Mano   I like hearing it. It's the "take me out to the ballgame" song of Mariachis everywhere. I'm not sure I noticed how beautiful it was until now.

He leans over and kisses her passionately.

Espy   What is that for?

Mano   A warning.

Espy   For what?

Mano   You know what.

Espy   No I don't.

Mano   You don't think I noticed.

Espy   Stop.

Mano   It's a new blouse, right?

She looks down. Terror without showing it.

Espy   And?

Mano   And it's yellow. A color I have never seen you wear.

Espy   I'm sure I have worn yellow.

Mano   The color that Tony Orlando tied around the old oak tree.[4] The color of those marshmallow peeps. But that's not why you're wearing it. You despise yellow.

Espy   No, I don't. Stop trying to make me self-conscious.

Mano   You already are. I remember I made a painting for you in yellow. You told me you would leave me if I ever did that again. And now you're wearing it.

Espy *feigns a laugh.*

Mano   But I like it.

Espy   You do?

Mano   Yes. You're changing. Your smile is making a comeback. I don't think I have anything to do with it, but I am happy to see you this way.

Espy *ignores it.*

Mano   You also wore your bright red Doc Martens last week. You haven't worn those in years.

Espy   Sure, I have.

Mano   No, you haven't. You're flirting.

Espy   You're dreaming.

Mano   The painting upstairs. It's waiting. It's my seventh of you. Seven, can you believe it? It's time to move on. You're different in each one. Something exposed,

---

4   "Tie a Yellow Ribbon Round the Ole Oak Tree" is a hugely popular 1973 pop song by L. Russell Brown and Irwin Levine, about signaling to a lover who has been in prison whether he is still welcome.

something being told. We almost have a complete story about us. It's also evidence. And I don't like that. But it is what it is.

Espy   It must have been the one with the Spanish artichoke. You've conquered texture. Congratulations.

Mano   Am I going to sound pathetic if I ask you again not to leave me again?

Espy   I never will. But why would you do that?

Mano   Tell you what I am feeling?

Espy   Ruin such a beautiful Sunday, in the middle of a plaza, with mariachis playing the most overplayed song ever.

Mano   He's back. The dead is fully in force. The clothes, the smile, the new outlook . . . But you haven't fucked him.

Espy   Stop!

Mano   He's stopped swimming, and now that he's back on dry land, he wants what he remembers. He's not smart enough to start completely over. He needs his past.

Espy   Clearly, I married an artist with great imagination.

Mano   Which one?

Espy   My God, please stop, I can't keep having these kind of conversations.

She throws the remaining churros to imaginary birds in the distance.

Just keep dreaming, my darling, it's what makes you money.

Mano   It's not what makes me money, it's what makes me happy. Don't worry. I love it. The new Kate Spade purse, so orange . . . I don't want any of this to stop. I will imagine it's for me.

Espy   Yes, enjoy it.

Mano   The only thing I can't stomach is the lying.

Espy   How have I lied?

Mano   Your hands.

Espy   What about them?

Mano   You're painting again.

Espy   And if I was.

Mano   If you were.

Espy   Do I need your permission?

Mano   Not at all. Make yourself happy. I just don't know that both of us can do it together. I can't wait to see what you dream up. Just don't settle for dull colors.

He gets up and walks away as **Espy** *watches him go.*

The Dead

The Beach House in Port Hueneme. **Espy** *and* **Cuauhtémoc** *stand apart.*

Espy   I love him.

Cuauhtémoc   I know. It makes me sad. It makes me jealous. It makes me a soap opera.

Espy   If you know, then you should step aside.

Cuauhtémoc   I can't. Someone always gets hurt in these things. But it's human nature. I love you. Otherwise, I wouldn't risk it.

Espy   Just grow up, Cuauhtémoc.

Cuauhtémoc   We both need to. You can't hold his poses forever.

Espy   That was mean. I don't just pose for him. I am a partner in his journey. Of being an artist. I help guide him. I am his gallery and his curator.

Cuauhtémoc   You're a transaction. I'm sorry, that was . . . mean. I can't help being cruel. I'm jealous of him. It's not his fault.

Espy   It's not.

Cuauhtémoc   We believe in two things that are always at battle with one another, the Buddhist concept of reincarnation, and the Chinese belief in the idea of a family line. It's why I am in it to win it. I've been reborn, reincarnated . . . as myself.

Espy   From a fake death, that makes no sense. There is nothing fake about him. He has this ability to see . . . This gift. To translate. But he's insecure, like you. He imagines the most amazing part of someone and gives it back in a painting.

Cuauhtémoc   Maybe we should be a throuple? I would hate sharing you, but I would accept it. I know, I know, sorry. Do you want to go back to him?

Espy   I haven't left. But the damage is done.

Cuauhtémoc   Then you want to be with me.

Espy   No, not at all.

Cuauhtémoc   No?

Espy   I need to help him finish his painting.

There is a knock at the door.

Real Estate

Raul *and* **Maribel** *in a booth at a Carrows Restaurant in Ventura. The sound of a seagull.*

Raul   You didn't go to the house? I had a surprise for you.

Maribel   I hate surprises.

Raul   I know, that's why I did it.

Maribel   Then I'm glad I wasn't there.

Raul   Where were you?

Maribel   I took a long walk down Victoria, alongside a bunch of plump Marines.

Raul   Plump Marines?

Maribel   Don't worry they're harmless, like seagulls. I was thinking about all the horrible things in the world right now, and a stupid house didn't rank high on that list. I'm sorry. I have been horrible to you and all you want is to make me happy. You know what? It's okay. It's not Malibu, but let's face it, we would never be able to afford Malibu. I would have to marry someone else for that, and the truth is, I love you. I love slightly above middle-class you. I also love your beard. I don't need to live in Malibu. I need to live with you. That's what marriage is. I'll make it work. We have two outlet malls. And the Panda Express always has something new on the menu. Port Hueneme tries. Just like you.

Raul   Oh no . . .

Maribel   You want a divorce?

Raul   I haven't even married you. Don't hate me, but I sold the house.

Maribel   You just bought it.

Raul   Someone else wanted it more than we did. He bought it sight unseen, like I did. Let's face it, we belong in downtown LA in some overpriced loft on urine-smelling Spring Street. We must risk our lives daily to walk to Little Tokyo to eat overpriced noodles that we can complain about. Now, we will finally have real things to complain about again.

Maribel   Yes, complain!

Raul   Let's complain about the larger than average rats, the aggressive panhandlers, the lack of fat in meatless burgers, the small amount of *carnitas* in our tacos, and the empty creamers at Starbucks, like we always do. We need to get back to that. But if we're going to complain, let's have something to really complain about, and living in LA is the place to do that. You can't complain here, it's nice, but not us. We are missing a big reason of why we are who we are. Complainers. It's no fun if we're not unhappy. And right now, we're kind of happy. I don't want that.

Maribel   Neither do I.

Raul   But, Maribel, we need to be unhappy together. About the same things.

Maribel   I agree. And we do. We hate the same things.

Raul   I know. You are going to be a great first wife.

Maribel   And you are going to be a great second husband.

Raul What?

Maribel What?

Raul Second husband?

Maribel I never told you.

Raul That you were married.

Maribel A long time ago.

Raul How long ago?

Maribel I don't know, a few years ago . . .

Raul We were already together a few years ago.

Maribel I love you.

Raul Was I the rebound?

Maribel I love you.

Raul Stop saying that.

Maribel You know you love it.

Raul I do, say it again.

Maribel I like you.

Raul Say it!

Maribel I love you.

Raul You're going to be mine.

Maribel No, you're going to be mine.

Raul Don't cut off my balls.

Maribel Don't take away my identity.

Raul Let's do what the ex-mayor did to his ex-wife.

Maribel What did he do?

Raul His name was Antonio Villa, and he took her name, Raigoza, when he married her. Well before he left her and started banging Lu Parker from Channel Five.

Maribel I love LA!

Raul Me too.

They kiss.

Raul Oh crap!

Maribel What?

Raul I hate it when we smoke pot and end up at Carrows eating a whole pie. I forget everything. Mano is at our former house waiting to paint you. It was my surprise, a portrait for our wedding. Just not a nude.

Maribel Ugh, Ven-Tuh-Rahhhhhh . . . It brings out the best in us. And we hate that.

They laugh, forget again, and eat pie.

The Brewery

Espy *enters* **Esteban***'s studio. He side-eyes her as best he can.*

Esteban I don't like you.

Espy I don't care.

Esteban You're a Disney villain.

Espy Grow up.

Esteban You're a snake.

Espy Oh, shut up. You're short.

Esteban You grow up.

Espy I see you haven't changed.

Esteban I've changed enough.

Espy So, you're the other woman.

Esteban Excuse me? You're the other faggot.

Espy Nice. I assume you know everything.

Esteban I know how cruel you've been, Cruella de Vil.

Espy What is this, the 1950s?

Esteban Everything old is new again.

Espy Well, we agree on something.

Esteban We are artists, after all. I know you know your art. I'll give you that much.

Espy Speak.

Esteban He loves you. He adores you. He lives for your every word. He's a puppy dog parading as a human. Complexity eludes him. It's not your fault. It's just who he is. You pulled him from the gutter. Even though you're from the gutter too. So, you pulled each other out of each other's mess. We all need to grow up sometime. I get it. It's just harder for some, more than others. Especially people like us. We're saturated in so much color, we forget how black and white this world is. I've never understood that, but . . . we take risks. We welcome the pain, otherwise we can't paint.

Espy   I don't want to hurt him.

Esteban   Too late.

Espy   It's more complicated than you imagine.

Esteban   I've been in relationships.

Espy   I'm not talking about one-night stands. Listen, I don't want him to be alone. He trusts you. Help me with him.

Esteban   Don't worry about us.

Espy   I don't. Take care of him. I give him to you. Emotionally, of course.

Esteban   I don't want your sloppy seconds.

Espy   Of course, you do. You know, we were all so happy once. The both of you just out of Cal-Arts. My MOCA days. Everything seemed on the cusp of something in LA. It still does. This city will always be so full of possibility. But it's overwhelming too. We must change. Whether we like it or not. You must feel that.

Esteban   I don't hate you, Es-Purrrr-ranzzzza.

Espy   I still don't like you. You're such a queen. You complain too much. It gets in the way of your work. And your color choices, my God, Wham! isn't even a group anymore.

Esteban   Bitch, please. Don't come in here and out-queer me. We should all go out sometime, like we used to.

Espy   No. We should all move on. Including you.

Esteban   Ooh, that's a Barbara Stanwyck line.

Espy   I am surprised you're still in this place. It reminds me of New Wave parties I used to go to in college.

Esteban   Well, listen, I am on a commission deadline, remember those? You can take off from your broom over there.

Espy   Be good to him. Please . . .

Esteban   He'll tell me what he needs.

Espy   I am sorry.

Esteban   Don't steal my art on your way out.

She sighs and goes.

Espy   Such an obnoxious queen.

Esteban   Thank you!

Menage

The Beach House. **Mano** *and* **Cuauhtémoc**, *standing on opposite ends of a room.*

Cuauhtémoc   You should go.

Mano   No, you should go.

Cuauhtémoc   I should go.

Mano   Yeah, you should go.

Cuauhtémoc   Listen, I'm sorry it didn't turn out the way you thought it would.

Mano   How do you know? We're not done.

Cuauhtémoc   We're not going to fight, are we?

Mano   That's up to you.

Cuauhtémoc   Good, I'm not a fighter, I'm a lover.

Mano   Do you make love the same way you fake your deaths?

Cuauhtémoc   Fuck you, dude. I'm being movie nice to you right now, and you're being a dick.

Mano   You don't look anything like I thought you would.

Cuauhtémoc   Neither do you.

Mano   I didn't realize she was into androgyny.

Cuauhtémoc   That was cheap. We're not going to play this, are we?

Mano   No, we're not.

Cuauhtémoc   We haven't done anything.

Mano   You've done too much.

Cuauhtémoc   Listen, man, I'm sorry for the damage. What's happened between us has nothing to do with you.

Mano   Destruction. You're sorry for the destruction. You don't have to explain. I get it. I see it in her face. I know what's up. You should go.

Cuauhtémoc   I should go.

Mano   It's a beautiful day. You should go out for a swim in that dangerous ocean that took you once. You're not afraid of it now, are you?

Cuauhtémoc   Of course not. It didn't kill me. It made me alive.

Mano   I need her, for my last painting.

Cuauhtémoc   Paint away.

Mano I need to finish it. Then I will never paint again. Then you can decide what you want to be to each other. I won't get in the way. You're a lucky fellow.

Cuauhtémoc Thanks, man.

Mano But the last pose belongs to me. I want her. Late in the morning. When the sun is clear about what it wants to be. You can have the night. That's her time. She's most alive then. Where do you live?

Cuauhtémoc Here.

Mano So close to the water . . . You never learn your lessons.

Cuauhtémoc I just bought this house.

Mano YOU bought it?

Cuauhtémoc Maribel convinced me they were selling it for almost nothing.

Mano Perfect.

Cuauhtémoc For us.

Mano Have a good swim. Go far . . .

Cuauhtémoc *looking at* **Mano** *who turns away.*

Patina

Espy *sitting on the edge of the fountain at Gloria Molina Grand Park. She is taping herself into her phone.*

Espy Hello, Olivia. I know you're gone. I'm so sad about it. As fan and confidante. There was just so much I wanted to tell you. You've become my patron saint. Every artist needs one. Look at me, I just called myself an artist again. Life has come calling. I'm doing a self-tape. You must know what these are. I'll look at it later, try and make sense of what I have said. It's cheap therapy. The phone doesn't judge me. Oh, Olivia, I've made a Zsa Zsa Gabor mistake. Not one, but both of my husbands are wrong for me. They don't need wives, they need themselves. But they don't know who they are. Were they ever right for me? I don't think so. Maybe that's not the way to look at this. Was I right for them? Maybe once it seemed so. But I gave up so much to be who they needed me to be. There's no blame, Olivia. I bought into this whole marriage thing, twice. I am freed now. He knows it and so do I. We just don't know what it will look like. The other one should go off and keep looking for himself. He won't of course, he's not an artist. He's a celebrity, he needs to be loved, and someone will see that in him and give up their life to make him happen. Thank God for autotune. I wish him the best. They are both afraid and depressed. Like the rest of the world is right now. It's a cruel and violent place to be these days. Not even a pandemic could remake us. But we survived. Maybe that was as good as we could expect. We survived. I wish you were Olivia Newton-John, you were why we sang along.

Just then, the fountain starts, jets of water fill the space behind her.

Oh. Okay. Thank you, Olivia!

Automatism

Esteban *is waiting in his studio. A rare moment, and figure of calm.* **Mano** *enters, anxious and destroyed.* **Esteban** *holds him for a moment.* **Mano** *pulls away.*

Mano   I knew this moment would come. I knew it for years. When I first met her. It was destined. I could feel it. She's not my art. She's my process. With every painting, I feel myself receiving a gift from her. She gives me everything. Shows me how. I knew nothing. I came into this with some intuition, some history, but I had no sense of the formal. The sharpness of the lines, the nuances. I didn't have words. She gave me everything. She is my brush.

Esteban   You gave her things too.

Mano   I was a canvas to work her ideas.

Esteban   You can make art without her.

Mano   But I don't want to. I want to be hers. Without condition.

He roams.

I remember when she took me to Spain. I fell in love. With her, with everything. It was something that I understood inside of me. Culture. Taste. Danger. But she was the one that had the defining experience. She was the one who understood the sacrifice of art. We went to a bullfighting arena, La Plaza de Toros, and she was terrified. But, still, we stayed. I held her and could feel her shaking. It was packed. A rite, a passage, ritual. The audience screaming, thirsty for blood. But as each stage went on, she eased into the matches. I could feel her slowly in my arms begin to understand the impact of what we were seeing. The primal nature of it. As if she was learning a language. Each bull, each *matador*, like a scumble, her own thirst quenched in understanding, each one better than the last. That's the way she taught me. From our experience in Spain. Before the afternoon was over, she was so moved she couldn't take her eyes off the spectacle. Each *picador*, piercing, drops of blood against the thick black skin of the bull, she would sigh and say, "Yes . . . that color." It was perfect. She understood it, even if I could not. This pain, a ritual giving a thirst for life, even if we lose something of ourselves in the process . . . She said it, "This is who I am. Now I can help you." We left La Plaza, and she was tormented, searching for something that could match that experience. She was still looking. For the right color. Finally, she paid a man in a restaurant to cook us a bull's heart. But first, she made him bring it out, raw and bleeding, so she could see it. We sat staring at it for the longest time. He showed us how to clean it, to take off the outer skin, to pull away the artery, and finally how to slice it, without effort, rich, deep full of color. The blade cut in so expertly, she smiled as she watched him prepare our feast. She loves me, but she loves the work more. And it's killing her. I think I have finished the painting. From memory.

Esteban May I see it?

Mano Yes. It's my best work. I want you to have it.

Esteban Really?

Mano Yes. All seven. They're yours. Don't sell them. Show them. Be a collector. It's the most that I will ever be able to give you of me. You need to be okay with that. I can't give you anything more than that. I love you.

He kisses **Esteban** *on the forehead and leaves.*

Hopelessly Devoted to You

Mano *and* **Espy** *in the loft. Standing apart for just a moment. "Hopelessly Devoted to You" plays in the background. Surprisingly, they smile at each other. Acceptance.* **Mano** *approaches* **Espy** *and kisses her lovingly on the lips and then takes her hand. He walks her to the big picture window in their loft.*

Mano No wonder my paintings were so big. This space is too much. I was trying to match the outsized vision. Although, I love how the light pours through here during the day. It's ours. We must never give it up. Promise me.

Espy I promise.

Mano Oh wow, right now the city looks almost—possible. It's so beautiful. L.A. is so damn naturally gorgeous. Even with its facelifts. But it's too much. You can't contain a thought in this metropolis. Ideas get lost. Too vast. Too big. That's the struggle. What we live for. Why we make the work. To make sense of this city, our lady.

He hugs her.

I found you the perfect color.

Espy You did?

Mano Yes. But now, you need to decide what it is you want to paint.

They turn and face the window. The light in the loft goes to black as the city skyline lights up. The sound of an ocean.

Pacific Rim

The Pacific Ocean at night. The house in Hueneme. **Cuauhtémoc** *sits with his back to us, staring out at the water. He stands and begins to take off his clothes. Again. He places them neatly in a pile. A ritual. When he is fully naked, he turns his head briefly to look at dry land. One last look. He gets good with himself. He goes toward the water. He jumps. The ocean. Waves.*

Painting in Red

Slowly, the lights begin to come back up on the loft, and we, once again, hear the first harp chords of "I Honestly Love You." It is now **Espy** *who sits on a stool in front of a canvas, painting a subject who sits on the chaise lounge. It is* **Mano**, *holding a raw bull's heart in his hand, bloody and stained. Like a Frida Kahlo painting, an IV drip stands guard next to* **Mano**, *holding a pouch full of his blood, attached by a tube to his wrist. The clear tube snakes across the loft, surging in plasma, taped to a palette held by* **Espy** *who dabs at it with her paint brush. The perfect color. They look at each other, and smile.*

EL FIN

FIXED

Boni B. Alvarez

FIXED

Introduction by Barbara Fuchs

Golden Tongues playwrights have often been attracted to tragedies as their source plays, recognizing the power of those predecessors, however problematic. Filipino-American playwright Boni B. Alvarez turns to Calderón's *El médico de su honra* (1637, variously translated as *The Doctor/Surgeon/Physician of His Own Honor*), skillfully dissecting it as he brings it into our own time.

The source features a noble lord erroneously convinced that his wife has betrayed him with a prince. Unable to tolerate even the possibility of his wife's infidelity, whatever her actual guilt, the husband is driven to violence. Despite the ambiguity of the situation, he finds no other means to safeguard his honor than to have his wife discreetly bled to death by a surgeon.

Alvarez's *FIXED* zeroes in on the costs of discretion, absolute certainty, and other supposed virtues, in an alternately moving and comical love story that also updates the preposterous, drastic medical "solution" of the source. First written in 2014, before the wave of repressive legislation targeting transgender people in many US states, the adaptation uncannily anticipates the violence of a politics that reaches into the bedroom.

Set in contemporary Los Angeles, *FIXED* focuses on Miracles Malacañang, a Filipino ladyboy who works in the House of Malacañang massage parlor. (The term "ladyboy," which Alvarez specifies in his list of characters, is used in Filipino slang, and more generally in Southeast Asia, to refer to drag queens or transgender sex workers.) Miracles is in love with Mariano Fernandez, a Chicano man whose brother, Hudson, is running for LA sheriff. No matter how hard he tries, Mariano can't stay away from the fabulous Miracles, even though the unconventional relationship might threaten his brother's electoral chances. Hudson's wife Dana, who is also his campaign manager, insists that voters cannot handle the confusion that Miracles represents to them. Mariano, meanwhile, is reluctant to recognize his own sexual preferences or embrace any label that might attach to his relationship with Miracles, and as the play proceeds it increasingly seems as though the pressures of heteronormativity and his brother's political careerism will keep him away from her. The tragic "fix" of the title comes with Miracles' attempts to resolve the contradictions of a body that does not match her gender identity, as she internalizes others' prejudice and convinces herself that Mariano would return to her if only they could be "like a normal couple" (p. 56). Though the tragedy is tightly focused on Miracles, the play ends with the ladyboys' extravagant, defiant drag ball at the House of Malacañang, strongly reminiscent of those immortalized in Jenny Livingston's 1990 *Paris Is Burning*, thereby insisting on Miracles' larger community and her place in her world.

Alvarez transposes the ambiguity of the wife's behavior in the Calderonian source into the sexual, bodily ambiguity that Dana targets and Miracles herself repudiates. Poignantly, from the very start Miracles expresses her desire to exist in a body unavailable to her, while others question whether she is just trying to satisfy Mariano. She desperately seeks authorization for gender-reassignment surgery, but is not considered psychologically fit to decide. Her own agency in her eventual fate does not change the larger truth that prejudice and intolerance force her hand.

In his adaptation, Alvarez faced the challenge of finding a contemporary context in which honor would become a matter of life and death, and of translating the external pressures of socially policed codes of chastity and shame to internalized and psychological ones. What configuration of sexuality and social opprobrium leads to tragedy, with so many fewer prohibitions left where sexuality is concerned? Who still cares about sexual mores, in a sexually permissive world? Like Mary Kamitaki in *The King of Maricopa County*, Alvarez found one brilliant solution to this dramatic quandary: *politicians* do, given their visibility in the public eye and their sensitivity to public opinion. Yet what might have seemed in 2014 like a daring gesture to center the marginal, by exploring Miracles' singular plight, has unfortunately become more widely relevant. In the time since *FIXED* was first written, the landscape of transgender rights has changed radically, with both greater visibility and dignity for transgender and LGBTQ+ people, and a violent backlash from the right to the mainstreaming of gender pluralism. What has unfortunately not changed, thus, is the unwarranted yoking of private decisions to public campaigns. Tragically, Miracles' impossible situation is more broadly relevant than a decade ago, and the sympathy and candor that Alvarez brings to his portrayal seem harder for the culture at large to achieve. *Fixed* seems ever more timely and probing as it updates Calderón's insight that the concern with appearances can be mobilized to terrible, repressive ends. Alvarez's deeper dive into Miracles' psyche centers the most vulnerable figure in the play to explore her own internalization of social expectations.

FIXED

Inspired by Caldeón de la Barca's *The Physician of His Own Honor*, FIXED premiered at Echo Theater Company (Chris Fields, Artistic Director) in Los Angeles. It was directed by Rodney To; set design by Amanda Knehans; costume design by Michael Mullen; sound design by Rebecca Kessin; lighting design by Matt Richter; and Haley Kellogg, stage manager.

The cast was as follows:

Hudson Fernandez: Joseph Valdez
Dana Fernandez: Renee-Marie Brewster
AJ Chavez: Adrián Gonzalez
Mariano Fernandez: Wade Allain-Marcus
Lizette Castro: Anna Lamadrid
Miracles Malacañang: Chris Aguila
Jenny Malacañang: Allen Lucky Weaver
Gigi Malacañang: Boni B. Alvarez
Carmie Malacañang: Tonatiuh

Setting: Los Angeles, CA

Characters

Hudson Fernandez, *40s, Mexican-American*	*Running for LA County Sheriff*
Dana Fernandez, *40s, African-American*	*Hudson's wife and campaign manager*
AJ Chavez, *30s, Mexican-American*	*Fernandez family friend*
Mariano Fernandez, *30, Mexican-American*	*Hudson's conflicted brother*
Lizette Castro, *20s, Guatemalan-American*	*Pines for Mariano*
Miracles Malacañang, *20s, Filipino-American*	*Hopeful and romantic ladyboy*
Jenny Malacañang, *30s, Filipino-American*	*Practical, God-fearing ladyboy*
Gigi Malacañang, *40s, Filipino-American*	*Head ladyboy-in-charge*
Carmie Malacañang, *20, Mexican-American*	*Hopes to be a fierce ladyboy*

Scene One

Sickenin' bright lights up on:

Miracles Malacañang *(20s, Filipino-American) standing in full drag—pretty, emotional, fiery.*

Her look is contemporary ladyboy. She wears her own hair, light beat of her mug. Her gown clings and caresses, dazzles, makes mouths salivate . . .

Percussive music launches **Miracles** *into a walk—a ball walk, elegant yet rough, daring the onlookers to gag. She stomps, then pauses with dramatic flair . . .*

Mariano Fernandez *(30, Mexican-American) slinks on, in the shadows, afraid of the light.*

Mariano   Yaaasss! Yass, Miracles, yass!

Miracles *registers a knowing smile, the glow filling her up, her pores like sequins. She swishes, stomps, sashays.*

Mariano   Walk it out, baby girl!

Mariano *approaches the "runway."* **Miracles** *continues her stomp—werking, flirting, slaying, with every percussive pose.*

Mariano   Dass my girl, stomp. Werrrrk, baby.

He punctuates **Miracles'** *steps with an "uh!", grunting out his approval.*

Mariano   Get it, girl, git it git it!

He follows **Miracles** *alongside the perimeter of the runway. She stomps, soaking in his adoration.*

Mariano   Beat fo' the Gawds, Miracles, eleganza extravaganza, you real, baby gurrrl. Serveitserveitserveit, baby! Ferocious, you fierce, you fi-re!

He is suddenly conscious of his gregarious over-excitement. He takes in the area anxiously . . . He retreats with his embarrassment into the shadows. As **Miracles** *does a runway turn,* **Mariano** *disappears.*

Miracles *scans the crowd for* **Mariano** *. . . her face hardens as she walks, not being able to locate him. She freezes, sadness taking over her.*

Lights and music transition to:

Malacañang Massage Parlor—Historic Filipinotown, Los Angeles.

The small reception area is cozily lit, soft rejuvenating music plays.

Jenny Malacañang *(30s, Filipino-American) sits on the floor, pinning the hem of* **Miracles'** *gown.*

54   FIXED

Jenny has a similar look to **Miracles**—*wearing her own hair and light make-up, definitely not as pretty. She is dressed in her work clothes—crisp white shorts, feminine white top.*

Jenny   You standin' on the train, Miracles.

Miracles *stands frozen in a daze.*

Jenny   Miracles? (*Beat.*) Miracles?

Miracles *is silent.*

Jenny   Lift yo' big boy feet, Miracles!

Miracles *snaps to attention. She lifts her feet.*

Jenny   God, so sorry for yellin' at Miracles. And for sayin' she has big boy feet.

She crosses herself, goes back to pinning.

What kinda heels you stompin' in?

Miracles   I don't know.

Jenny   The old-school studded Manolo's?

She inches around the gown.

Miracles, what you thinkin' for yo' feet?

Miracles   I don't care.

Jenny   You betta get to carin'. You got trophies to snatch. Gigi want trophies. You remember how salty she was last year? She was ready to kick us outta here. And that was with us snatchin' six trophies. Six!

Miracles   Trophies don't mean nothin'.

Jenny   House of Malacañang's got to sweep, honey. Sweep sweep sweep all the trophies. If we lose to Casita de Secretos Grandes again, she will flip—

Miracles   What's any of this shit matter anyways?

Jenny   Miracles, what is wrong wid you?

Miracles   I don't care 'bout no ball, 'bout no trophies. I could give a fuck 'bout what Gigi wants.

Jenny   Miracles, your language. God is listening.

She gets up, looks towards the heavens.

Please forgive Miracles for her language, God.

She backs up, appraises the gown.

My goodness, Miracles, I get so green wid you. Watchu think?

Miracles It's a fierce frock, Jenny.

Jenny Fierce? I'm completely gagging. What you think Motha Gigi gonna say?

Miracles Who knows with her? She's so pre-menopausal.

Jenny *circles* **Miracles**, *putting on the airs of* **Gigi**.

Jenny It's ovaaaaahhhhhhhh! Ovah and done! Done and done and done! Ovah-done, I say! Hand over the trophies, all of 'em cuz it's a wrap! House of Malacañang done wrapped you up. They lost, lost in the Malacañang shade. Can't find they way home. It's the Filipino tea, the Filipino glamor. Filipino realnessssssss.

Miracles *cries.*

Jenny My goodness, girl, if you don't like the dress, you ain't gotta cry about it. I'll make you somethin' else.

Miracles No, no, I'm—I . . .

Jenny Why you cryin'?

Miracles It's—I . . .

Jenny Oh girl, LaShawndra's death done really shook you up.

Miracles What?

Jenny House o' Vanderbilt been a mess since they Mama Larissa was called back.

Miracles LaShawndra lucky. She dead.

Jenny Miracles!

Miracles LaShawndra Vanderbilt was a tacky ho and you know it. Methed out, turnin' tricks at the bus stop on Highland and Santa Monica.

Jenny They was gettin' evicted. She was doin' what she—

Miracles You really shocked some psycho john smashed her tits in?

Jenny Don't be talkin' 'bout a fallen sista that way.

Miracles I don't give a fuck 'bout dem Vanderbilt whores.

Jenny Miracles! Lord, she didn't mean it. She did not.

Miracles *cries.*

Jenny *goes to hug her.*

Miracles *pushes her away.*

Jenny What in God's name is wrong wid you?!

Miracles *cries, shakes her head.*

Jenny Miracles!

Miracles I went to the doctor. I—I didn't pass.

Jenny Oh goodness, what's wrong? What do you have?

Miracles What?

Jenny What kinda bug you got? Oh heavens, is it *the* bug? My goodness gracious, Lord Have Mercy, Miracles!

Miracles I didn't pass the psych evaluation. She won't let me—
Doctor Kim won't clear me for gender re-assignment surgery.

Jenny Oh God!

Miracles She won't let me.

Jenny You just made me take the Lord's name in vain! I'm sorry, God.

Miracles Jenny, I haven't seen Mariano in like six months.

Jenny I heard y'all FaceTimin' the other night.

Miracles For like a minute here and a minute there. It's not the same.

Jenny I know you goin' thru it.

Miracles My life! My life don't mean nothin'.

Jenny Miracles, you do not need a sex change!

Miracles If I could get the surgery, then maybe things would work out and we could be like a normal couple. Then his brother and his wife wouldn't—wouldn't be so against me.

Jenny They're jerks. Jerkfaces.

Miracles I gotta keep lookin', lookin' for a doctor that understands me.

Jenny Any legit doctor's gonna tell you no.

Miracles You don't understand, Jenny. You just like Doctor Kim.

Jenny Doctor Kim's not the problem. Yo' problem is Mariano. What does it say 'bout yo' man that he's listenin' to his jerkface brother?

Miracles I love him.

Jenny Miracles.

Miracles My heart hurts.

Jenny Really, girl?

Miracles It's broken inside me and cuttin' me all up.

Jenny Really, Miracles? Can't you just write a poem and move on?

Miracles Don't be a heifer.

Jenny Okay, so go to him.

Miracles Gigi would beat me, bust my head open wid her wide-ass wedges.

Jenny Yeah, she prolly would.

Miracles And then I'ma be just like LaShawndra.

Jenny You bite your tongue, Miracles.

Miracles Homeless, turnin' tricks in the Chik-fil-a parking lot and I'ma get HPV and chlamydia—

Jenny You are soooo dramatic.

Miracles Why can't we just be together?

Jenny You can. You just have to leave the House of Malacañang.

Miracles *is quiet.*

Jenny You need to pull yo'self together. We have a ball comin' and we need you read' to stomp.

Miracles You think Mariano will come?

Jenny Girl, how am I s'posed to know?

Miracles You think he thinks about me?

Jenny Maybe you should be thinkin' 'bout other men.

Miracles Log off, bitch.

Jenny Why you always talkin' 'bout runnin' off to him? I ain't seen him try to come here in the last six months.

Miracles He did! That one night real real late. Throwin' quarters at my window?

Jenny 'Cept it wasn't your window!

Miracles Gigi threw the skillet at 'im.

Jenny And the tea pot and the waffle maker. We need to get another waffle maker.

Miracles Mariano, his poor head.

Jenny *laughs.*

Miracles Jenny! Don't laugh. He was hurt real bad.

Jenny It's too much, Miracles. I can't.

Miracles We're meant to be together.

Jenny I can't witchu. I can't.

Miracles You don't never have my back!

Jenny My goodness, look, if you two are meant to be together, God will put you together. You need to pray for guidance, girl.

Carmie Malacañang *(early 20s, Mexican-American) bustles in with laundry baskets. She's a boy, rough around the edges, desperately trying to find her inner femininity—dressed in tight shorts, frilly top, light make-up—very early "baby" drag.*

Carmie   Damn, Miracles, gag! You look off the hook!

Jenny   Carmie! Is that my blouse?

Carmie   Uhh, no.

Jenny   Stretchin' it out wid yo' big Messican shoulders, you know betta!

Gigi *(offstage)*   Carmieeeee!

Carmie   Shit.

Carmie *scurries out the front door.*

Jenny   You gonna be fine, Miracles. God's got you. He keep everything right and tight.

Jenny *dabs at* **Miracles'** *eyes with a Kleenex.*

Gigi Malacañang *(40s, Filipino-American) parades in, an entourage of fabulous air blasting in with her. She is the head ladyboy in charge. She sports an oversized sequinned white shirt, belted of course. The ensemble is finished with white capris and white wedge sandals.*

Carmie *scampers in behind her with more laundry baskets.*

Gigi   Oh myyyy, *susmariosep*[1] my heavens and the stars, what is this I see?

She takes off her white sunglasses.

Such glamour on display in the front parlor? Baring our armoires, exposing ourselves for the whole neighborhood? Why not have Carmie deliver it straight to Casita de Secretos Grandes? Just hand over all the trophies!

Jenny   So sorry, Gigi, I was just—

Gigi   You wasn't thinkin'. Again. What if one of those tranny-chasin' thugs happened by and peeped this? Use your damn heads. What do I always tell you?

Carmie   A dumb girl is not a pretty girl.

Gigi   I do not expend my energy on ugly girls. Do I look like I have time to deal with ugly girls?

Carmie   Nope, no time for ugly girls.

Gigi *circles* **Miracles***, studying the gown.*

Jenny   It has walkability. The train moves nice. Red carpet fierce.

Gigi   It is fierce.

---

[1] A mild Filipino oath: Jesús, María, José.

Jenny Yeah?

Gigi Very Badgley Mischka, ohhh yasss, Jenny.

Jenny Fierce, right? You like it?

Gigi Badgley Mischka . . . circa 2002.

Jenny's *face drops.*

Silence.

Carmie So . . . it's retro?

Gigi Carmie, what did I say about dumb girls?

Carmie They not pretty?

Gigi Yes, you are having a very ugly moment.

Miracles It don't even matter. I'm not gonna be walkin' the ball noways.

Carmie Ooooo, lemme walk for Miracles.

Gigi You plannin' on movin'?

Miracles Uh, no.

Gigi I just came from outside and I swore there was a sign out there that said Malacañang Massage.

Miracles You sayin' I don't earn my keep here?

Gigi Carmie, what's—what's my last name?

Carmie Malacañang.

Gigi And this is the House of Malacañang, am I correct?

Carmie 'Sho is. When I'ma get the name, Gigi?

Gigi House of Malacañang, girls. House of Malacañang. You took the name, you walk for the house. I can't make it any more basic.

Miracles We're not yo' damn slaves.

Gigi Okay, Miracles Tubman, you just love to get it twisted.

Miracles Ain't nothin' twisted, *Lola.*

Gigi You keep spikin' my blood pressure, tryin' to kill me with your faggotry. The exhaustion you heap upon me.

Miracles That's called menopause.

Gigi Little miss, you betta get yo' *pek-pek*[2] in order.

---

2 Tagalog term for vagina.

Gigi *heads for the back.*

Miracles   I swear you so obsessed wid my *pek-pek*, it's like—

Gigi   Bitch, get that damn frock in the back!

Lights fade as **Gigi** *huffs off.*

Scene Two

Fernandez Home—Echo Park, Los Angeles

Hudson Fernandez *(40s, Mexican-American) stands, facing his audience of one:*

Dana Hernandez *(40s, Black), fast and pointed, judges from a distance.*

Hudson *tucks his crisp shirt into his pants.*

Hudson   I'm truly very honored to be here.

Dana   You're not accepting some prize.

Hudson   I am . . . humbled?

Dana   I don't know. Are you?

Hudson   I'm humbled by this incredible privilege. The grand opening of this state-of-the-art Boys and Girls Club, it—it touches my heart.

Dana   Sounds gay.

Hudson   It touches me.

Dana   Creepy.

Hudson   Look, why can't I—I'ma just try bein' real, all right?

Dana *nods.* **Hudson** *resumes.*

Hudson   If it wasn't for the Echo Park Boys and Girls Club when I was comin' up, I wouldn't be who I am now. This club kept me straight, on the right path. Now, look at me. With a lot of hard work, a lot of long hours, I'm Assistant Sheriff of Custody Ops. Without this club in my youth, I'd probably be *in* custody today.

He places a tie around his neck.

Dana   No tie.

Hudson   No?

Dana   These are homeless kids. They—

Hudson   Dana, this is the Boys and Girls Club. They're not homeless.

Dana   You know what I mean. Be like them. You're "of the people."

Hudson   I like that.

Dana   I like the way that shirt clings to your big ol' muscles.

Hudson   Yeah?

Dana   Keep going.

Hudson   My young brothers and sisters, this is your club. Look to these mentors to keep you on track. You need to treat them with—

Dana   Don't lecture.

Hudson   This club will help shape you into honorable men and women who contribute to the success and pride of our community.

Dana   Right before you cut the ribbon, when you're posing for the camera, give 'em that dolphin smile.

Hudson   Dolphin?

She nods. He smiles boyishly.

Dana   That's it. Give 'em that look.

Hudson   We haven't played dolphin in a while.

He glides to her, leans in for a kiss.

She pushes him away.

Dana   Focus.

Hudson   You don't think I'm sexy anymore.

Dana   Hudson, you're sexy.

Hudson   Sexy enough to get elected LA County Sheriff?

Dana   Hideous men have been elected to bigger offices.

Hudson   So I'm hideous?

Dana   Did I say that?

Hudson   I should wear the sheriff dress uniform, don't you think? Look more official?

Dana   No need to flash the dress uniform. Right now, you're an Assistant Sheriff. You're the man they want to put *in* the fancy sheriff get-up.

Hudson   "Of the people."

Dana   That's right. You're "of the people," baby.

She rewards him with a kiss.

Los Angeles Magazine wants twenty minutes before the ribbon cutting.

Hudson   What the—*Los Angeles Magazine*?!

Dana Work your angle, man of the people.

Hudson What about *Opinión*? They gonna be there?

Dana Maybe. They don't really matter.

Hudson Sure they do.

Dana Their readers are gonna vote for you regardless.

Hudson Let's not take them for granted.

Dana Hello, loads of campaign experience here. Don't take that for granted.

He kisses her, pawing her all over.

AJ Chavez (*30s, Mexican-American*) *hurries in dutifully.*

AJ Oh shit, my bad.

Hudson *and* **Dana** *break.*

Hudson Hey, AJ.

AJ Ready to go?

Dana Mariano in the car?

AJ Uh . . .

Dana Uh what?

AJ I don't think he can make it.

Dana What?

AJ He had an accident.

Dana What has he gotten himself into now?

AJ It was—he had a riding injury last night.

Hudson Man, I told him to get rid of that motorcycle!

Dana He's not bailing on us. Not today. Mariano!

AJ He's not here.

Dana Where is that fool?

AJ The hospital?

Hudson Shit, he's hurt that bad?

Dana Hudson, your brother is grown. You need to stop coddling him.

Hudson Is he okay?

AJ His back, he could hardly move it last night.

Hudson Was he wearing a helmet?

Dana His head's hard as a coconut. I'm sure he's fine.

Hudson He could have spinal injuries. We have to go see him.

Dana Huh-uh, no. They are expecting us at the Boys and Girls Club.

Hudson We can swing by the hospital before.

Dana Hudson, I busted my ass to get *Los Angeles Magazine*.

Hudson He's my brother, baby.

She counters with a kiss.

Hudson What hospital, AJ?

AJ I don't—I think he's—

Dana Fuckin' Christ, I'd like to see him come through for you just one time. One fuckin' time.

Hudson He knows how important this campaign is.

Dana These last six months, it's been one thing after another.

Hudson It's been hard on him.

Dana We're in the middle of a campaign. It's hard on everybody.

AJ He's been tryin'. He's been—

Dana No trying. He needs to be doing. I mean, why can't he be more like you, AJ?

AJ Uh, I don't know.

Hudson Mariano's doing his part.

Dana We should ship him off somewhere. AJ can play your brother.

Hudson AJ practically is.

Dana Dependable. Solid. A head that actually has a brain in it.

Hudson Babe, c'mon now.

Dana He's useless.

Hudson Mariano's held up his part of the agreement. He hasn't been there.

Dana We can't be one hundred percent sure.

Hudson AJ's been watching him. Just like you wanted.

AJ I been lookin' out. He hasn't seen—

Dana Don't you even say it! That place, those people, they're the sty in our eyes. The humps on our backs. The giant pus-filled boils on our damn butts.

Lights fade.

Scene Three

Malacañang Massage—Reception Area

Carmie *folds towels at the reception desk.*

After a few moments, she takes a step from behind the counter. She walks the runway. Her walk is ruff, urban catalog at best.

She turns, walks back to the counter.

Carmie   Stomp. Stomp. Stomp. Stomp. "You fierce, Carmie!" Meowmeow, bitch. I know it.

Mariano *winces in. He watches* **Carmie** *for a second.*

Mariano   Uh, hey.

Carmie *turns quickly, appraises* **Mariano**.

Carmie   Who're you?

Mariano   Didn't mean to interrupt your stomp.

Carmie   I didn't see you. Cuz I—I was turnt the other way.

Mariano   Uh, is Miracles, is she—

Carmie   How you know Miracles?

Mariano   She here?

Carmie   Miracles is available. (*Beat.*) I think. Watchu lookin' for?

Mariano   What?

Carmie   Deep tissue? Reflexology? Hot rocks?

Mariano *stares at her, confused.*

Mariano   You—are you . . . you like Miracles?

Carmie   She fierce. But one day, I'ma be fiercer than her.

Mariano   No, I mean, are you, you Filipino?

Carmie   No. I'm Mexican.

Mariano   Why you not wid Casita?

Carmie   Watchu know 'bout it?

Mariano   Nothin'.

Carmie   Just cuz I'm Mexican, I'm s'posed to be wid those cha-cha bitches?

Mariano   Fine, it's fine.

Carmie   Betta be.

Mariano   Forget I asked.

Carmie Miracles, she ain't even full, she only part Filipino.

Mariano You got good skin.

Carmie Me?

Mariano Yeah. Look smooth and soft.

Carmie Really?

Mariano Got nice hair too.

Carmie (*laughing awkwardly*) You lyin'.

Mariano So, is Miracles available?

Carmie Yeah. I mean, no, I'ma check.

Carmie *scrambles to the back.* **Mariano** *waits anxiously.*

Miracles *emerges—she has changed into her massage parlor whites—short white shorts, white halter.*

Miracles Mariano?

Carmie This is Mariano?

Miracles What you doin' here?

Mariano I need a massage.

Carmie He can't be here. Can he be here?

Miracles *moves towards* **Mariano**. *She stops.*

Mariano Miracles.

Carmie You want me to call the popo?

Mariano Why?

Carmie You s'posed to be dangerous.

Mariano I'm not dangerous. I just need a massage.

Jenny *sneaks in from the back.*

Jenny Bwisit,[3] it is you.

Mariano Hey, Jenny.

Jenny (*crossing herself*) Gigi is here. You need to go.

Mariano I just came for a massage.

Jenny Oh God, please help us.

---

3 Tagalog interjection of frustration.

Carmie   Should I call 9-1-1 or not?

Jenny   Get out, go.

Mariano   I hurt my back.

Miracles is silent.

Mariano   I did, for reals.

Jenny   Then go to a doctor.

Mariano   Miracles?

Jenny   Miracles, he gotta go.

Miracles   He need a massage. He's—he's a customer.

Jenny   Gigi will cut him. She'll cut you both.

Carmie   Maybe you should keep it movin'.

Miracles   If God wants us to be together, he will bring us together. That's what you said, Jenny.

Jenny   Huh-uh, don't be puttin' me in the middle o' this.

Miracles *takes his hand. Everyone holds their breath from the contact.*

Miracles   Hold yo' roll, Jenny.

Jenny   Go 'head, get yo' life.

Miracles *walks* **Mariano** *towards the back.*

Miracles   Carmie, keep your mouth shut.

Carmie *shakes her head yes.*

Miracles *and* **Mariano** *disappear into the back.*

Jenny   God help us, Carmie.

Carmie   Should I call 5-0?

Jenny   You really think we need the cops in here?

Carmie   You right, you right. I can handle him.

Jenny   She don't never be thinkin'.

Carmie   He ain't even all that.

Jenny   He not even that.

Lights crossfade to the:

Massage Room.

Mariano *lays face-down on the massage table, a towel draped over his butt.*

Miracles *rubs her palms together, warming her hands.*

She places her hands on his back, presses.

Miracles You was wearin' your helmet, right?

Mariano Wasn't on the Harley.

Miracles You got another bike?

Mariano Nope.

Miracles Then what were you drivin'?

Mariano Do it matter?

Miracles Oh, I get it. You was fuckin' some chuntara[4] so hard, you jacked up yo' back.

Mariano I was ridin' a bull, all right?

Miracles What ratchet pussy you lay into last night?

Mariano A big ol' wild bull.

Miracles Mariano, you think I'ma . . . oh my God, you was ridin' the bull at Saddle Ranch!

He laughs.

Miracles Shhh.

Mariano Why you bein' so gentle?

Miracles Thought you was injured.

Mariano Dig in, baby.

She applies more pressure.

Mariano That's right. It's all yours, Mami.

Miracles Mine?

Mariano You don't miss me?

She doesn't answer—massages quietly.

Mariano You look beautiful, Miracles. More beautiful than before.

Miracles Uh-huh.

Mariano *reaches under the towel.*

Miracles Watchu doin'?

---

4 Mexican Spanish, insult, low-class or vulgar.

Mariano Tryin' to get more comfortable.

Miracles Huh-uh, keep yo' panties on.

Mariano I don't wear panties.

Miracles I'm not playin', Mariano.

Mariano I'm not playin' either. You ever see panties on my junk?

Miracles Whatever.

Mariano *reaches under the towel.*

Miracles I told you I ain't playin'. Your boxers stay on.

Mariano You act like you don't want it.

Miracles You need to stop.

He pulls her to him.

Miracles Quit.

She slaps his back.

Mariano Shit!

Miracles Shhh. You want Gigi to hear you?

Mariano C'mon, ain't it time for me to turn over yet?

Miracles This not gonna be that kinda massage.

Mariano I coulda got a real happy ending somewhere else.

Miracles That's all you came here for?

Mariano No.

Miracles Yes it is.

Mariano I thought you'd—I don't know. Maybe treat me like you in love with me or somethin'.

Miracles It's been six months, I don't hardly remember you.

Mariano It's gonna be like that?

Miracles You come here, unbothered, like we see each other all the—

Mariano I texted you and was FaceTimin' you.

Miracles Cuz you was drunk. That's real romantic.

Mariano *gets off the table.*

Mariano So, what, you not in love wid me no more?!

Miracles Shhhh!

Mariano *moves to her. She scrambles to the other side of the table.*

Mariano You didn't feel me thinkin' 'bout you? You didn't feel me in yo' heart, baby?

Miracles Heartburn. That's all I be feelin'.

Mariano I think about you all the time.

Miracles You a lie.

Mariano Look, I'm here now.

He goes to her.

C'mon, Miracles.

Miracles You want a massage or not?

Mariano You don't miss me?

She's silent.

Mariano You act like I wanted to be away from you.

He inches toward her. She lets him.

Mariano I thought about you. I did.

Miracles Yeah?

Mariano All the time. You didn't think about me?

Miracles You know I do.

Mariano All the time?

Miracles I think about you, all right? I can't stop thinkin' 'bout you. You so addicting.

Mariano So why haven't I gotten a kiss yet?

She kisses him lightly. She pulls away.

He grabs her by the waist.

Miracles You need to cool down.

Mariano It don't feel good?

Miracles No. Yeah. It does. But not here.

Mariano We'll be quiet.

Miracles Mariano, we can't.

He plants his lips on hers. They kiss, breathing life into each other.

She pulls away, crying.

70   FIXED

Mariano   Baby, what's wrong?

She wipes away tears.

Mariano   Why you gotta be so sentimental?

Miracles   I went to—to the ...

Mariano   Where?

Miracles   Doctor Kim.

Mariano   For what?

Miracles   For, you know.

Mariano   You pregnant?

He laughs. She shoves him.

Miracles   I hate you.

Mariano   It was a joke, Miracles.

Miracles   I went to Doctor Kim to see 'bout the surgery.

Mariano   Oh.

Miracles   She said she couldn't approve me.

Mariano   All right.

Miracles   All right? (*Beat.*) That's it?

Mariano   What you want me to say?

Miracles   You don't even care.

Mariano   Who said that?

Miracles   Isn't that what you wanted? For me to get the surgery?

Mariano   You the one brought that mess up.

Miracles   Mess?

Mariano   That's not what I mean.

Miracles   You don't care cuz you never had any intention of bein' with me or stayin' with me or lovin' me.

Mariano   Why you gotta be so much drama?

Miracles   I'm just tryin' to figure out what you want.

Mariano   I'm here wid you. That's it. Done.

Miracles   For the moment. One tiny little—

Mariano   Comin' here, it's not as easy as you make it out to be.

Miracles   It's easy if you know what you want.

Mariano   Things are complicated.

Miracles   But things would be easier if I had the surgery. That's what you said.

Mariano   No. I said it would be easier if—

Miracles   If I was a girl.

Mariano   Yeah.

Miracles   So I just told you, that's not gonna happen.

Mariano   I heard you the first time.

Miracles   See! You don't care!

Mariano   Where you get that from?

Miracles   You don't care about me.

Mariano   Would you stop being such a damn girl?!

She raises her hand to hit him.

He grabs her wrists, pulls her to him.

They lock lips.

Scene Four

Outside of the Boys and Girls Club

AJ *walks ahead of* **Hudson** *and* **Dana**.

AJ   You slayed, Hudson.

Hudson   You think?

Dana   Everybody was feelin' you. The boys, the girls, their parents. You killed, baby.

Hudson   I did, didn't I?

Dana   *Los Angeles Magazine*! Man of the people, they ate every syllable of that shit.

Hudson   All because of you, babe.

Dana *stops, gives him a long deep kiss.*

Hudson   Dolphin?

Dana   Unless you wanna play Jungle.

Hudson   For reals?

She rewards him with another kiss.

Hudson AJ, get us home A-SAP.

Lizette Castro *(20s, Guatemalan-American) swoops in like a pigeon on a french fry.*

Lizette Mariano!

AJ Lizette!

Lizette Where is he?!

Dana Hot damn.

AJ You did yo' hair different?

Lizette Shut up, AJ.

AJ Looks good. I'm sayin', it—you, you look good.

Lizette You always coverin' for Mariano.

Dana Mariano's not here. There's no cover-up.

Lizette Why wasn't he at Saddle Ranch last night? Mariano texted me, tellin' me to meet his ass there. I got all done up. And where was he, huh? Where was he?!

Dana Saddle Ranch, really? This crazed tirade is seriously about Saddle Ranch?

Lizette This about his word. About doin' what you say you gonna do. That's what this is about, bitch.

Dana Okay, look, stop it.

She takes **Lizette**'s *arm, pulls her away from the Boys and Girls Club.*

Lizette Get yo' hands off me.

Dana You need to turn your volume down.

Lizette This a free country, bitch.

Hudson There's no need to make a scene, Lizette.

Lizette Scene?! You think this is a scene?!

Hudson Tell me, what do you need?

Lizette You guys act like he does nothin' wrong. Like he's some perfect Santo Mariano or somethin'. But he's not. He's not, all right?

Dana Lizette, you still haven't told us what you need.

Lizette I told you, he stood me up.

AJ He didn't really stand—

Lizette He doesn't text me back.

Dana This fit, this is really about some texts?

Lizette *tears up.*

Lizette He keep playin' wid me, playin' wid my heart.

Hudson He's been very busy.

Lizette Bullshit! He never calls when he say he's gonna call. He always set up times so we can kick back and then what? Nothing, that's what!

Dana I'm sure he's got good—good reasons as to why—

Lizette My heart is not some kinda toy, all right?!

AJ Nobody said it was.

Lizette Why do I even bother?

AJ I don't want you thinkin' that I—that uh, that we don't care 'bout—

Lizette You guys gonna back him up no matter what.

Dana That's not true.

Lizette So tell me where he is.

AJ I'll hit you up later. Find out if he's—I'll come by. I'll come thru, Lizette.

Lizette I took Lyft to Saddle Ranch and then back. You know how much that cost from K-Town?

AJ He got in a accident. He was really hurt.

Lizette Don't lie to me. He found some skanky chunt—

AJ Lizette, on the real now, he got injured in the bar and I took him home. That's why he wasn't there when you came thru.

Lizette So why didn't he text me that he was—

AJ I shoulda told him to. But you know, he was like dead weight. I had my hands full. I was basically draggin' him to the car.

Lizette You lyin'.

AJ No, I swear. I took him home. Put him in bed and gave him some stuff for his pain.

Dana Mariano's pathetic. He's a pathetic man-baby.

Hudson Lizette, I will tell him to call you.

She stares him down.

Lizette Yeah?

Hudson Yes. You have my word.

Lizette I hope your word's worth more than your brother's.

Dana Do I look like a woman that gets things done?

Lizette *nods.*

Dana   I will make sure you hear from him by the close of business.

Lizette   When's that?

Hudson   Before tonight, Lizette. You'll hear from him.

Dana *pulls some cash from her purse.*

Lizette   What's this for?

Dana   For your Lyft last night.

Lizette   It was over forty dollars. Both ways, remember?

Dana *pulls out more cash.*

Lizette   Tonight, right?

Dana   Yes, Lizette.

And she heads off.

Dana   Your brother's a damn mess.

Hudson   He said they only hooked up once.

Dana   Not even here and still makin' a shit show of things.

Hudson   It's not Mariano's fault she got attached.

Dana   Hudson, did you not see her? That girl is crazy.

AJ   She's not crazy.

Hudson   She's just really sprung for Mariano.

Dana   Exactly. She's crazy.

Dana *stares* **AJ** *down.*

AJ   What?

Dana *slaps* **AJ***'s arm.*

AJ   Owww.

Dana   You said he got in a motorcycle accident.

AJ *is quiet.*

Dana   Don't play stupid, AJ. Where is he?

AJ   I don't know.

Hudson (*laughing*)   He was riding that mechanical bull again, wasn't he?

AJ   Yeah.

Hudson   How long did he last?

AJ   Almost three minutes.

Hudson *laughs proudly.*

Dana   I'm glad you find this funny.

Hudson   C'mon, Dana, he was just havin' fun.

Dana   All his fun, it's gonna cost you this election.

Hudson   I'll talk to him.

Dana   We've worked too hard for this.

Hudson   We're good. It's all good.

He leans in for a kiss. She averts.

Hudson   C'mon, babe.

Dana   No, Hudson. He done fucked up the mood.

Lights fade.

Scene Five

Malacañang Massage—Massage Room

The lights are dim.

Mariano *and* **Miracles** *on the massage table, catching their breath.*

Miracles   Don't move. Leave it . . .

Mariano   I knew you missed me.

Miracles   Hold me, stupid.

*They spoon—***Mariano***'s the big spoon.*

Mariano   Tell me you missed me.

Miracles   I missed you.

Mariano   How much?

Miracles   I missed you so much.

Mariano *squeezes her tight.*

Mariano   You feel that?

Miracles   What?

Mariano   They swimmin' all up in you.

Miracles (*laughing*)   You so dumb.

Mariano   You'd be a good mami.

Miracles I would?

Mariano But don't be spoilin' all of 'em.

Miracles How many you want?

Mariano Gotta have more than one.

Miracles A boy and a girl?

Mariano Maybe.

Miracles What you wanna name 'em?

Mariano *is quiet.*

Miracles I always liked the name Savannah. For a girl. You like that? Savannah Fernandez.

Mariano *gives her neck a quick kiss.*

Miracles For a boy, I like Gallagher. I know it sound a lil funny, but—oh, but if we only have one boy, then he would have to be Junior. Mariano Fernandez Junior.

Mariano *starts to pull away.*

Miracles Nooo.

Mariano I gotta go.

He extracts himself. As he wipes down, the afterglow fades.

Miracles Why you gotta rush off so fast?

Mariano *pulls his jeans on quickly.*

Mariano Where's my tank top?

Miracles *turns up the lights.*

Mariano Damn, that's bright.

Miracles *picks up* **Mariano***'s tank top.*

Miracles Here.

Mariano *eyes* **Miracles***, turns away, puts on his tank top.*

Miracles What?

Mariano Nothin'.

Miracles What, Mariano?

Mariano Put yo'self together.

Miracles *looks down at herself.*

Mariano Put your shit away.

Miracles You didn't have a problem with my shit a few minutes ago.

Mariano   Why you tryin' to piss all over the good time we just had?

Miracles   Sooo good you can't wait to bounce.

Mariano   You really gonna start up?

Miracles   You can't even look at me.

Mariano *is silent.*

Miracles   Why do I bother with you? Why? I just let you come in here and use me for—

Mariano *slides his feet into his shoes.*

Mariano   I'm not tryin' to fight wid you, boo.

Miracles   Go. Ain't nobody tryin' to hold you here.

Mariano   Okay then, gimme some sugar.

Miracles   Just go already.

Mariano   Gimme a kiss, a hug, somethin'.

He pulls her to him. She cries.

Mariano   Man, why you gotta be so dramatic?

She kisses his cheek.

Miracles   Bye.

Mariano   Why you gotta do this?

Miracles   You bookin' outta here so quick like you embarrassed.

Mariano   Of what?

Miracles   You tell me. Cuz when you leave, I don't feel nothin' but cheap.

Mariano   Really, Miracles?

Miracles   You don't love me.

Mariano   I do.

Miracles   You don't act like it.

Mariano   We just spent some quality time and shit.

Miracles   How many months I gotta wait before I see you again?

Mariano   You worse than a *novela*.

Miracles   You make me this way!

Mariano *hits the massage table in frustration.*

Miracles   What? You wanna hit me?

Mariano I want you to not be so much drama.

Miracles I'm sorry, all right? Sorry for carin' for likin' for lovin' you.

Mariano Listen, I'm just tryin' to do my brother a solid. Til he gets elected.

Miracles We don't have to be nowhere near his campaign.

Mariano That's what I said, but you know.

Miracles Let's go away together.

Mariano I can't right now. But after Hudson gets elected—

Miracles I'm not talkin' for a trip. I'm sayin' we move.

Mariano Move?

Miracles Remember when we was in San Francisco?

Mariano When you was tryin' to push me off the trolley?

Miracles Shouldn'ta been tryin' to give me a wedgie.

Mariano *laughs.*

Miracles You loved that clam chowder.

Mariano Dem sourdough bread bowls—

Miracles Off the chain, right?

Mariano S-F was good times.

Miracles Remember when we was havin' happy hour in the Castro?

Mariano In that old man bar.

Miracles You lifted your lemon drop and you said, "We should live here. We should get old together here." You said that. You remember?

He nods.

Miracles You held my hand every day we was there. Everywhere we went.

Mariano It's different there.

Miracles That was the real us.

Mariano The real us?

Miracles I want that. What we had up there.

Mariano We don't know nobody in S-F.

Miracles That's the point, baby. It would be a fresh start for us. Make up our own rules. We'll have new friends. People who are nice, really really nice. They won't care what we look like, what we used to look like, what we wanna look like. We can do us and it'll be all right by them.

Scene Five

Mariano Where would we even live?

Miracles We could live in the Castro. Next to the old man bar.

Mariano Get a job bartendin' there.

Miracles Those old men would tip you like crazy. I could work at one of those shops. The ones with the clothes made from repurposed stuff.

Mariano Naw, I don't want you dressin' all hippie-dippie.

Miracles (*laughing*) I can get a job at the gelato place we went.

Mariano Mmmm.

Miracles I'd bring home some mocha rocky road for you every night.

Mariano And those lavender basil cookies.

Miracles You can see it, baby, right? You and me in San Francisco. With gelato and cookies. Happy.

Mariano They got that good air. Not all this smog we got.

Miracles Exactly. We can breathe up there.

She wraps her arms around **Mariano**'s *waist, rests her head on his chest.*

Mariano Watchu doin'?

Miracles Dancin'.

Mariano Dancin', huh?

Miracles We'd dance, Mariano. Every day. In our new life. In our Victorian apartment, in the Muni station, on the wharf. Shit, we'd dance on the Golden Gate Bridge.

They dance quietly, side-to-side, side-to-side.

Miracles We should just pack our shit up.

Mariano And do what?

Miracles And go. Be together. You and me.

Silence.

You don't want all that?

Mariano Did I say that?

Miracles You didn't say nothin'.

Mariano Cuz I was thinkin'.

Miracles Take you that long?

Mariano Bitch, you need to quit.

80   FIXED

Miracles   So I'm a bitch now?

Mariano   Why you like doin' this?

Miracles   Doin' what?

Mariano   Makin' me mad.

Miracles   You mad? What you think I am? I ain't seen you in how long? Then you just come by like nothin'—

Mariano *slams his fists into the massage table.*

Miracles (*cont'd*)   Go 'head, hit me!

Mariano   Man, fuck you.

Miracles   You know you want to. Hit me.

Mariano   Man, shut your damn mouth!

Miracles   Do it, Mariano!

The curtain goes flying open. **Gigi** *barrels into the room,* **Carmie** *in tow.*

Miracles   Oh God, oh God!

Gigi   You got some big ass balls, huh, Mariano?

Gigi *tasers* **Mariano**.

Mariano   Shit! What the fuck?!

Miracles   Noooo!

Gigi   Big hairy Messican balls! They must be bulletproof the way you done swung 'em into my house.

She tasers him again. **Mariano** *screams.*

Miracles   Gigi, stop it!

Gigi   What's it gonna take for you to pull your *pek-pek* together?

Miracles   You a little cunt, Carmie.

Carmie   I didn't say shit. (*Beat.*) I didn't mean to, but—

Gigi *goes for* **Mariano** *again. He runs behind* **Miracles**.

Mariano   You fuckin' crazy, man!

Miracles   Gigi, how you gonna be like this?

Gigi   Pray tell, like what, you little harlot?

Miracles   We are in love.

Carmie   Aww, damn.

Gigi   This is not love, Carmie. This is delusion.

Scene Five   81

Miracles   You so old, don't know what love is. It could knock you in yo' fat face and you wouldn't—

Gigi   You love her, Mariano?

Mariano   Huh?

Miracles   Mariano loves me.

Gigi   Maybe in the confines of this room. In the dark. Where no one sees him kissing and licking and dicking a girly boy.

Carmie   You love 'er or what?

Mariano *goes for the exit.*

Gigi *holds up the taser.* **Mariano** *retreats behind* **Miracles***.*

Gigi   This is what you're in love with? This faggot?

Mariano   I'm not a faggot, you old cunt.

Carmie   You best mind yo' words.

Gigi   I'm not the one cowering behind a ladyboy.

Miracles   It's a new day, Gigi. A girl can protect her man.

She blocks **Mariano** *from* **Gigi***, clearing him to the door. He rushes out.*

Gigi   He leaves you defenseless. No honor, Miracles. No chivalry.

Miracles *lunges.* **Gigi** *lifts the taser.* **Miracles** *grabs a handful of taser.*

She screams.

Miracles   I hate you! You fuckin' bitch, Gigi, I hate you!

Gigi   Take note, Carmie. A man that loves you, he wouldn't run out leaving you exposed, half-naked, victim to someone you supposedly hate.

Carmie *appraises* **Miracles***.*

Miracles   Keep listenin' to her ancient secret life lessons, you gonna dry up, unhappy, growin' ooold all by yo'self.

Carmie   I'ma—I'ma find somethin' fo' yer hand.

Carmie *slinks out.*

Miracles   Who screwed you over so bad, Gigi?

Gigi   I beg your pardon, sir?

Miracles   Someone done hurt you so bad, you can't let no one be happy.

Gigi   You think Mariano gonna fill yo' life wid picket fences and a pocket full o' posies? That the show in yo' head? Daydreams rarely play out according to plan, baby girl. You old 'nough to know that.

Miracles   You a sad lonely old man.

Gigi   I'm single. That don't mean sad. It don't mean lonely.

Miracles   I'd rather die than be like you.

Gigi   You think I ain't been where you at? I had me a slew of Mr. Wonderfuls. Teams, gangs, armies of 'em. And there was one. One of 'em always gotta be special, right? The one, the one and only. He wanted girly show twenty-four seven. I'd be a fool to offer what I don't have.

I had to slap my dick in his face. Remind him what program he was tuned in to. I didn't like the show I was starring in, little miss, so I flipped the channel.

Miracles   My life ain't no show. All real, all tea.

Gigi   He's not bringin' you home, Miracles.

Miracles   We can make our own home.

Gigi   Mariano's not the type. (*Beat.*) None of 'em are. Not the ones that come thru here.

Miracles   He's different.

She heads for the exit. **Gigi** *blocks.*

Gigi   You a bright girl, Miracles, but you was always dumb as shit when it come to dick.

Miracles   Oh, cuz you some kinda expert, Lady Lonely?

Gigi   You love chasin' the unavailable. You the bitch who knows the number's disconnected, but you keep on dialin'.

Miracles   Thank you, you done wid yo' basic-ass after-school drag special?

Gigi   I'll be done when you pull yo' head out yo' *pek-pek*.

Miracles   Yo' *pek-pek* so damn clogged wid dust bunnies—

Gigi   Why don't you ever listen?!

Miracles   You're not my mama, all right?!

Gigi   You right, I'm not some strung-out white-trash meth head. Not yo' daddy neither. Didn't run back to the Philippines when I found out you like takin' dick up yo' ass.

Silence, then . . . **Miracles** *screams, charges at* **Gigi**. **Gigi** *holds up the Taser threateningly.*

Miracles *collapses on the massage table, slapping it—in frustration, sadness, defeat.*

Miracles   Fuuuuck! Fuck my life!

Gigi   I gave you all the rules, Miracles. From the get-go. A client comes back within the first week, don't make that second massage so good. Cuz all those men, they got shows in they heads too and you do not wanna be the star of those twisted stories. (*Pause.*) You got the head for studyin', for doin' somethin'. You was thinkin' 'bout nail school.

Miracles   I don't wanna do nails all my life.

Gigi   You should be watchin' Jenny, learnin' how to make stuff.
Get that sewing down and you could try out for—

Miracles   I could be on *Drag Race* if I wanted to. Ain't no thing.

Gigi   Maybe. But if you wanna win, it's not just 'bout the runway. You got dem challenges where you gotta sew all kindsa looks. Gotta have fierce lip synchs, death drops—

Miracles   You just tryin' to live out some squashed dream through me.

Gigi   I'm tryin' to get you some real dreams. Mariano, he the one squashin' yo' shit.

Miracles   You don't know him.

Gigi   They happy endings for a reason, Miracles. Lil tugs of happiness and it ends. It's done. There's no life for it outside this room.

Lights fade.

Scene Six

Fernandez Home—Living Area

AJ *holds up his phone for* **Dana** *and* **Hudson** *to read.*

Mariano *sulks on the sofa, holding an ice pack to his burns.*

Dana   What is this madness?

AJ   Lizette's been postin' non-stop for a hour.

Dana   We need to lock her down, get her under control.

AJ   She's not a problem.

Dana   Yes, she is.

Hudson   She's saying Mariano is a womanizer, an adulterer, a—what did she say?

AJ   Dirty diseased man whore.

Hudson   This is not good.

Dana   Well, at least she's a girl.

Mariano   What's that s'posed to mean?

Dana   She has a pussy! Makes you look virile, like some kinda playboy.

Mariano Man, why you gotta be such a bitch?

Dana She's a loose cannon. She could go straight to Mickelson's camp with these accusations.

Mariano She's lyin'.

AJ She's upset. Her feelings are hurt.

Mariano Nobody's gonna believe anything she says.

Dana Are you stupid? She knows about Miracles.

Mariano I'm not stupid.

Dana You need to go to Lizette and make nice.

Mariano For what?

Dana Bring her candy. Hold her hand, whisper in her damn ear.

AJ She's not Mariano's girlfriend.

Dana Would it kill you to cuddle with the bitch?

Mariano Man, you go cuddle her.

Dana Do you think about anybody but yourself?

Hudson AJ, can you get Mariano more ice?

Dana Stop babying him, Hudson.

Mariano I'm not a baby.

Hudson AJ, please.

AJ *rushes off.*

Dana *stands over* **Mariano**.

Dana Does anything register in that thick head of yours?

Mariano Back off.

Hudson He's really injured, Dana.

Dana Hudson asked you not to patronize that establishment.

Mariano This was the first time.

Dana Oh my God, how basic do we have to get? Stay away from—

Mariano One time in six months!

Dana No times. None. Not until Hudson gets elected. That's what you agreed to.

Hudson Everybody, let's stay calm.

Dana Hudson, he's a child. A man child. Just draining us of—

Mariano Do you have a off switch?

Dana   Mariano, why do you do it? I mean, what kinda spell has she cast on your dick?

Hudson   Dana.

Mariano   Go to hell!

Hudson   Mariano.

Dana   Grow up! You can't be some tranny chaser your whole life!

Mariano *lunges for* **Dana**. **Hudson** *grabs him by the arms.*

Dana   So offended by the truth?

Mariano   Fuck off!

Hudson   Mariano, c'mon, relax!

Mariano   You should bang your wife, bro.

Hudson *throws* **Mariano** *onto the sofa.*

Hudson   One thing, Mariano! That's all! I can't force you. But I asked you and you agreed. One thing.

Mariano   You wanna ask me a favor, cool. Telling me how to live my life is a whole different thing.

Dana   Nobody would have to tell you anything if you would just grow up.

Mariano   Don't talk to me.

Hudson   We're not telling you how to live your life.

Mariano   You don't hear yourself?

Dana   Why do you want to destroy all the hard work Hudson has done?

Mariano   I don't.

Dana   All of his achievements, they're a joke to you.

Mariano   No.

Dana   Yes. He's worked so hard for you both.

Mariano   Why does my life—*my* life—that should have nothing to do with him.

Hudson   It shouldn't, but it does, Mariano.

Mariano   You the one runnin'. It's not me.

Hudson   It's not that simple.

Mariano   They can't judge you by what I do.

Dana   Of course they can. And they will. If you're gay—

Mariano   I'm not gay!

Dana   I'm just sayin'. If you're gay—

Hudson Babe, he already said he's not gay.

Dana If he is, then people get that.

Mariano If you don't quit, I'm gonna punch you in the face.

Dana You're a man and if you were with Miracles as a man, then people get it. Gay couple. A gay relationship. People, voters, they can get behind that or not. If that was the scenario—if you were a gay couple—a loving gay couple, I could make that work.

Mariano *is silent.*

Dana You as a man in a relationship with a transsexual, I could possibly sell that. Tougher sell, but there's a chance. You're a man who fell in love with a woman, and maybe you didn't know. You didn't know. That woman, it just so happened that she used to be a man. She's pretty. It's conceivable. People may look at you as a straight couple. Possibly. But like I said, tough.

Mariano *is silent.*

Dana But you, a straight man sneaking off visits to a drag queen in a massage parlor, that—that, people don't understand. You have sex with—or are you dating—or are you with that—that girl? A boy kinda dressed as a girl . . . no, she's a boy? Too many questions. People don't know. When they don't know, they're afraid. And then they distance themselves. They distance themselves and then they don't vote for your brother. That would be the best outcome.

Mariano Best?

Dana Worst is they talk mad shit about you. Online and taunting Hudson at appearances, attacking him, me, you. Physically. And then running again? Forget it.

Hudson It may be a tough way of looking at things, but it's the truth.

Dana The other option is the one we agreed upon, Mariano. Just hold off until Hudson wins and then you can go back to her. Him. You know.

Mariano It shouldn't have to be that way.

Dana Go make nice with Lizette.

Mariano Man, you don't know—

Hudson Mariano, *por favor*, you agreed!

Mariano What the hell?

AJ *hurries* **Gigi** *and* **Carmie** *into the room.*

Gigi You best lift your paws from my person, Juan Jose Enrique Maria!

Carmie Oww!

Hudson Gigi, what are you doing here?

Dana Oh Lord, did anyone see them coming in?

Gigi   Did anyone see us coming in?!

Dana   Don't be so loud, you tacky heifer.

Gigi   Tacky is that nineties lesbian ensemble you got on, hunty.

Dana   What couldn't you and your supposed fabulousness convey over the phone?

Gigi   Keep you and yours in check and I won't have to stomp out here.

Carmie   Mariano was at the parlor today.

Dana   We know, ladyboy.

Carmie   Me? A lady? For reals?

Dana   You turned your parlor into a homeless shelter?

Gigi *marches on* **Dana**. **AJ** *inserts himself between them.*

Gigi   Why's your thug brother-in-law comin' round my place of business?

Hudson   He's not a thug.

Gigi *marches toward* **Mariano**.

Mariano   Back up, Gigi.

Gigi   I thought we had an agreement.

Hudson   We were just addressing the issue.

Gigi   Address it a lil harder, Hudson. He's got my girl all loose in the head.

Mariano   Is Miracles alright?

Carmie   She just got tasered once.

Mariano   Damn, Gigi.

Gigi   Oh, now you care?

Dana   Wow, gotta taser 'em to keep 'em in your brothel?

Gigi   Massage parlor, sir.

Dana   Hookers.

Carmie   Hookers? Really, bitch?

Hudson   Mariano will not be over there anymore.

Mariano   Don't speak for me.

Gigi   You hear that?!

Dana   You need to keep a better eye on that Miracle girl. Boy. It.

Gigi   You need to keep a better eye on your moustache.

Hudson   Gigi, you forget I could shut you down in a minute?

Gigi This again? Really?

Dana We can have the whole sheriff's department on your bra stuffing in no time.

Gigi All these years and my titties still intimidate you.

Dana Bitch, please.

Gigi I wish you would let it go already. You act like I conjured your man over to my place or somethin'. He was the one who stumbled into the House of Malacañang. Drunk wid all his homie homeboy thugs.

Carmie Mmmm, the tea.

Gigi No shade.

Carmie Just pink lemonade.

Hudson I didn't know! Besides, that was years and years ago, decades!

Gigi But you liked it, didn't you?

Hudson It was one time! How long I gotta pay for that?

Gigi Residuals, baby doll. I know you still dreamin' 'bout it.

Hudson It wasn't even my idea. My friends took me there.

Gigi As I remember, every single *vato*[5] liked the service they got, including Hudson.

Dana You tricked him.

Gigi Yeah, I cast a spell. Tricked the nectar outta his stick.

Dana *charges at* **Gigi**. **AJ** *intercepts.*

Dana I will burn your house to the ground.

Gigi Bring it, manly girl. Bring it.

Dana Throw your ass in jail for prostitution.

Gigi So salty cuz yo' husband and his brother are a tranny-chasin' duo.

Dana *charges at* **Gigi**. **Carmie** *pushes her back.* **Dana** *shoves* **Carmie** *to the ground.*

Carmie Damn, you a strong bitch!

Gigi *pulls off her wedge, launches it at* **Dana**. **Hudson** *catches it.*

As **Gigi** *takes off her other wedge,* **Mariano** *sneaks away.* **AJ** *follows.*

---

5 Mexican-Spanish, slang, guy, man.

Dana Do not touch me, ratchet boy!

Gigi Put your manly hands on me again, try it.

Hudson Back off, Gigi.

Dana I swear, don't you get tired of this circus show you call a life?

AJ Mariano, where you goin'?

Mariano I can't handle this shit.

AJ We gotta figure this out, bro.

Mariano Naw man, it's too much.

Mariano *runs off.*

Gigi What looks worse? A drag queen working as a masseuse or the guy running for sheriff who once partook in said drag queen's services?

Carmie I'ma say the sheriff.

Dana *takes a swing at* **Gigi**. **Gigi** *averts.*

Hudson Dana, no!

Dana Close her down, Hudson! I want you to shut that syphilis-infested hell hole down once and for all!

Gigi Do I really have to get Councilman Hansford on the phone? (*Beat.*) Or Judge Gutierrez? That's the one.

Hudson You don't need to call anyone.

Gigi You see, your husband ain't but one little slice of chorizo on Gigi's list. You wanna shut me down? Go 'head, try it.

Dana *advances on* **Gigi**.

Hudson Dana!

AJ *grabs her, faces her towards* **Carmie**.

Carmie *holds up her phone, filming.*

Carmie Oooh, you not ready for yo' close-up.

Dana *backs away.*

Hudson We've sorted this all out. Mariano will not be bothering your girls anymore. Right, Mariano?

Silence. They look around the room.

AJ Mariano's gone.

Dana Where the fuck did he go?

Gigi If he sets foot near Miracles, I swear I'ma tase his dick off.

AJ Would it be so horrible to just let them be together?

Dana Yes, AJ, it would.

AJ Why?

Carmie Yeah, why?

AJ Look, it's a lot of gay people these days.

Carmie Gays everywhere.

Hudson Mariano said he's not gay.

Gigi Take note, Carmie, denial is fuckin' contagious.

Hudson He's not gay, all right? My brother is not gay!

Carmie Oooh, she doth protest too hard.

AJ All I'm sayin' is maybe ya'll tryin' to control him too much.

Dana If we let him cavort around town as he pleases, it would be disastrous.

Gigi For once, I concur.

AJ I mean, look around. You guys are the ones goin' crazy. Crazy for what? Mariano isn't even here. Neither is Miracles.

Lights fade.

Scene Seven

Malacañang Massage—Reception Area

Jenny *applies ointment to* **Miracles'** *hand.*

Jenny You not gonna be able to work so good for 'bout a week.

Miracles I need a break anyways.

Jenny The privileges of being pretty.

Miracles What you sayin'?

Jenny I actually know the difference between deep tissue and Swedish and Thai. I don't just tap-tap, push-push.

Miracles You act like I don't haveta work for my coins.

Jenny Not as hard as I do.

Miracles Girl, bye.

Jenny *grabs* **Miracles'** *hand, starts bandaging.*

Miracles Oww, don't be so rough.

Jenny Oops, sorry.

Miracles People don't tip me just cuz I'm pretty, Jenny.

Jenny Pretty privilege, I ain't never had that. My coins depend on my skillz.

Miracles I got skillz too.

Jenny I got better hands.

Miracles You best pray to God for all yo' boastin' and shit.

Jenny *releases* **Miracles***' hand. She pats it harder than she should.*

Jenny There you go. All wrapped up.

Miracles Owww, Jenny! Why you hatin' so hard?

Jenny You be livin' in some lil fantasy world. Like you blind to reality.

Miracles Why you so pressed 'bout my life?

Jenny Cuz you be draggin' all o' us in. Into your dramatics.

Miracles You really be exaggeratin'.

Jenny Uh-huh, look at yo' hand.

Miracles You sayin' this my fault? You on her side?

Jenny You put yo'self in that situation, Miracles. You. Nobody else. It was you, girl.

Miracles I didn't know she'd come out with a Taser, Jenny!

Jenny You know full well what Gigi is capable of.

Miracles I didn't know she was gonna—

Jenny Honey, God can hear the lies you about to release.

Miracles Well, God is the one who brought all these guys to us in the first place.

Jenny Or the devil.

Miracles The first time I walked into the room and saw him lyin' on my table, I thanked God.

Jenny Maybe you spoke too soon.

Miracles The scoop in his lower back. His shoulders? Oh my God, his shoulder blades. His muscles, his beautiful skin. I rubbed my palms together and I placed them on him and he shivered. There was this shock. It went through my whole body, chargin' from my wrists to my elbows, shimmerin' past my nipples down into my stomach and into—

Jenny I don't wanna hear it. I don't wanna hear it.

Miracles His energy filled me up, Jenny. I was soo nervous the whole massage.

Jenny Nervous cuz God was tryin' to tell you somethin'.

Miracles Me and Mariano, that's God's work, Jenny.

Jenny Girl, bye!

Miracles Betta watch yo'self, gettin' so bitter. You gonna look up one day and realize you just like Gigi. A old angry spinster who lives to make everybody else—

Jenny I don't need a man to make me happy, Miracles.

Miracles Be for real, Jenny.

Jenny You be for real, bitch.

Miracles Look at you, gettin' soo salty.

Jenny If you don't get outta my face right now, I swear to God above, I'ma—

Miracles What? We just ki-ki'ing, right? Can't handle the tea?

Jenny *takes a deep breath, exhales. Another deep breath.*

Miracles Y'all don't never think 'bout what it's like for me. Like maybe, maybe I might be trans.

Jenny Really, Miracles?

Miracles You don't know my insides, Jenny.

Jenny Bitch, you ain't trans. You just tryin' to find some solution to the mess that is Mariano.

Miracles I never felt right in my life. Always felt weird, like I don't belong.

Jenny And that's why you a tranny?

Miracles You so wrong, usin' that word.

Jenny Girl, log off! Who here ain't felt like they don't fit in? Kick yo' heels off, cuz that's a long fuckin' line.

Miracles Don't nobody in this house treat me serious.

Jenny God, God, God, pleeease help me!

She crosses herself.

Gigi *and* **Carmie** *bustle through the front door.*

Gigi I hope you're done playin' hide-n-seek wid your common sense, Missy.

Gigi *eyes* **Miracles**' *bandaged hand.*

Miracles I'm fine. Ain't no thing.

Gigi It's not just your money you playin' wid, baby girl.

Miracles Oh, I'm sorry. I'm sorry you Tasered my hand, Gigi.

Carmie It was a accident.

Miracles Oh, I'm sorry you a fuckin' snitch, bitch.

Carmie   I'm not a snitch.

Miracles   I can't. I can't wid none o' y'all.

Gigi   The drama is ovah, Miracles. It's ovah and done.

Carmie   Mariano, he won't be comin' 'round here no more.

Jenny   Thank goodness in the heavens.

Miracles   Why?

Carmie   Hudson and Dana said they gonna make sure.

Miracles   You went over there?

Gigi   To clean up your mess.

Miracles   Why can't y'all just leave us alone?

Gigi   Because you two are addicted to drama.

Miracles   We don't even make no drama. It's you and Hudson and Dana, you the ones always instigatin'.

Gigi   Oooooo, I can't.

Miracles   You so jealous of us. Jealous of our happiness, of us bein'—

Gigi   I can't, I can't, I can't. I can't take it anymore.

She heads for the back. **Miracles** *blocks her way.*

Gigi   Lil boy in drag, you best sashay to the right.

Carmie   Step off, Miracles.

Jenny   This not the time to get crazy, Miracles.

Miracles   I'm sick o' everybody puttin' demselves in my shit. I'm sick o' this shit! Y'all don't see it? How y'all all be—

Gigi   You don't like it here? Then drop the name and get outta my house.

Carmie   Don't we need her?

Gigi   Pray tell, for what?

Carmie   To stomp. Miracles, she our best walker.

Miracles   Carmie know the tea.

Gigi   She's lost it. Ain't nothin' miraculous 'bout her.

Miracles   You the reason we all so miserable.

Gigi   You miserable? Really? Cuz I can give you some Kathy Bates realness, give your mug some real misery.

Miracles If you hadn't taken our money, I'da been gone a long—

Gigi Your money?

Jenny You do take a big cut outta our fees.

Miracles What we s'posed to do wid forty per cent?

Gigi That ain't no different from any massage place in LA and you know it.

Jenny Yeah, but—

Gigi Do I really have to remind you that you live rent-free?

Miracles By forcin' us to be drag queens.

Gigi Where on earth you think I met your ratchet heels? At the balls, that's where. Tweakin' sixteen-year-old, two nickels away from turnin' tricks. Get yo' head right cuz this early Alzheimer's is not a good look for you.

Miracles I'm tired of the drag.

Gigi Then don't do it. Buy a pair of Dickies, throw on a wife beater. Don't beat yo' face. I don't give a fuck.

Miracles We all know you'd kick us out wid the quickness.

Gigi You still gotta bring in your percentage of business. If you can do it as a boy, then by all means. Be a boy. You not such a ugly boy.

Carmie You prolly a real pretty boy, huh?

Jenny You need to get dat trans thing outta yo' head.

Gigi Trans? Who trans?

Jenny Miracles say she is.

Miracles You don't never know when to shut yo' fat mouth.

Jenny Wasn't you just schoolin' me on yo' tea?

Gigi You a fierce ball queen. Everythin' from banjee[6] to couture. Shit, on a good day, I even give you butch queen realness. But trans, that ain't a category you just pick.

Miracles Shut yo' hole, Gigi. I'm not in the mood.

Gigi There is true sadness and pain in needin' gender reassignment. It's for little boys and girls that are trapped. Trapped in the wrong bodies.

Miracles *heads off.* **Gigi** *grabs her by the arm.*

Gigi You act like drag is some kinda evil frock that's been thrust upon you. Drag was always a part of the equation. You tired of it now, I get it, but it's done good by you. Drag gives you license. You beat that face and give yourself whatever

---

6 Street style or swagger. The term originated in the balls.

personality you want. Your mug is your bullhorn, ladies. And when you stomp a ball, people take notice. Who's this bitch? They whisper, they ki-ki. They dicks are tucked, but they still pee a little cuz they scurrred o' your stomp.

Jenny   I know that feeling.

Carmie   Damn, when I'ma feel dat?

Jenny   You live for the runway.

Miracles   Not no more.

Gigi   Then hang your heels up, Michael.

Jenny *and* **Carmie** *gasp.*

Gigi   You don't know which way yo' nuts hang since Mariano done twisted yo' panties up. You a boy and he a boy, that mean you gay. You not special. Just two faggots that don't know how to be faggots together.

Miracles   Y'all ain't experts on Miracles, all right?! I'm the one an' only Miracles!

She runs off.

Jenny *crosses herself.*

Gigi   That's right, Jenny, pray for us. Mother was rough round the edges, but God knows the tea.

Lights fade.

Scene Eight

Fernandez Home

Mariano *hurries for the door—quickly, quietly.*

Hudson (*offstage*)   Where you off to?

Mariano   What?

Hudson *approaches.*

Hudson   You never had any self-control.

Mariano   It's gettin' old, bro, you bein' all up in my biz.

Hudson   Biz? Is that what this is? This is your business?

Mariano   I'm not in the mood for a lecture, all right?

Hudson   Look, Mariano, you tryin' to make somethin' work that—

Mariano   Man, can this damn election be over already?!

Hudson   I'm not talking just 'bout the election. I'm talking about you.

Mariano *heads for the door.* **Hudson** *blocks.*

Hudson   You tried it out, dabbled in it. Yeah, it can feel good. It's different, it seems like—

Mariano   Just stop. Stop talkin' like you—

Hudson   You can't live your life like this.

Mariano   Like what?

Hudson   You can't be with her.

Mariano   Do I ever get in your business? You don't hear me tryin' to dictate to you what you should and shouldn't be doin'.

Hudson   It's not a normal—

Mariano   Yo', just stop policin' every detail of—

Hudson   If it was a normal kind of thing, if you could live together, if you would be happy bein' wid her for the rest of your life, you woulda decided. You would have made a choice already.

Mariano   When nobody wanted you to be seein' Dana, I didn't jump on that train.

Hudson   How you gonna compare my marriage to what you and this Miracles have?

Mariano   Everybody else, they was givin' you all kindsa grief. Hatin' on the two o' you. I had your back, Hudson!

Hudson   Dana and me—people came around. Cuz they knew that it was right.

Mariano   The problem here is you want what you want when it ain't even about you. Maybe I love her.

Hudson   You don't love her.

Mariano   You don't know.

Hudson   You wouldn't have all this back and forth.

Mariano   You don' know anything about us.

Hudson   Sneaking around, this embarrassment, and so much drama, Mariano—all this drama because you know it's not right.

Mariano   Man, this is some bullshit.

He goes for the door. **Hudson** *grabs him by the shirt.*

Mariano   I'm not some criminal you got locked up, can't be forcin' me to—

Hudson   Grow up, Mariano!

Dana *comes in, wrapped in a robe.*

Dana   What he do now?

Mariano   Nothin'.

He heads for the door.

Dana   Where you think you goin'?

Mariano   None o' yer damn business.

Hudson *grabs him by the shoulders, pulls him away from the door.*

Mariano   Get the fuck off me!

Dana   You sneakin' off to that damn—

Hudson   Dana, I got this.

Dana   Hudson, I've had enough of his—

Hudson   Dana! (*Beat.*) I said I got this.

Dana *stares* **Mariano** *down, takes a beat of pride in her husband, then leaves.*

Mariano   I'm not property. You don't "got" me, bro.

Hudson *shoves* **Mariano**.

Mariano   Oh, so you gonna do the big ol' macho cop thing now? Gonna flex your muscle?

Hudson   You are property, Mariano.

Mariano   Fuck you.

Hudson   Look at you. Can't hold down a job for more than a month. No schooling. No family, goals. Nothing. Wid you, I got a big pile of nothing. Thank God Mami's not here to see what you've become.

Mariano   Don't bring her into this.

Hudson   Seriously, what would she think? I mean if she's watching us, watching you—

Mariano   That's your problem. You can't let go. It's like you like bein' over me, controlling me.

Hudson   I want you to control yourself.

Mariano   It's not my fault Mami died and you had to step up, all right?

Hudson   I ain't never blamed you for that.

Mariano   You always holdin' it over me. Like I should kiss yo' feet every time I see you, thank you over and over for—

Hudson   You think I wanna take care of you forever? I don't wanna be your mother.

Mariano   So quit! Quit tryin' to run my—

Hudson I'm waitin' for you to show up. You thirty and everything, Mariano, everything in your life—the bed you lie in, the car you drive, the tortillas you eat, the *chones* around your little confused dick, you have all of that because of me. So, when I'm trying to do better for me and my wife, when I ask you for one favor while we're in this campaign, you shouldn't even have to think about it. Be grateful and just do it.

He heads off. He stops.

If you decide you can't honor my request, you let me know.

Lights fade.

Scene Nine

Lizette*'s House*

AJ *holds on to* **Lizette***'s phone.* **Lizette** *grabs his arm, trying to snatch it back.*

Lizette Give it here!

AJ You gotta stop with all the posting, Lizette.

Lizette *screams in frustration.*

AJ I'll give it back. Just please, stop with the crazy posts.

Lizette Dana said he'd be here when business was finished.

AJ What?

Lizette The end of the day! She said Mariano would be here. It's already eleven. The day is gone. It's over!

AJ *hands back her phone.*

Lizette Where is he?

AJ I don't know.

Lizette You always know.

AJ I got my own life too, you know. I'm not alive just to be watchin' Mariano.

She advances on him.

Lizette Did he go back to her?

AJ Who?

Lizette Don't treat me like I'm stupid, AJ! I can read between two lines.

AJ He seen her, yeah.

Lizette Whyyyyyyyyyyyyyyyyy????????????

AJ Calm down.

Lizette My life is crumbling around me an' you tellin' me to calm down?!

AJ You—don't you got other dudes?

Lizette Watchu talkin' 'bout?

AJ Other guys you talkin' to.

Lizette I'm a chunt to you?

AJ No! I just—I was—I'm sorry.

Lizette Is—is she pretty?

AJ C'mon, don't do this.

Lizette You seen her in person, what's she like?

AJ I don't know.

Lizette She be usin' all kindsa filters on her Instagram. She not that hot, is she?

AJ It's hard to explain.

Lizette She real fancy? Like she speak good?

AJ I guess. (*Beat.*) She's—I don't really know nobody like her.

Lizette Oh, so you tellin' me she real special. Like she precious, like one in a infinity and that kinda shit.

AJ She's pretty.

Lizette You don't have to pour salt into my eye, AJ.

AJ She's not as pretty as you. She has no ass.

Lizette I'm not just a ass, AJ.

AJ No, that's not what I meant.

She goes for the door.

AJ Where you goin'?

He takes her arm.

Lizette Let go of me, AJ.

AJ Look, just cuz he went to see her, it don't—

Lizette He would rather have that flat-ass Filipina over me? Why why why why why? I don't get it. I mean, look at me!

AJ I'm lookin' at you.

Lizette Why wouldn't he want this?

AJ I don't know.

Lizette You have to bring 'im here, AJ, please. Bring 'im to me.

AJ You're a beautiful girl.

Lizette Tell Mariano that! You two are tight. He'll listen to you.

AJ Look Lizette, I think you're beautiful. You're funny. A little wild, but—

Lizette Don't say stuff just to make me feel better.

AJ I'm not. Everything I say is on the real. You're beautiful.

She stops, sizes him up.

Lizette Why can't Mariano see what you see?

AJ Cuz he's—cuz he might be that way?

Lizette What way?

AJ C'mon, you know.

Lizette You mean like . . . like only likin' Asian hos?

AJ Uh, I was thinkin' more like—

Lizette There's no way he only like dem Filipina *putas*. We went on a date, okay? A date!

AJ One date don't mean nothin'.

Lizette It does to me.

AJ Okay, the sex couldn't have been that good. So good that it's got this grip on you.

Lizette We didn't have sex.

AJ You didn't?

Lizette You think I'm some ratchet ho?

AJ No, but I thought you woulda—

Lizette That's what made me fall in love with him.

AJ You are not in love.

Lizette Don't tell me how I feel.

AJ How could you possibly be in love?

Lizette He's so nice. He was a gentleman. He didn't even make a move on me.

AJ And that don't tell you nothin'?

Lizette Tells me he respects me. He was bein' romantic. He held my hand for a few minutes during the movie. And at the end of the date, we kissed.

AJ Besides that, you didn't do nothin'?

Lizette It was the most perfect kiss.

AJ Okay.

Lizette Now what am I gonna do when I see pandas?

AJ Pandas?

Lizette They were my favorite animal, but now, now I gotta get rid of all my stuffed pandas. My posters and magnets and figurines.

AJ Why?

Lizette Cuz we went to see Kung Fu Panda 9, hello? Now, I'm evicting all pandas from my life.

AJ *laughs.*

Lizette This is not funny.

AJ I'm sorry, you right. It's not funny.

Lizette It's not.

AJ You're—you're—

Lizette What?

AJ You're cute when you get mad.

Lizette Don't condescend me, AJ!

Pulls out her phone.

Maybe if I post this sonogram, he'll come lookin' for me.

AJ Sonogram?!

Lizette It's my cousin's. But it'll get his attention. Hudson will make him do right. He wouldn't let Mariano just abandon his kid.

AJ But there's no kid.

Lizette I got a sonogram.

AJ You're talkin' crazy.

Lizette I'm not!

AJ You're makin' up a baby!

Lizette It's a real baby. It's just my cousin's.

AJ Lizette!

Lizette Why doesn't he want me?

AJ You're crazy for some guy you kissed once. Once!

Lizette We held hands!

AJ Open your eyes, Lizette. Check out the guy in front of you who actually likes you. The one who wouldn't leave you hangin'. The one who would text you back and come thru when he says he will.

Lizette *is silent.*

AJ There, I said it.

Lizette You like me?

AJ Ain't that what I said?

Lizette You really like me?

He hugs her.

Lizette You really like me.

AJ Yeah, I'm not playin'.

Lizette This—this feels nice.

AJ Yeah?

Lizette I think so.

They linger in the hug.

AJ Uh, I'ma—Lizette, can I . . .

Lizette What?

AJ I'ma kiss you, okay?

Lizette *hesitates, then nods.* **AJ** *goes in* . . .

Mariano (*offstage*) Lizette?

Lizette Mariano?

Mariano *comes in with a bouquet of flowers.*

Mariano (*to* **AJ**) What you doin' here?

Lizette Those for me, Papi?

Mariano Uh, I got 'em-- yeah, these for you.

Lizette *takes the flowers, throws herself in his arms.*

Lizette Oh my God, Mariano, you're here! You got me flowers!

AJ Lizette, what about what we—

Lizette AJ, you such a loyal friend. Puttin' yo'self on the line for Mariano like that.

Mariano What you two been doin'?

Silence.

Lizette He was comfortin' me, Papi. AJ told me you was gonna come thru.

AJ Lizette, I wasn't kidding about what I—

Lizette I shoulda been patient. Dana and Hudson said you'd come.

Mariano Watchu talkin' to Dana and my brother for?

Lizette I gotta work on my trust issues. My trust issues and my patience.

Mariano *pulls away from* **Lizette**.

Lizette Shit, I shoulda cooked you somethin'. You hungry, Mariano? I can make us some quesadillas. Or we can go out, you wanna go out?

Mariano *inches towards the door.*

Mariano Naw, I'm— I have to . . .

Lizette Mariano, you got a taste for chicken? We could get Pollo Campero.

Mariano This—naw, this was a bad idea.

Lizette Watchu want? You want pupusas?!

Mariano I can't. I can't do this. I shouldn'ta come.

And he rushes out.

Lizette Mariano! No! Mariano!

She runs to the door. **AJ** *grabs her arm.*

Lizette Let go o' me, AJ!

AJ You don't need to be chasin' him.

Lizette You ruined everything!

AJ Me? What I—

She shoves him, rushes out.

AJ Shit, Lizette! Lizette!

He runs out.

Scene Ten

Malacañang Massage—Reception Area

Carmie *lugs a big suitcase from the back. After a few moments,* **Miracles** *hurries in from the back with a bag and giant purse,* **Jenny** *hot on her heels.*

Miracles' *face is wiped clean—she is dressed as a boy.*

Jenny You just gonna go? Just like this?

Miracles I'm pushin' through, Jenny. Gonna have a fresh start.

Jenny Who just springs packed bags on someone?

Miracles Mariano and me, we both want this.

Jenny You need to cool yo' cha-cha heels a minute and think this through. Like where you even stayin'?

Miracles We ain't pressed. We'll figure it out.

Carmie You don't have nowhere to stay?

Jenny She don't know nobody there.

Carmie Girl, homeless ain't a good look.

Miracles I got Mariano.

Jenny Yeah, so unbothered wid him at yo' side.

Miracles Whatever, hater, bye.

She grabs all her luggage, struggles to the door.

Jenny Girl can't even handle her baggage.

Carmie Miracles, don't be leavin' all angry-like.

Miracles San Francisco's not far, Carmie. Once we settled, you can come visit.

Carmie Don't be pretendin' you don't know me when I pop up on yo' doorstep.

Miracles Please, I ain't like that.

Jenny She ain't goin' nowhere, Carmie.

Miracles You don't even want me here.

Carmie Why not?

Miracles She want all the clients to herself, Carmie.

Jenny You a lie and a half. We was havin' a sisterly argument. Things come up that—

Miracles All that shit you was mouthin' off, you meant it, Jenny. Own it.

Carmie What you say, Jenny?

Jenny I know my truth. Do you know yours?

Miracles Heifer, please.

Jenny Riddle me this, girl. Wid yo' clothes and face like this, you think Mariano gonna be comfortable walkin' down the street wid you?

Carmie Wait, he seen you like a boy, right?

Miracles *evaluates her boy clothes.*

Miracles It's complete realness.

Carmie Girrl, some people can't handle realness.

Jenny Ain't that the tea!

Miracles Mariano loves me.

Jenny You are not bein' smart, Miracles!

She grabs **Miracles** *by the arms.*

Miracles Bitch, quit!

Jenny You make me wanna shake you. I just wanna shake you, girl. Shake some sense into you.

Carmie Jenny!

Miracles *yanks herself out of* **Jenny***'s grasp.*

Miracles You gone crazy.

Jenny Lord, forgive me for my frustration, but you are not lettin' me thru! I need you to send this girl some kinda sign that—

Miracles I can conversate wid God on my own.

Jenny Boy or girl, Miracles? How you gonna live yo' life? You really gonna drag it up every day in S-F? All kindsa hats and sunglasses, a thousand pounds of make-up so that man, that *boy* can continue lyin' to himself? Goin' to sleep in a lace-front wid a full beat every night?

Miracles *is quiet.*

Carmie Maybe you should find someone else.

Miracles He loves me. However. Whichever. Whatever.

Jenny Sorry, did I miss the news flash? He outta the closet now?

Miracles You don't know how strong our love is.

Jenny Do you know how strong the closet is?

Carmie That shit is strong.

Jenny He's just using you, Miracles.

Miracles Hash tag real love, bitch.

Jenny I know you wanna be in love. I know. I swear as God's my witness, I will help you. I'll hit all the bars, all the clubs wid you.

Carmie I wanna come.

Jenny We will find you someone.

Miracles I'm not on the market!

Carmie We'll put yo' mug up online. I'll find us all some mens. Shit, I'll even find

106   FIXED

Gigi a old man.

Jenny   We can go to one o' dem gay churches. Or those mixers they have at—

Mariano *comes in, stops at the sight of* **Miracles**.

Mariano   Miracles?

Carmie   Damn. Look what the fish swam in.

Miracles *runs to him, hugs him. He pulls away, studies* **Miracles**' *appearance.*

Jenny   You feelin' this look?

Miracles   Shut up, Jenny.

Mariano *touches* **Miracles**' *hair.*

Mariano   I, uh—it's different.

Miracles   Baby, it's me.

Mariano   Yeah, I know. But . . .

Jenny   Lights different in the massage rooms.

Mariano *touches* **Miracles**' *face.*

Mariano   Never seen you wid no make-up.

Jenny   You like a girl to beat her face, right?

Miracles   Jenny, if you don't quit.

Mariano *clocks the luggage.*

Mariano   What's all this?

Miracles   My bags. I wanna go. Tonight.

Mariano   Where you goin'?

Miracles   Us, baby. San Francisco.

Mariano *is silent.*

Miracles   Lavender basil cookies, baby. Sourdough bread. The Golden Gate Bridge.

Lizette *appears in the doorway.*

Lizette   Mariano!

Jenny   Lord, help us.

Mariano   What you doin' here?

Carmie   Who da hell is this?

Lizette   I'm his woman, bitch.

Miracles   You betta get her the hell outta here.

Lizette (*rushing towards* **Miracles**)   You need to mind yo' own . . .

Lizette *slows, the light bulb going off.*

Lizette   Wait. (*Beat.*) Nooo. (*Beat.*) No, this is . . .

Carmie   No, what?

Jenny   Wait for it, gurl.

Lizette   You Miracles?

Jenny   Here we go.

Lizette   Miracles is a boy?

Miracles   Baby, get 'er outta here.

Lizette   I thought Miracles was—she not a girl?

Miracles   More girl than you'll ever be.

Lizette   Mariano, you gay?

Mariano   No.

Carmie   Wow, for real?

Lizette   Ya'll together?

Jenny   You ain't figured it out yet?

Lizette   Bitch, shut yo' face!

Jenny   God, don't make me have to fight her.

Mariano   Lizette, man, you should leave. You don't need to be here.

Lizette   You takin' up wid this or not?

Miracles   Ain't no takin' up. We been together. Get it straight.

Lizette   What you do to him? Turned him out wid yo' nasty ways.

Miracles   I'm nasty? Have you seen yo'self?

Lizette   Why you gotta do me like this, Mariano? Whyyyyyy? Why you haveta seduce me—if you gay, you shoulda never asked me—

Mariano   I'm not gay!

AJ *hurries in.*

AJ   Lizette!

Lizette   Stop stalkin' me, AJ!

Jenny   Okay, everybody, all the Messicans need to get out.

Carmie   I live here.

Jenny   Y'all need to leave.

Lizette   Is this yo' man or not?

Miracles   You already know I am.

Lizette   I wanna hear Mariano say it.

Mariano *takes* **Lizette** *by the arm.*

Lizette   Let go o' me!

AJ   Let 'er go. I'll handle her.

Lizette *charges at* **Mariano**, *slapping him.*

Carmie   Aw, shit!

Jenny   Ratchet, just ratchet everywhere.

AJ *pulls* **Lizette** *away from* **Mariano**. **Lizette** *swings her arms—thunderous windmills.*

Lizette   I hate you. You and yo' nasty freak.

Mariano   Man, shut up!

Lizette   Tryin' to kick it to me wid yo' AIDS-ridden dick!

Miracles   Get out!

Lizette   I shoulda known! I shoulda known!

Gigi *rushes in from the back.*

Gigi   What the hell kinda faggotry is goin' on in my house?!

Mariano *moves to the wall, cowering.*

Lizette *struggles to break free of* **AJ**'s *grasp.*

Lizette   I'ma kick his ass. Kick 'im in the nuts. See how his boyfriend freak like 'im when his nuts all smashed!

Gigi *advances on* **Lizette**.

Gigi   This is a massage parlor, hunty. Not some Messican swap meet.

Lizette   I'm Guatemalan, you ugly beast!

Gigi *shoves her towards the door.*

Gigi   Get yo' ratchet ass outta my place of business!

Lizette *gathers herself, seems like she's going for the door, then she charges at* **Gigi**.

Lizette   Ugly fuckin' *puta*, don't be—

AJ *intercepts.*

AJ   Shit, Lizette, it's not worth it.

Lizette   Mariano Fernandez is a faggot!

Gigi   Tell us somethin' we don't know!

AJ   Let's go, Lizette!

Lizette   You gonna see! The whole world gonna know!

Mariano   Man, shut your hole!

AJ   Leave her be. I got this.

Lizette   Gaaaayyyyyy! You faggoty gay faggot!

AJ   Lizette, bring it down.

Lizette   Why'd he have to bring me into all this mess?

AJ   You good, you good.

Lizette   I wish I never met you!

And **AJ** *takes her out.*

Gigi *stares* **Miracles** *and* **Mariano** *down.*

Miracles   What?

Gigi   Nothin' to say fo' yo'self?

Miracles   I wasn't the one actin' crazy.

Carmie   That was some crazy tilapia.

Jenny   Rotten fish. Bait.

Gigi   She ain't the root of the madness here.

She moves towards **Mariano**.

Mariano   I didn't bring her here, Gigi. She followed me. I didn't know she was gonna—

Gigi   You not s'posed to be here either, fool.

Mariano   Right, but Miracles—

Gigi   You done promised Hudson and Dana to stay away from Miracles til the campaign was over.

Miracles   Why you always gotta instigate?

Gigi   You here cuz you love her? Love Miracles so much, you wanna be wid her forever and ever? Is that why you here, Mariano?

Miracles   We done arguin', tryin' to convince you that—

Gigi   It's a simple question. You either love her or you don't.

Mariano *is silent.*

Miracles We done wid this shit. No pimps and politicians bossin' us, makin' rules for us. We choose, right, Mariano?

Gigi It's all about him. What he wants, what he's hidin' from, all the shit he's afraid of. It ain't never gonna be 'bout you, baby girl.

Miracles I got the real tea, old lady. I'm leavin'.

Gigi *Putang ina,*[7] Miracles! His silence, it's deafening. It says everything you need to know.

Miracles Baby, get the suitcase please.

Carmie Miracles, no.

Miracles *hugs* **Carmie**.

Miracles You get outta dis place soon as you can.

Jenny You can't just leave like this.

Miracles We too good to be hookers, Jenny.

Carmie Who be hookin'?

Miracles What we do here, it ain't but a millimeter o' difference.

She grabs a bag, heads for the door.

Gigi *grabs the bag from her.*

Gigi It's not talk just to talk, Miracles. What I'm tryin' to shout in yo' head is truth. On the real, it's the mothafuckin' tea.

Miracles Preach to the next girl, Gigi. I'm done.

Gigi What am I gonna do wid you? I am-- I have been tryin'-- Mariano, he's the worst-quality crab, Miracles. I am begging you, for once in yo' life, choose the best. The best quality, Miracles. You deserve it.

Miracles Don't pay her no mind, baby. Get the suitcase. We out.

Mariano *takes a couple steps towards the suitcase.*

He stops, looks at **Miracles**.

Miracles Mariano?

Mariano *bolts!*

Jenny Oh God, help us!

Miracles Mariano!

She rushes out the door.

---

7 Tagalog profanity/interjection, "whore mother."

Carmie   Fuck!

Gigi   Without a single word.

Silence.

Jenny *takes hold of the suitcase.*

Gigi   What you doin', Jenny?

Jenny   Might as well put it back in her room.

Gigi *watches as* **Jenny** *drags the suitcase towards the back.*

Gigi   Put it out front.

Carmie   Out front?

Jenny   Gigi, you—you can't just kick her out.

Gigi   She quit the house, Jenny.

Jenny   We do not want her endin' up like one o' dem Vanderbilt girls.

Carmie   Oh God.

Gigi   Carmie, put it out front.

Carmie   She gonna be homeless, Gigi.

Gigi   Carmie.

Carmie   No, Gigi. No.

Gigi *rolls the suitcase towards the door.*

Jenny   Gigi!

Jenny *and* **Carmie** *block the door.*

Gigi   She's cancerous. She stays here, he'll be back again. I ain't got time for that mini-series.

Jenny   You gotta forgive her.

Carmie   Ain't we her family?

Gigi   How many times we s'posed to rescue her?

Jenny   You know how she is.

Gigi   Yes, she's a addict. She loves drama, the unavailable, abandonment.

Carmie   So you just give up?

Gigi   What else we gonna tell her? I gave her a job, a home. I gave her my name. Everything.

She rolls the suitcase past **Carmie** *and* **Jenny**.

Lights fade.

Scene Eleven

Miracles' *Car*

Miracles *sits in the car half-naked, beating her face with blush.*

She evaluates her handiwork in the rearview mirror.

She dials on her phone, puts it on speaker.

Mariano (*voiceover*)   Leave a message. Yo' digits too.

Miracles   I'm outside, Mariano. You almost ready? Come out soon, baby.

She hangs up.

She expertly lines her lips, then applies lipstick.

She hooks on a bra.

She digs through a bag on the passenger seat. She takes her cutlets, stuffs them in her bra.

Fishy. Real fish. They can't tell.

She dials again.

Mariano (*voiceover*)   Leave a message. Yo' digits too.

Miracles   Papi, almost 'read to go. Come out.

She hangs up.

She slides into a blouse, adjusts her rack. She stares into the mirror.

She gets out of the car—stands in front of the side mirror in her blue briefs.

Shit.

She reaches into her briefs and tucks.

It's tucked, ain't nobody gonna clock . . . it's tucked.

She smooths down her crotch.

There. Smooth.

She examines her tuck in the mirror.

I don't even really have to. Cuz you love me any which way. But I'ma do it anyways.

She dials.

Mariano (*voiceover*)   Leave a message. Yo' digits too.

Miracles   I know you not—you not gonna leave me hangin', Mariano. Hurry up, get out here.

She studies her tuck.

What do you see? (*Beat.*) Can you tell?

Disappointment fills her face.

She digs in her bag, pulls out a pair of manicure scissors.

I'ma fix it, don't you worry. I'm gonna fix it.

She reaches into her briefs and untucks.

Lights fade as she brings the scissors towards her crotch.

In darkness, we hear **Miracles** *scream—a very pained, masculine scream.*

Scene Twelve

The Ball

Gigi *stands in a black gown, holding a microphone. She emcees the ball.*

Gigi   Where's the banjee girlz? Category is. Vogue fem! Come thru!

Ball vogue music pulses. **Carmie** *works the start of the runway, dressed in banjee girl realness—arms flailing, shoulders windmilling, hands slapping the air.*

Gigi   From the House of Malacañang, givin' you banjee girl realness.

Jenny *rushes on in her best eleganza, sidelining the runway like a crazed fan.*

Jenny   Yassss, girrrl, give it to 'em!

Spin, bitch, spin! Serve it serve it!

Percussion drops in hard. **Carmie** *struts forward, voguing.*

Gigi   Banjee girl, what?

Give it to me give it to me, what?

Give it to me give it to me.

Carmie *punctuates every move with a hand, a kick, a pelvic thrust, a back arch.*

Gigi   Eat it eat it! Serve it, serve it!

Serve it, Miracles! Miracles Malacañang, servin' you. You gonna gag!

Carmie *stops nervously, look up at* **Gigi**.

Jenny *hurries to* **Gigi**, *is about to step up on the platform. After a few beats,* **Gigi** *gathers herself, resumes.*

Gigi   Ladies and gentlemen, from the House of Malacañang, Carmie Malacañang!

Bring it to the floor.

Bring it to the runway.

On cue, **Carmie** *resumes. She obliges with a dramatic death drop.*

Jenny *Yassss,*
you betta drop!
You got it, chola!
Hips don't lie. Serve it, bitch!

Carmie *vogues, getting to her feet, giving all kinds of angles and contortions.*

Gigi School is in session. You are experiencin' the legendary House of Malacañang. Are you living? We live. Live, I say. Live.

Lights fade as **Carmie** *lives for the runway.*

END OF PLAY

School for Witches, or Friendship Betrayed!

Madhuri Shekar

School for Witches, or Friendship Betrayed!

Introduction by Barbara Fuchs

Madhuri Shekar's subtitle winks at her source text, *La traición en la amistad* (*Friendship Betrayed*, c. 1618–32), by the noted protofeminist María de Zayas (c. 1590–1661). In that comedy of amorous intrigue, four young women—Marcia, Fenisa, Belisa, and Laura—must negotiate their loves for three gallants, Liseo, Gerardo, and Juan. The betrayal involves Fenisa pursuing Liseo, whom Marcia loved first. Shekar's *Witches* picks up on *Traición* as a play about and among women, where friendship and desire are considered from multiple female perspectives.

Shekar goes beyond Zayas' focus on women to present an entirely female universe, with nary a male character to be seen. Abstracting from Zayas a more generalized concern with women's power and patriarchy's response to it, she sets her play "At a reform school—a juvenile detention facility—for witches" (p. 119). The school is a sort of Hogwarts-meets-*Mädchen in Uniform*, with magic as a stand-in for the sexual intensity of the teenagers.

Shekar's all-female world magnifies Zayas' portrayal of female friendship that shades into homoeroticism. In the source play, women constantly express their admiration for each other's beauty, while in the adaptation they frankly lust for and sleep with each other. The adaptation's focus on witchcraft as a metaphor for female power picks up on a small but significant detail in the source, where the *gracioso* [comic sidekick] offers Liseo a spell to solve the problems born of his infidelity (ll. 224–5). Though this remains immaterial to the plot of *Traición*, it invokes the famous figure of La Celestina, and a rich universe of female power in witchcraft, magic, and medicine. From these threads, Shekar weaves a humorous yet trenchant fantasy of restored female agency.

In *School for Witches*, the idea of a "normal" heterosexual union towards which the play and its protagonists inexorably career becomes a running joke from the start, as Marcia tries to divine who her husband will be by using a head of lettuce, to great comic effect. In fact, Marcia has no real interest in men, but only in being "normal," whatever her actual desires. Heterosexuality as default is immediately satirized, long before there is any actual partner for Marcia to engage. Fenisa instead conjures her own magic to visualize a free-floating soulmate—possibly Marcia's, possibly her own—and thereby introduces Lisea. She will become the source of friction between the two friends as they compete for the newcomer's attentions, much as they do for the male Liseo in Zayas' original.

Shekar introduces two antiheroines—Lisea and Fenisa—only one of whom corresponds to a female character in Zayas' original. Lisea is an interesting composite: as the adaptation only gradually reveals, she is fundamentally untrustworthy, and has done great harm to other witches. The most serious damage—again, as in Zayas' original—is to Laura, who has been irreversibly transformed by her encounter with Lisea. But whereas in *Traición* Laura has lost her virginity to Liseo, in the adaptation she has been more wholly transformed—into a frog.

At the same time, Lisea is a fiery, uncompromising revolutionary. A new arrival at the school, she constantly goads the others towards rebellion and violence: the residents should blow up the school, join the revolution, take over the world. Yet she is also the one who voices uncomfortable truths about the status of women under patriarchy, as she encourages the others to break out of the passivity that their indoctrination has imposed. When Fenisa notes, "This place has a way of making us feel not so great about ourselves," Lisea responds, "That's what it's designed to do. Take two strong, beautiful, women like yourselves, and make you feel like you're less than. You're deviant. You're wrong" (p. 129). Instead of representing a patriarchal, heterosexual alternative to gynocentrism, as her counterpart Liseo does in the original play, Lisea introduces the possibility that those whose personal behaviour is reprehensible might nonetheless offer important political alternatives. In this female universe, allegiances are complicated and gender offers no reliable guide to character.

Shekar's Fenisa also illuminates Zayas' original in fascinating ways. In the source text, Fenisa functions as a female Don Juan—a cautionary counter-exemplar of unbridled female sexuality—or, conversely, as a defiant example of a woman who refuses to abide by patriarchal limitations. In the adaptation, Fenisa is similarly complex: sexually liberated, she announces her relationship with Lisea to Marcia by listing all the places the two have had sex, even though she knows that it will devastate her scandalized friend.

Despite this rather spectacular breach, Shekar's purely female universe recuperates Fenisa: there are no nuptials here to exclude her or leave her out in the cold to receive her comeuppance, as in the original. Whereas in Zayas' the women come together to enforce Laura's "claim" to Liseo and punish Fenisa for her insatiable sexual appetite, reinforcing patriarchal mores, in Shekar's version the betrayal in Marcia and Fenisa's friendship is overcome and repaired, in an ending that restores the bonds between the women.

Shekar's comic adaptation thus makes visible crucial tensions and unspoken ironies in Zayas' original. As a strong reading, the adaptation expands upon the original's ideological potential, underscoring its most pressing questions: what particular kind of threat does a female Don Juan pose, and to whom? What is the value of female solidarity if it only serves to police female sexuality? How does homosociality shade into homoeroticism, and how can those attachments be expressed within a patriarchal, heteronormative context, on the one hand, or beyond it, on the other? *School for Witches* does not merely update *La traición en la amistad*, although it certainly does that, with freshness and charm. It also revitalizes our reading of the complex gender politics of the original, finding new possibilities between the lines.

School for Witches, or Friendship Betrayed!

A play by Madhuri Shekar

Inspired by *La traición en la amistad* by Maria de Zayas y Sotomayor.

Characters

THE WITCHES
Marcia, *female, 17*   *Trying to be good. Trying to be Normal.*
Fenisa, *female, 17*   *Trying to be discreet. Will never be Normal.*
Lisea, *female, 17*   *A very attractive mystery.*
Laura, *female*   *A voice in the vents.*

Setting

At a reform school—a juvenile detention facility—for witches.

Scene One

*Marcia and **Fenisa** hang out in their dorm room. Spare. Drab. It's a dorm. **Fenisa** is lying on her bed, reading a book. **Marcia** looks backwards into a mirror holding a head of lettuce. **Marcia** is still in her school uniform, wearing a shiny, glinty, prefect's badge.*

Marcia (*singsong*)

> Tell me now oh mirror white
> Who will grace my dreams at night
> My soul to dream, my heart to call
> To the man who'll win it all.

She kisses the head of lettuce, throws it up in the air, and spins around to check herself out in the mirror. She picks up the lettuce, kisses it, and tries tossing it again.

Fenisa *turns from side to side, trying to ignore her, finally—*

Fenisa Marcia, what the fuck are you doing?

Marcia One of the new girls told me this is what the Normals are doing in the village.

Fenisa Making out with vegetables?

Marcia This is how Normals are finding out who they're going to marry. When you say the rhyme and kiss the lettuce and throw it up and then you look at yourself in the mirror, you should see the face of the man you're meant to be with.

Fenisa Normals are trying to do magic?

Marcia Well, it's not magic though. It's like. . . it's like . . .

Fenisa A superstition?

Marcia Maybe. So that's why it's safe. It all feels very normal. In fact, it doesn't seem to be working.

Fenisa You don't even like boys.

Marcia I will like boys, when I finally get to meet them. In fact, that is on the top five list of the things I will do as soon as I get out. I will find a boy, and use his penis to make a baby.

Fenisa We don't need a penis to make a baby.

Marcia Normals do.

Fenisa Just seems messy.

Marcia Yeah, well.

Fenisa I made a baby once.

Marcia You did?

Fenisa I was six. Really wanted a little sister. My mom was like, I'm never touching your dad's penis again. So I went into the garden, rolled up a ball of soil and grass, and made a baby.

Marcia When you were six?

Fenisa Yeah.

Marcia Was that when your parents . . . knew?

Fenisa Yep.

Marcia What happened to the baby?

Fenisa She was cool. I named her Dirt. She didn't last long. She turned back into soil and grass a couple of days later.

*A beep, and then an announcement through the **PA System**. These announcements are routine and regular.*

PA System (*beep*) It is now 8pm. All students must return to their dorms. Any student seen outside or in the halls will be subject to detention. Remember. You are not special. Good night.

Marcia *sits down on the edge of* **Fenisa**'*s bed.*

Marcia Hey . . . don't tell your story to anyone else. Your baby story.

Fenisa Of course I won't. Think I'm crazy or something?

Marcia I'm gonna miss you.

All these years together and you still surprise me.

Fenisa *chuckles.*

Fenisa Right back atcha milady.

Bet you never thought we'd still be here, huh?

Marcia   . . . You, maybe.

Me? Of course not.

I'm gonna pass this time. I'm gonna be out of here.

She crosses her legs.

Fenisa You're thinking about the grass under your feet, aren't you?

Marcia Yes. But only how I'm going to control myself.

Fenisa Thinking about the fresh, dewy, moist—

Marcia Stop it—

Fenisa Cool, soft, earth under your feet—

Marcia Stop it—

Fenisa Feeling that warmth rise up through your toes, your heels, your ankles, your calves, your thighs—

Marcia Stop—stop it, it's not cute—

Fenisa All the way up through your arms until it bursts out in one ecstatic—

Marcia (*really upset*) STOP IT.

(*Pause.*)

I'm going to pass it this time. I'm going to pass the test. I'm going to stay Normal. And I'm going to go home.

Fenisa Sorry.

Marcia You should be. That's not nice.

Fenisa *shifts in bed.*

Marcia Don't you want to go home?

Fenisa Of course not. I turn eighteen in six months. They have to let me out either way.

Marcia But how are you going to survive out there if you haven't passed the half-yearlies? If you haven't learned to be Normal?

Fenisa I'll figure it out. We've been around as long as Normals have been around, and... we've survived.

Marcia Well, I'm getting out. I've gone five months and twenty-nine days with no incident demerits—they actually made me a prefect this year—and I'm going to pass —I'm going to crush the half-yearlies. I'm gonna be so Normal, I'm gonna be, like, stupid. The wardens are gonna be, like, how did she even get in? Oh my God. We must've made a mistake, six years ago. And my mom and dad and brothers and sisters are going to be super-happy to see me. And I'm going to marry the man that the lettuce shows me, and use his penis to make a baby!

She grabs the lettuce and starts the ritual again.

(*Singsong.*)

> Tell me now oh mirror white
> Who will grace my dreams at night
> My soul to dream, my heart to call
> To the man who'll—

Fenisa (*interrupting*) Christ, Marcia. There's an easier way.

She sits up in bed, a familiar glint in her eye. She starts looking around the room.

Marcia Nope. Nope.

Fenisa I'll do it for you.

She pulls out a bucket from underneath her bed.

Marcia   Fenisa, no. No. Come on, I'm standing right here.

Fenisa   You gonna rat me out?

She grabs a kettle that's on the stove. Hot water.

Marcia   Of course not. But the wardens can smell it. They say they can smell the magic on us. They say we reek of it.

Fenisa   They're bluffing. You can't smell magic.

Marcia   They'll put you in solitary!

Fenisa   We both know there's no such thing.

She starts dragging out various implements from around the room. Roots, tubers, worms . . .

Marcia   We wouldn't know! Would we! What are you doing?

Fenisa   Making a potion.

Marcia *flips out.*

Marcia   We can't make a potion, are you insane!

Fenisa *grabs tea bags and drops them into the bucket along with everything else.*

Fenisa   I have my bath bucket, I have some tea bags, not as good as tea leaves, but they'll do.

Marcia   Divination is the worst form of magic.

Fenisa   I do it all the time.

Marcia   You do?

Fenisa *pours in the hot water.*

Fenisa   Sure. Is the sewing class going to be cancelled on Monday? What mood is Warden Jones gonna be in tonight? Will I still be sleeping with Griselda next week? The bucket tells me everything I need to know.

Marcia   But—

Fenisa *starts stirring the "cauldron"—the bucket.*

Fenisa   Come on. The cauldron is ready. Gimme the lettuce—

Marcia   What do you need this for?

Fenisa   It's a fresh head of lettuce. It's green and leafy. Where did you get it?

Marcia   The vegetable patch.

*A moment as **Fenisa** falls silent. **Marcia** knows why.*

Fenisa (*casual*)   It's a wonder you even got it in here. How did you get it in here?

Marcia   I'm a prefect. The wardens trust me. They don't trust you.

Fenisa   Gimme the lettuce.

Marcia   No . . .

Fenisa   Do you wanna find out who your soulmate is or not?
Look.
I'm doing the spell, not you. Your record will be fine.

She beckons. **Marcia** *reluctantly hands over the lettuce.* **Fenisa** *drops it into the potion.*

Fenisa   No silly rhymes. We're not children. Just . . .

HMMMMM . . .

She has her arms extended out over the potion. Her eyes are closed in concentration.

Magic is always accompanied by a strong humming, a throbbing. Either from the witch herself or from the air around her.

HMMMMM . . .

Potion . . .

We're looking for a soulmate.

Show us who Marcia's soulmate is.

The humming gets louder, now it seems to be coming from outside **Fenisa**. *Slowly, a slight, shimmering apparition appears before the two of them. Transparent, no, translucent.*

They both stare at the apparition.

Marcia   Ohhh. Wow.

Fenisa   Oh, yes.

Marcia   He's . . . handsome.

Fenisa   He's . . . a girl.

Marcia *does a double take.*

Marcia   No.

Fenisa   That's a girl.

Yep, definitely a girl.

The apparition spins around for them obligingly.

Marcia   But . . . but no.

Fenisa   It's okay. Some Normals like girls too, you know.

Marcia   But . . . but . . . I—I need to be a normal Normal.

Fenisa Oh, sweetie. (*She turns her attention back to the apparition.*) Mmmm. She is . . . she is . . .

Marcia She is . . .

A moment as they admire the figure. **Fenisa** *realizes—*

Fenisa   . . . She goes here.

Marcia What?

Fenisa She's new. She goes here.

Marcia What do you mean?

Fenisa This morning. I saw her from the window. She was dropped off at the front gate in a big black car. The wardens took her in. We'll probably see her at lunch tomorrow.

Marcia (*hardly believing her luck*)   . . . No.

Fenisa Oh yes.

They both sigh at the same time. They both reach out for the apparition. It shimmers and fades. They groan in disappointment.

Marcia (*pause*)   I'm going to turn in.

Fenisa (*quickly*)   So am I, good night!

They both dive into their respective beds.

Scene Two

Lunch room. It's drab. A very, very depressing cafeteria.

Marcia *and* **Fenisa** *stand to the side, holding their trays.* **Lisea** *sits by herself—the very apparition they'd seen the previous day, now in full flesh, bone, and hair. A very striking young lady.* **Marcia** *clutches her tray, staring at* **Lisea.**

Marcia Oh gosh. Golly. Gee willikers.

You were right. She does go here.

Fenisa I told you.

Marcia She seems . . . like . . . our age.

Fenisa Yeah.

Marcia I've never heard of someone joining the institute so late in life! Most of us know by the time we're eleven.

Fenisa Some don't realize it till later. Some think they can still live like Normals. Some try their best to hide it.

Marcia Isn't it obvious though?

Fenisa   Not always.

PA System (*beep*)   A reminder that today is the last day to register for the half-yearlies. The next visitation day has been moved to December 15th. Tryouts for the cooking and baking team are today at 3 p.m. in the home-sciences studio. Remember. You are not special.

Marcia *looks around.*

Marcia   We should go sit with her. But just to be polite.

Fenisa   Whatever you say, Marcia, she's your soulmate.

Marcia   Stop saying that.

Fenisa   Wow, blush any harder and you'll turn into a tomato.

Marcia   Shut up.

They go up to the table.

Lisea *looks up at them.*

Marcia   Hi.

H-hi-

Hh-hhhaaahhhhhhh

Marcia*'s mouth goes dry.*

Fenisa   Can we sit with you?

Lisea   Sure.

They sit down.

Fenisa   I'm Fenisa. And that quivering hunk of jelly over there is Marcia.

Lisea   I'm Lisea. Nice to meet you both.

Fenisa   Not from around here, are you?

Lisea   I've been places.

Fenisa   I saw you getting dropped off yesterday. What year are you in?

Lisea   They said I'm in Year 6.

Fenisa   Oh, that's what we are. Just the two of us left in Year 6, actually. Most people get out much earlier, cuz, you know, they start when they're pretty young. And it doesn't take most people half a decade to get Normalized.

Lisea   And yet, you are still here.

Fenisa   I'm biding my time. I'm almost eighteen anyway. This one though—oh, it's not for lack of trying.

Marcia   I have . . . control issues.

I just, I . . .

I get so close to staying Normal. And then something happens, inside me, and I—pfff.

Lisea *reaches out and puts a hand on* **Marcia's**.

Lisea   It's all right.

Marcia   Hhhh—hhhhahhaahhhhhhhh—

Fenisa   Marcia, save the drool for the sandwich.

Marcia *dabs her mouth with a napkin.*

Fenisa   So how come they got you in so late?

Lisea   I've been in and out of a few schools.

Fenisa (*intrigued*)   Oh, that's . . . that's interesting.

Marcia   Are you doing the half-yearlies next week?

Fenisa   Do you even know what the half-yearlies are?

Lisea   They are the exams, here, I'm assuming.

Fenisa   Yeah, every six months. Ergo, half-yearlies. You just got here though. Are they gonna let you take it?

Lisea   It was told it would be in my best interest to pass the half-yearlies, yes.

Marcia   That's great. That means you might be able to get out as early as next week.

Fenisa   If that's what you want.

Lisea   You're free to go, if you pass?

Fenisa   Well, free, like, they send you back to your family.

Lisea   What's the exam?

Marcia   Um, they take us all out into the woods, and we stand barefoot in the grass for an hour, and they watch us for any signs of magic. Even tiny things can disqualify us—like a blade of grass shooting out between your toes, or a little levitation, or you know . . . if we look. . . like . . . too happy.

Fenisa   They try to provoke us too. Try to make it really uncomfortable, really painful sometimes, to just stand there, to see if our instincts take over. They're about this close to tying us to the stake.

Marcia   You're exaggerating.

Fenisa   I tell the truth.

Lisea   Sounds terrible.

Marcia   It's really hard, but I can help you prepare.

Lisea   That's a very kind offer.

Marcia (*blushing*)   Well . . .

Lisea (*low and deep*)   Is that where you lose control, my dear? When we're out in the woods.

Marcia   Hhhhhh—

Fenisa   It's amazing, Lisea. It's epic, every time. You don't see a goodier two shoes than Marcia here, but man, the moment her bare feet touch the earth—the wardens don't even have to do anything—beams of energy shoot out of her eyeballs and turn squirrels into blue birds.

Lisea   You're powerful.

Marcia (*surprised*)   No, I'm weak. That's why that happens.

Lisea   You're powerful. (*To* **Fenisa**.) And so are you. I can feel it.

Fenisa   This place has a way of making us feel not so great about ourselves.

Lisea   That's what it's designed to do. Take two strong, beautiful, women like yourselves, and make you feel like you're less than. You're deviant. You're wrong. (*Pause.*) How long have you been here?

Fenisa   Six years.

Lisea   Everything about this is evil. They bring you into the woods, into the heart of nature, into the bosom of our mother—

Marcia   Shh. (*Pause.*) We can't—we can't say things like that. The earth is not our mother.

Lisea   The earth gives us power, gives us life, gives us reason to be here, doesn't she? They bring you to her beating heart, and pour concrete over it, barely giving us a window to look out of—imprisoning us when we have committed no crime other than embrace our full power, our worth, our destiny as witc—

Marcia *gasps.*

Lisea   Witches.

Fenisa   Witches.

Marcia *half gets up, then sits down again.* **Lisea** *takes her hand.* **Marcia** *melts.*

Lisea   My dear Marcia. Can you not see the irony inherent in this situation? They want to strip away our magic. To deny us our humanity. To make us forget that we are powerful. And so instead, they send us to live with each other. Where we come to see that together, there is nothing wrong with us. Together, we are beautiful and perfect. Together, we are powerful—so powerful—that it terrifies them.

Marcia (*enraptured*)   It does?

Lisea   It does.

Fenisa   Lisea, what's it like outside? Is it . . . safe?

Lisea There are tens of thousands of us around the world.

Fenisa Tens of thousands?

Lisea And we live—openly. Happily. In full control of our powers.

Marcia They're not . . . killing us?

Lisea Is that what they tell you? Those were in the Middle Ages, dear Marcia. Times have changed.

Marcia Why are you here?

Lisea I got caught.

But we won't be here long.

Marcia Yes, the exam's only a few days away.

Lisea *leans forward, and quietly, seriously—thrillingly—*

Lisea Fuck the exams.

Marcia What?

Lisea Fuck the exams.

They look around to see if anyone's listening in. No one is.

Lisea It's time to end this bullshit once and for all.

Fenisa What do you mean?

Lisea They take us all out into the woods? Together? (*She counts the people at lunch.*) 100–20 witches all together? With the source of our power at our feet? Our heels connected to the earth?

Marcia Uhm . . .

Fenisa What are you thinking, exactly? Because we'd still be on school property. The walls are 80 feet high. It's impossible to levitate that far. They'd catch us.

They'd—they'd shoot us down if they had to.

Marcia (*quietly*) I saw it once.

Lisea We blow up the school.

Marcia What?!

Lisea We blow up the school. Boom. And leave.

Marcia With . . . what?

Lisea With these.

She touches **Marcia** *and* **Fenisa**'s *hands for a second.* **Marcia** *melts again.* **Fenisa** *gets charged up.*

Fenisa Can you do that? Yourself? Blow something up?

Lisea Have you ever tried combining your powers with another witch?

I can show you.

Fenisa I'm into that.

Heat. **Marcia** *clears her throat.*

Marcia And then what?

Fenisa What?

Marcia What next? They might not be shooting us on sight any more, but what do you think they're going to do to a bunch of witches who just blew up a school? If that's even possible.

Lisea My dear Marcia, this is only the first step of the revolution.

Marcia The revolution?

Lisea It's happening around the world. We're organizing. We're fighting back. We're saying, this is bullshit. We're saying, this is unfair. We're saying, you hate us because you fear us. And now, we're going to give you a real reason to.

Fenisa It's happening?

Lisea This is the first step. This charade has gone on long enough. We're going to take over the world. It's our birthright.

Fenisa Fuck. Yes.

Lisea Will you join us, Marcia?

Marcia I don't know.

Lisea *gently touches* **Marcia***'s wrist, then rubs her finger on the inside of it as she speaks.*

Lisea I would so love for you to join.

Marcia (*melting*) Hhhh—hhhhhh—

As **Marcia** *melts,* **Lisea** *and* **Fenisa** *lock eyes. Heat.*

Scene Three

In an empty classroom. **Marcia** *sweeps up while* **Fenisa** *flicks things into cupboards with a flick of her wrist.*

Marcia Revolution is messy. (*Sweeping.*) I was so nervous the wardens might pop in. I mean. Technically we booked this room for study hall. But what if they popped in? And you know, we might be future potential revolutionaries, but people should still pick up after themselves. You know. Next underground meeting I'm assigning cleanup duties. (*She looks at* **Fenisa** *magicking things away.*) Fenisa please. You're just tempting fate when you use magic like that.

Fenisa   The whole point of revolution is for you to be free to be yourself. Now come on. Let the broom clean up by itself. Make it clean the room.

Marcia   You know I can't do that.

Fenisa   Can't or won't?

Marcia   Can't. You know I—I never learned how.

Fenisa   It's time to start trying.

Marcia   I can't shake the feeling that it's wrong.

Fenisa   Get angry Marcia. It's time to start getting angry. Doesn't this whole situation make you furious? That we're even in here?

Marcia   I just . . . sure. Yes. It's unfair. But what good is getting angry?

Fenisa   You can't be a part of the revolution if you're not angry.

Marcia   Maybe we should let Lisea decide that.

Fenisa   Yeah. Fine.

They keep cleaning.

Marcia   The way she looked at me today. Oh. It was a wonder I could stand up, my knees were shaking so hard. She's so . . . handsome. Isn't she?

Fenisa   Mmm.

Marcia   When she looks at me, it's like we're the only two people in the world. The only two people who ever lived. She is more charming, more beautiful . . . I imagine she's what a goddess might look like, if goddesses existed. She's made my soul her life's work, and now it is impossible for me to exist without Lisea. She is the prize I desire with every breath I take.

Fenisa   So you . . . you've given up on your lettuce man, huh?

Marcia   Duh. She's my soulmate. Like some Normal could ever compare. That's what excites me about the revolution. About life after the revolution. Just picturing me and Lisea . . . living in a villa in Spain . . . walking barefoot on the grass . . . every night.

Fenisa   See, I wasn't quite sure if you were still interested in her.

Marcia   I'm in love with her.

Fenisa (*sigh*)   Well, you see. That's a problem.

Marcia   Why?

Fenisa   I'm in love with her too.

Marcia *stops sweeping, then keeps sweeping.*

Marcia (*pause*)   Well.

Fenisa Yes?

Marcia That's unfortunate.

Fenisa For you?

Marcia For you. For us. What do you mean for me?

Fenisa Well, there's a simple solution.

Marcia There is?

Fenisa Stop being in love with her.

Marcia Wait, why should I stop being in love with her? She's my soulmate!

Fenisa The thing is, you think she's your soulmate, but she doesn't think she's yours.

Marcia How would you know?

Fenisa I'm her Lieutenant.

Marcia I'll have you know that the Second Under Secretary of the Revolution is also a very privileged position.

Fenisa She just doesn't see you that way.

Marcia She will see me that way, in time. The spell very clearly indicates that she's my soulmate.

Fenisa I mean, maybe. Maybe the spell just assumed it was meant for me. I was the one who performed it, after all.

Marcia No. (*Pause. She sits down on a table, depressed.*) Oh, no. You think so?

Fenisa Why not?

Marcia I—I mean—

It doesn't matter anyway. Divination is stupid. No one can tell the future, not really. The important thing is that I'm in love with her, and we're meant to be together, and we're perfect for each other.

Fenisa See, but Marcia, I don't think you are.

Marcia Oh, so you think you are?

Fenisa Well, yeah. Lisea is a fiery revolutionary rabble rouser, and she and I are perfectly, intellectually in sync. She and I believe in exactly the same things. Whereas you . . . you are a goody-two-shoes.

Marcia Stop calling me that. I can change. I am changing!

Fenisa I'm just telling you, as a friend, that it's a lost cause.

Marcia And I'm telling you as a friend that as a friend you should be nicer about it! And not make a move on her!

Fenisa   What? Why not?

Marcia   Because friends don't do that!

Fenisa   But that's not fair. I like her, she likes me, she doesn't like you, so why shouldn't we get together?

Marcia   What makes you so sure that she likes you?

Fenisa   Because we've had sex a bunch of times!

Marcia   W-what?

Fenisa   Yeah, like, in her room, in the science lab, behind the gym, on that table—

Marcia *jumps off the table.*

Fenisa   In the kitchens, in the locker room, on your bed that one time when there was laundry on my bed—

Marcia   WHAT?

A loud HMMMM fills the room. We hear thunder. See flashes of lightning.

Fenisa   Woah, Marcia—

Marcia   ON MY BED?

Thunder rumbles loudly.

Fenisa   Chill, girl. Oops. There we go.

It's now raining inside.

Marcia   Oh, dangit.

It continues to rain. There's a sharp rapping on the door. They look at it.

Scene Four

Detention. A bare room with a few beds and tables.

Marcia *is soaking wet and shivering. She sneezes.*

Marcia   Can't believe I got detention. Me. A prefect. A PREFECT, getting detention. Six years of never coming near this place. Five months and twenty-nine days—record gone. Poof. Great. Awesome. And my only friend here has betrayed me. Betrayed me down to my wet, shivering bones. They're probably having sex right now. They've probably had sex here, and here and here, and—

A voice from within the walls . . .

Laura   Hello there.

Marcia *jumps.*

Marcia   Hello?

Laura   I heard you got detention.

Marcia Hello? Who's talking?

Laura Hi. My name's Laura.

Marcia Where are you . . . Laura?

Laura In the ceiling. Above you. In the vents.

Marcia What?

Laura Hello.

Marcia *slowly looks up, almost afraid.*

Marcia How . . . Why are you in the vents?

Laura I heard you got detention, and I just had to come talk to you. I've been hearing some interesting chatter lately, you see.

Marcia How are you in the vents? How could you fit there?

Laura I turned myself into a talking frog. It's kind of my specialty.

Marcia Okay . . .

Um . . .

We could just talk at lunch tomorrow if you want. Laura, you said?

Laura Ah. I don't go to lunch.

I'm kept in solitary.

Marcia Wait . . . what?

Wait, no.

Solitary's not real.

Laura Now we're getting philosophical. Is anything real, really?

Marcia They don't put people in solitary here. It's not that kind of school.

Laura Oh, but they do.

Pause.

Marcia Are you . . . Prisoner X?

Laura Mmm. I've heard people talk about me that way.

Marcia You're Prisoner X. Holy shit. I thought that was a myth.

Oh my God. Laura. That's awful.

Laura It's not too bad. They don't know I can get through the vents, you see. It's almost like they've forgotten I have frog powers. So. Tell me. Why are you in here?

Marcia Uh.

Well.

I . . . I got my heart broken by my best friend. Well, not by her. But she was involved.

Laura   And then what happened?

Marcia   I made it rain. Inside.

Laura   That's pretty impressive.

Marcia   No, it's not. It's not. It was a moment of weakness. Won't happen again. The exams are tomorrow. I have to pass.

Laura   You're eager to get out, aren't you.

Marcia   I just . . .

I just want to be normal.

I just want to live.

I bet Normal girls don't betray their friends. (*Pause.*) Why are you in here? Why are you in solitary?

Laura   I turned a whole village into frogs.

Marcia   That's . . . that's impossible.

Laura   Oh, it's possible.

I was young. And totally in love. With this beautiful girl who moved to our village. I thought I was the only one who was like . . . me, you know. I didn't know there was a word for it. I didn't know I was actually part of a tribe. And then I met her, and she showed me the full extent of my powers. She showed me what we could do together. But for us to be ourselves, she said, we needed to get rid of the Normals. All of them. Starting with my parents. My brothers. My neighbors. The shopkeepers. The mayor. Turned 'em all. (*Pause.*) It was . . . intoxicating. What we were able to do.

Marcia   Were they . . . talking frogs?

Laura   No, they were just regular frogs.

Marcia   So . . . you . . . you—you—basically—you basically ended their lives! As humans!

Laura (*pause*)   Yes.

Marcia   How could you do that?

Laura   It seemed like the right thing to do at the time.
She can be very convincing.

But of course, when the police came—because they'd heard an entire village turned into frogs—she was nowhere to be seen. She slipped away without me. And I was caught.

Marcia   Laura . . . I'm so sorry.

No matter what, no witch should ever do that to another witch. That is . . . that is unforgivable. (*Pause.*) Laura?

Laura   Yes.

Marcia At least here you'll learn to be Normal, right? Do they teach you that in solitary?

Laura Oh, I am beyond hope. I'm kept here for my own safety. That's what they tell me.

Marcia Laura, who did this to you?

Laura You know her. (*Pause.*) I hear everything through these vents you know.

A beat.

Marcia Not Lisea.

Laura Ribbit. (*Pause.*) Sorry, animal urges come out when I hear her name.

Marcia Is that why you wanted to talk to me? To warn me?

Laura I'm not surprised she's here. I knew she'd get caught eventually.

And I'm not too surprised she's up to her old ways.

Don't fall for it.

No matter how lovely she is.

Marcia We need to get you out, Laura. This isn't all your fault. We need to tell the wardens what really happened. You need to confront her.

Laura I'm much safer in solitary.

Marcia Safer? From who?

Laura From Lisea. (*Hiccup, ribbit.*) I can't trust myself around her. Good luck.

We hear a hop hop hop. **Marcia** *stands on a chair, trying to get closer to the vent.*

Marcia Laura, Laura wait!

Laura (*echoing*)   What?

Marcia In the spirit of female solidarity, Laura, I vow to stop loving Lisea, and expose her for the person she truly is.

Laura Loving her? Uh. Sure.

Marcia You sound skeptical.

Laura I mean, it's not really necessary. She's fucking your friend, like, everywhere.

Marcia (*annoyed*)   Shut up.

Scene Five

Outside the classroom from earlier, where the revolutionaries hold their meetings. **Marcia** *catches up with* **Fenisa** *just as* **Fenisa** *is about to enter the secret meeting.*

Marcia Hey, wait!

138   School for Witches, or Friendship Betrayed!

Fenisa *looks back.*

Fenisa   Look who's out.

Marcia   Fenisa, wait. Don't go in.

Fenisa   The meeting's about to start. Are you coming?

Marcia   Wait. We have to talk.

Fenisa   About what?

Marcia   What do you think? Look. I'm going to forgive you for what you did.

Fenisa (*sigh*)   Marcia.

Marcia   And in a show of female solidarity, I'm going to cast aside my feelings for Lisea to warn you.

Fenisa   Warn me?

Marcia   That she's not who you think she is.

Fenisa   What is she then? A potato? A hyacinth? A Normal?

Marcia   She's a duplicitous, deceptive woman. She'll use you and lose you.

Fenisa   I'm a big girl, Marcia. I can handle my own relationships.

She tries to go in, **Marcia** *stops her again.*

Marcia   It's not about her breaking your heart, which, by the way, she will totally do anyway, and you totally deserve after all the hearts you've broken, but it's much worse than that.

Fenisa   I have to go—

Marcia   I met Prisoner X. She's in here because of Lisea.

Fenisa   Prisoner X is a myth.

Marcia   She's a girl. Like us. Her name is Laura. I heard her through the vents when I was in detention. They keep her in solitary because she turned a whole village into frogs.

Fenisa   Really.

Marcia   She and Lisea were in love. They were partners—they did the whole thing together. But Lisea abandoned her, and Laura got caught. And now she's Prisoner X.

Fenisa *stares at her.*

Fenisa   I never thought you'd be one to fall for propaganda, Marcia.

Marcia   What?

Fenisa   I thought you were smarter than that.

Marcia   Fenisa—

Fenisa   There is no Prisoner X. It's a myth. I don't know what you were hearing in the vents, maybe voices in your head.

Marcia   It was real!

Fenisa   Then probably it was an enemy spy out to sabotage the revolution.

Marcia   There isn't going to be a revolution, can't you see, she's just using you to escape the school!

Fenisa   Stop talking like that or we can't be friends anymore. I mean it.

Marcia *takes a step back. Shocked.* **Fenisa** *softens.*

Fenisa   Come in. Join us. I don't want to leave you behind.

Lisea is the real deal. I know it. I believe it.

Please.

Marcia   . . . Okay.

Fenisa *opens the door. They enter the classroom. The meeting is in progress. We don't see the other girls, just* **Lisea**, *who looks up as they come in.* **Lisea** *is in mid-speech.*

Lisea   Good! Lieutenant Fenisa. Second Under Secretary Marcia. You're here. We were just going through the battle plans.

Fenisa *and* **Marcia** *sit on either side of* **Lisea**. **Marcia** *eyes her warily.*

Marcia   Battle plans?

Lisea (*to the group, whom we don't see*)   Now remember, girls. They have pushed us around long and hard enough. They have rigged the game and decked the cards against us. They've made us think that if we play by their rules, be good, obedient, quasi-Normals, we'll be rewarded—but with what? "A good and decent life," they say? They are smart, you see. They know that they could never win an outright war against us, so they turn us into our own worst enemies. They make us think we belong inside—concrete walls, tiled floors, low ceilings, instead of breathing free and easy, power coursing through our limbs, our heels dug into the earth.

PA System (*beep*)

*The group—***Fenisa** *and* **Lisea** *included—starts booing loudly.*

PA System   This is a reminder that . . .

The group is booing so loudly that we can't even hear the announcement. Only **Marcia** *hesitates, worried, looking at the group with growing anxiety. They boo till the announcement ends.* **Lisea** *continues with renewed energy.*

Lisea   They indoctrinate and brainwash us into believing a Normal life is what is true and desirable—that we are wrong, deviant, and weak. What are we?

The group responds as a chorus. **Marcia** *is uneasy and just watches.*

Group   Powerful!

Lisea Who are we?

Group Witches!

Lisea Never forget that! Because when we are together . . . (*She holds hands with* **Fenisa** *and* **Marcia***,* **Marcia** *holds hands with the "group" (our SD reader)—the group hums with power.*) We are strong!

HMMMMMM. The furniture rattles in the room.

Marcia Girls! Stop! They'll catch us!

The humming stops. The furniture stops rattling. Everyone turns to look at **Marcia***.*

Marcia They can hear us if we're this loud. They're cracking down extra hard on magic. I just got sent to detention for that.

Lisea (*using it as a talking point*) They send you to detention for simply being who you are.

That wasn't just detention, Marcia. That was civil resistance to a corrupt system.

Fenisa Hear, hear.

Lisea Not exactly what we're going for in our revolution, but still a good attempt.

Fenisa Marcia does have a point, we should be careful until we're out there.

Lisea Our days of being careful will soon be behind us, ladies. Let's get to the battle plan. (*She starts gesturing towards a map of the campus, probably a crudely hand-drawn one.*) So we will arrange ourselves here—

Marcia Who?

Everyone looks at **Marcia** *again.*

Lisea All of us in this room. So, when the announcement goes in a few hours to assemble on the grounds, we—

Marcia Why is the group so much smaller? The last meeting had more people.

The group groans at the interruptions.

Fenisa Not everyone has the guts for revolution, Marcia. Not everyone is a true believer.

Lisea Which is a good thing. The last thing we need are flip-floppers. Wishy-washy allies of the establishment.

"Burn them!" someone shouts from the crowd.

Lisea All in good time.

Marcia What?

Lisea So we find ourselves on the grounds, in the woods, sorted by year. Our first move is to find each other. Take a good look at your sisters here. We must find each other quickly and discreetly. When the timer goes off for the exam, we take three quick steps—1-2-3—and join hands. Close our eyes. Combine our powers. And blow up the school.

Marcia   WHAT?

Lisea *sighs.*

Lisea   You have a question?

Marcia   We're actually blowing up the school?

If there were crickets in that room, they would chirp.

Fenisa   Yes, Marcia. That's what we've been talking about this whole time.

Marcia   I thought you meant like metaphorically.

Fenisa   How do you metaphorically blow up a school?

Marcia   I don't know. With . . . thoughtful debate? Democratic reforms? (*The group groans and boos.*) You're talking . . . explosion! Rubble! Carnage! ("*Yes!*" *the group shouts.*) People might get hurt.

Lisea   Who, the wardens? Who grind us under their heels every day? Whose entire mission is to crush and break our spirits?

Marcia   They're just doing their jobs.

Fenisa   They are part of an evil corrupt system and must fall with it.

Marcia   What about the other girls? The students taking the exams who don't know what's coming? Our sisters?

Fenisa   If they're not in this room, if they haven't joined the revolution, then they're not true witches. They're not our sisters.

Marcia   How can you just decide who's a true witch or not?

Fenisa   Marcia, what the hell, we have to finish the battle plan.

Lisea   It's all right, Fenisa.

Marcia, no revolution comes without its cost. But we must be committed to our goal of true liberation.

Marcia   But—

Fenisa   Marcia, stop it.

Marcia   BUT WHAT DO YOU DO AFTER?

Pause.

What is the plan after you blow up the school?

Fenisa   We run deep into the woods to establish the home base of our new utopian society.

142   School for Witches, or Friendship Betrayed!

Marcia   But what does that mean? Who's going to be in charge? What are the rules going to be?

Fenisa   There will be no rules. No one will be in charge.

Marcia   What about when the Normals come after us?

Lisea   We'll take care of them.

Marcia   Like . . . kill them?

Lisea   If we have to.

It's never stopped them before, when it comes to us.

Marcia   But you said it yourself—we're living in different times now.

Fenisa   Marcia, what are you talking about? Do you think it's right, the way we're living now? Do you think it's fair?

Marcia   N-no, but—

Fenisa   THEN WHAT ARE YOU TALKING ABOUT?

Marcia   You just don't seem to have a plan.

Lisea   And you don't sound like a true believer, Marcia. In fact, you don't sound like a true witch. (*The group murmurs affirmations.*) No one escapes complicity in an unjust system.

Marcia   Look, girls—

Lisea   Sisters.

Marcia   Sisters. Fine. Look I can't let you do this.

Fenisa (*a warning*)   What do you mean by that.

Marcia (*to* **Fenisa**)   Just think it through, please. I don't want you to get into trouble.

Lisea   She's one of those lost causes. She's been completely brainwashed. There's no hope for her. She's hoping to live a Normal life, maybe even make babies using penises.

The group goes "Ewwww."

Marcia   I'm not brainwashed! I just see right through you! She will abandon you when it's convenient to her—she's done it before!

Prisoner X told me everything! Remember Laura, Lisea? Remember what you did to her? She's here.

Lisea *goes white.*

Fenisa   You're starting to sound like a crazy person.

Marcia   You let Laura get put into solitary, you bitch. (*The group gasps.*) And I'm not gonna let you do that to my friend.

Lisea   She is a dangerous renegade. A spy. An enemy implant.

Marcia *heads to the door.* **Lisea** *extends her wrist and flicks it.*

Marcia   I'm not gonna let you do this.

She jiggles the doorknob but it's locked.

What?

Lisea *has magically locked it.*

Lisea   Not so fast. We need to take care of you first.

Marcia   What?

Lisea   Fenisa, make sure she doesn't cause trouble.

Marcia   What?

Lisea   Immobilize her.

Marcia   No, Fenisa, no.

Lisea   You can fight back if you want. But you won't. Because you don't know how to control your own magic, do you? You've bought into their brainwashing so hard, you don't even know how to use your own powers. Can't have dead weight like you hanging around. Fenisa, take care of her. Unless you want me to.

She flicks her wrist and **Marcia** *grabs her throat and gasps.*

Fenisa (*quickly*)   I'll take care of her.

Marcia   Fenisa, stop, don't—

MMMMMMMM

Marcia's *mouth has been magically shut. She tries to pry it open.* **Fenisa** *flicks her wrist again and* **Marcia**'s *wrists and feet get magically bound before her. She squeals and squirms.*

Lisea   Take her somewhere out of the way.

Fenisa *goes up to* **Marcia** *and grabs her arm.*

Fenisa   I'm sorry, Marcia.

I really didn't want to leave you behind.

But you're forcing us to.

I'll take you to our room.

She hoglifts **Marcia** *onto her shoulder, as she squeals.* **Fenisa** *takes her out of the classroom, exiting.*

Lisea *turns to the group, dusting off her hands.*

Lisea (*chirpy*)   Remember, sisters. We're all in this together!

Scene Six

A few hours later in her dorm room. **Marcia** *twists and turns in her dorm room, still magically bound up.*

PA System (*beep*)   This is the last call for all eligible students to assemble on the grounds through the North Gate for the half-yearlies. All late students will be disqualified.

Marcia *squeals. Then, a voice . . .*

Laura   Oh goodness. It's you!

Marcia *looks up. There's a vent in her dorm room.* **Laura**'s *voice comes through.*

Laura   I thought there was a cat loose in the building. That would be something, huh. A cat loose in a school full of witches.

Marcia *squeals.*

Laura   Hmm. An immobilization spell, I see. Haven't come across one of those in ages.

Marcia *squeals.*

Laura   Need a hand?

"*Yes,*" **Marcia** *squeals. A faint hum.* **Marcia** *is released. She topples to the floor, stretching and shaking her limbs. She stretches her jaw.*

Marcia   Oh, oh my - oh my face - oh my God. Thank you, Laura. Oh my God. The exams. Ohmygodohmygodohmygod. I can't believe Fenisa. I cannot believe her. (**Marcia** *runs around the room gathering her things.*) Forget their stupid revolution. I don't give a shit. I can't believe Fenisa made me miss the exams! THE EXAMS, Laura!

Laura   You may not need to worry about that.

Suddenly an alarm goes off. Bars slam down on the windows. **Marcia** *covers her ears.*

PA System (*beep beep beep*)   EMERGENCY CURFEW. All students gather indoors immediately. All students on the grounds return within the main building immediately. No students may be seen outside. This is an EMERGENCY CURFEW. All prefects report to the head office immediately.

Marcia *uncovers her ears, shocked.*

Marcia   What . . . what happened?

Laura   Revolutions are messy.

Scene Seven

In the darkness. Rustling. We're in the woods. Flashlights. Dogs barking in the distance. **Marcia**'s *voice gets louder till she appears. Wearing a special prefect's hat, a reflective vest, holding a flashlight. She wears boots and gloves.*

We notice **Fenisa**, *scrambling, hiding. Her feet are bare.*

Marcia Fenisa!

Fenisa . . .

Fenisa!

The flashlight lands on **Fenisa**. *She's hiding in a vegetable patch.*

Fenisa I thought it was you.

Marcia All the prefects are searching for you. All the wardens are searching for you. They have, like, sniffer dogs out on the grounds.

Fenisa I know. How did you find me?

Marcia This was the place you discovered. The vegetable patch, behind the fertilizers. Where it smells terrible. That crack in the wall. The place you discovered the last time you tried to escape.

Her flashlight swings over to illuminate the crack in the wall. Just large enough for a tiny girl to slip through. Neither of them are tiny anymore.

Fenisa When we were twelve.

Marcia Yeah.

Fenisa Why didn't I run?

Marcia You didn't have a place to run to. So you came back.

A moment. Neither makes a move.

Fenisa You gonna turn me in?

Marcia I should. That's why I'm out here. Those were our orders. To find the . . . You know.

Where's Lisea now, huh?

Fenisa (*quiet*) You were right.

Marcia What's that?

Fenisa You. Were. Right.

We have no idea where she is.

She split as soon as we tried to blow up the school. She split in the confusion. We're all scattered now.

Marcia So much for your revolution.

Fenisa I am so, so, so sorry. For what I did to you. I feel like shit. I don't know what came over me.

Marcia *takes it in.*

Marcia Eh. You fell in love. People do shitty things when they fall in love.

Fenisa Not always.

A moment.

Marcia Come back with me. Just . . . it's not that bad. Come back, right now, apologize, do some detention . . . leave in six months. Just . . . you know. Stick to your original plan.

Fenisa They won't just give me detention, Marcia.

Marcia I'll vouch for you.

Fenisa Stop being nice to me. I don't deserve it.

Marcia Oh for crying out loud. Snap out of it, Fenisa. You're not acting like yourself.

Look, you can either come back with me, or let one of the wardens find you, with their dogs. What would you prefer?

A moment.

Fenisa Come . . . with me.

Marcia What?

Fenisa That crack in the wall.

Marcia It's not big enough anyway.

Fenisa We can try.

Marcia No. No, Fenisa. I'm giving you a second chance here.

Fenisa So am I.

Marcia What?

Fenisa Lisea might be a piece of shit, but all that stuff she was saying. About the world. Our lives. What they do to us. That wasn't all lies. None of it was lies. And you know it.

Marcia They just want us to be Normal. Just be . . . regular women, you know.

Fenisa There's nothing wrong with us.

Well.

There's definitely nothing wrong with you.

You're way too good for any of this.

Marcia . . .

Take off your boots.

Marcia I can't.

Fenisa You can. It feels right. Take them off.

Take off your gloves.

Feel the earth.

Please.

Just . . . do this for me.

While we're here.

Together.

Just . . . feel the earth with me.

Marcia *slowly, cautiously takes off her gloves. She touches the earth.*

Fenisa   Does anything feel more right than this?

Does anything feel more normal than this?

Marcia *has her hands planted on the earth. The air around them seems to hum. Suddenly dogs barking, a voice crying out—"I think I see something!" And flashlights land right on their faces.* **Fenisa** *gasps.* **Marcia** *plunges her hands into the earth and goes—*

Marcia   NO.

Suddenly a hissing, buzzing, distorted sound, like the crackling of electricity. The lights distort around them. The dogs and flashlights pass them by. The footsteps pass them by.

Fenisa   What . . .

Marcia   Shh . . .

Fenisa   What's happening?

Marcia   Shh . . .

Fenisa *reaches out and touches the air—it sizzles.*

Fenisa   This is . . .

This is an invisibility dome.

Marcia   Shh. I'm concentrating.

Fenisa   Holy shit. You're doing this. You're deliberately doing this. Magic. Incredible magic. Marcia. You just saved us.

Marcia *breathes heavily.*

Fenisa   I think they're gone.

Marcia *collapses.* **Fenisa** *hugs her, tight.*

Fenisa   You saved me.

You did magic.

Can't you see . . . how powerful you are?

I can't leave you.

Marcia This is wrong.

Fenisa *strokes her hair.*

Fenisa You don't have to listen to me. You don't have to listen to anyone. Just listen to yourself. Trust yourself. For once. There's nothing wrong with you.

Marcia We can't stay out here. We have to go back.

Fenisa Never. Dear God—

Marcia Can't you see I'm trying to save you?

Fenisa Can't you see I'm trying to save you?

Marcia I'm so close. I'm so close to graduating with honors.

Fenisa But that's not going to change a thing. Passing their stupid exam is not going to change a bit of who you really are.

Marcia It's something.

Fenisa You'd rather live a half life, in fear, forever out of sync, than just . . . leave . . . with me . . . and find a place where we can live. Just live? Full lives. Full, free, complete—

Marcia We have to—

Fenisa Do you really want to go back.

Marcia . . . No.

Fenisa We can do this. (*Pause.*) Look at me.

The revolution might not be real. But you're real. I'm real. We can't change everything all at once. We can't blow up the school. We can't upend the way the world works. Not today. Not right now. But we can start. We can start today. With ourselves. We are so close.

Marcia *plants her hands on the ground, the air hums around them, and the crack in the wall slowly widens.* **Fenisa** *looks at it excitedly. And tugs on* **Marcia**'s *sleeve.*

Fenisa Yes. Yes.

Come on.

Let's go.

Marcia Not me.

Fenisa What?

Marcia Go ahead. Just go.

Fenisa Marcia . . .

Marcia I can't.

Dogs and footsteps coming closer.

Fenisa I won't go far.

Marcia You have to. Please.

Go!

Footsteps coming closer. **Fenisa** *shoots* **Marcia** *a pained glance, and slips through the crack. As flashlights get nearer,* **Marcia** *collapses in a heap and pretends to gasp for breath. She talks to one of the "wardens."*

Marcia I saw one! She hit me with a spell of some sort. She ran off that way. Hurry!

She points in the opposite direction. The dogs and footsteps recede.

She slowly gets up and dusts herself off. She puts on her gloves. Or tries to. She just . . . can't . . . quite . . .

She flings her gloves on the ground. She takes off her boots.

She stands barefoot on the earth, feeling her natural power course through her limbs. The air hums around her.

She runs to the wall.

Marcia Fenisa?

Fenisa *reappears at the crack and sticks her arm through, reaching out to* **Marcia**.

Fenisa Told you I wouldn't go far.

Hurry.

She pulls **Marcia** *through the crack in the wall, and we hear their bare, soft footsteps recede into the woods.*

END OF PLAY

The King of Maricopa County

Mary Lyon Kamitaki

The King of Maricopa County

Introduction by Barbara Fuchs

Mary Lyon Kamitaki's adaptation queers Lope de Vega's *El castigo sin venganza* (*Punishment without Revenge*, 1631), widely regarded as his mature masterpiece. Lope's play is a study in the relation between public and private lives: by focusing on the ethical perversions to which the honor code leads its most ruthless and hypocritical enforcers, it exposes the moral failings of those in power. Kamitaki's *The King of Maricopa County* adapts *Castigo* to examine the personal implications of political hypocrisy and, conversely, the political effects of personal insincerity in our own time. Crucially, *King* also explores the (in)visibility of transgression when heterosexuality is assumed as the generalized norm and homophobia makes it difficult to recognize queer loves.

The source text follows the Duke of Ferrara, who after years of sexual excess finally decides to take a wife, the noble Casandra, for political expediency. His illegitimate son, Count Federico, falls for his new stepmother, who reciprocates his love. When the Duke eventually learns of their liaison, he decides to punish their transgression discreetly, so as to avoid the political fallout. He forces Federico to stab a supposed traitor who is bound, gagged, and disguised by a cloth; when it is revealed that Federico has actually killed Casandra, the Duke has his courtiers kill Federico in turn.

King, written in the period of intense political turmoil between the US 2018 midterm elections and the 2020 presidential contest, focuses on the rapidly transforming state of Arizona. Maricopa, its most populous county, was for decades terrorized by Joe Arpaio, an elected official who styled himself "America's Toughest Sheriff." Arpaio's electoral defeat in 2016 was widely regarded as a bellwether of Arizona's political transformation, with a growing Latinx electorate unwilling to tolerate his strongman tactics, but the state continues to be deeply divided. In Maricopa as in many corners of the US, moreover, the defense of gay rights often pits libertarian-minded Republicans against religious conservatives. Kamitaki's adaptation, with a "Duke" who is Sheriff of Maricopa County, is thus set in an unevenly conservative terrain full of evasions and contradictions.

Kamitaki updates the central love triangle of Lope's play by giving her Duke a daughter instead of son. Reprising the "meet cute" of Lope's original, in which Count Federico rescues Casandra from a carriage, Kamitaki's Casandra accidentally crashes her car into Freddie's in the middle of the desert. After a passionate encounter, she is shocked to discover that Freddie is the daughter of the man she is about to marry. Her distress is compounded as she gradually realizes that Freddie is not out to her father or anyone else in her conservative milieu. Instead, Freddie constantly evades them and drinks copiously in her misery.

As a person of color, Casandra does not feel particularly welcome in Duke's gated community. While her "exotic" (p. 170) difference is visible and indeed even attractive to Duke, her bisexuality is completely illegible in this conservative context. Similarly, Freddie's homosexuality cannot be spoken and goes unnoticed even by her friends: Duke's sharp assistant Dawn (to match Lope's Aurora), and his hapless deputy Buzz. As Kamitaki's adaptation explores the attraction between Freddie and her new "mom," as Buzz jokingly calls her, it examines the stakes of this invisibility and adds the burden of a second secret to the already formidable tension in Lope's original.

Yet even in a conservative setting certain questions cannot be permanently elided. Duke's visibility in the public eye and his growing ambitions all raise the stakes of his personal life and how it is perceived, much as it does for the Duke of Ferrara in Lope's original. When Duke leaves for Washington, DC, to prepare his next career move—as Lope's Duke leaves to aid the Pope in his wars—Casandra is left alone in the house with Freddie. As Dawn gradually recognizes the actual relationship between the two women, Freddie desperately tries to distract her by insisting on her own heterosexuality. She is convinced that the unthinkability of homosexuality will provide cover, yet Kamitaki shows us how even the most conservative locales can no longer discount queer lives. Even when Dawn recounts what she has witnessed, however, Duke continues to ignore the liaison.

Like Shekar's *School for Witches*, *King* ends with the women making their escape from an unbearably repressive situation. When Casandra decides to leave, on the very day of her wedding, Freddie begs to come along. Whereas Shekar's play ends on a note of hope, however, Kamitaki's has a *Thelma-and-Louise* flavor, with the final scene entitled "Off a Cliff." The lovers fail to get away unnoticed, and Freddie must therefore face her father. Duke fails to dissuade her, and directs her to take Casandra's car, falsely claiming that it has now been repaired from the initial crash. Its faulty fuel line will serve as his dissimulated murder weapon, in an ending abundantly signaled yet unstaged.

As in Lope's *Castigo*, the child's transgression must remain hidden to ensure the father's political survival. Duke engineers the lovers' escape in the deadly vehicle, secure in the knowledge that its destruction will cover up all tracks, or at least provide plausible deniability. His only mistake is a brief grammatical slip-up, as he unintentionally reveals to Dawn, who is searching for Casandra, that he knows Freddie is with the missing bride. This small moment brings home to Dawn the depths of Duke's ruthlessness: he is privy to the joint escape and presumably the choice of vehicle. The exchange pithily signals to Dawn as to the audience the ethical cost of supporting Duke. The enormity of the women's deaths, should they meet their end in Casandra's car, hangs heavy over Dawn.

In Kamitaki's open-ended version of Lope's tragedy, the death of Casandra and Freddie is both imminent and endlessly suspended, directly Duke's responsibility and yet indirectly achieved. The adaptation glaringly reveals the ruthlessness of the Duke's verdict in *Castigo*, which Lope renders in just a few verses. Lope's Duke blames the heavens for the punishment he will mete out, arguing that it is their "divine rod" that will come down on the lovers. Kamitaki's unresolved yet clearly signaled ending highlights the fundamental evasion of responsibility in the source: what would it mean to insist that only Heaven is responsible for the death of Casandra and Freddie, when the modern Duke sends them away in a rolling time-bomb? *King* thus reveals the bad faith of Lope's protagonist, who invokes religion as a cover for his all-too-human *castigo*. It also cannily avoids the revelation of the dead bodies that is a key part of Lope's conclusion, thereby refusing to stage any sort of punishment for the lovers.

The adaptation brings home the blinkered logic of patriarchs and political leaders, establishing a direct line from one Duke to the other. The pragmatism of their response, as they seek to avoid political fallout and private shame, is entirely Machiavellian: any ethical consideration is subsumed to the central goal of preserving power by maintaining appearances.

The King of Maricopa County

By Mary Lyon Kamitaki
Adapted from *El castigo sin venganza* by Lope de Vega.
Commissioned by Playwrights' Arena and UCLA.

Characters

Casandra, *25, impulsive and lonely* — *Former teacher. BIPOC. Engaged to Duke.*

Freddie, *26, wild child. Loyal, and trying her best* — *Daughter to Duke. White or white passing.*

Duke, *47, conservative, but not out of touch* — *Sheriff of Maricopa County with greater ambitions. Father to Freddie. White.*

Dawn, *26, willful and decisive, but sensitive* — *Duke's assistant and Freddie's best friend.*

Buzz, *24, a kid with grown-up responsibilities* — *Duke's deputy, childhood friends with Freddie and Dawn.*

Note

When characters are on the phone, they should not hold actual phones in their hands or mime speaking into anything. Instead, they can address the audience. Phone sounds are okay.

Time

Now.

Place

A deserted stretch of highway south of Phoenix. The Starlight: a dive bar with neon lights and a jukebox. Duke's house in a white housing development.

St Elmo's Fire

The crackle of static on the radio. A man's voice emerges, low and measured. He sounds like he could be speaking from another era, but still right in your ear—intimate and unsettling.

Duke   I want to begin today as I begin every day: with gratitude. I know it must seem strange. Many of you are asking, what is there to be thankful for, with everything going on in the world? I say, look no further than your home. What is there on this Earth more important than family? I thank God each morning for mine. A man is nothing without it.

The sound of a crash, and he is gone.

Lights up on the purple desert at dusk, with the crackle of electricity in the air.

Casandra *enters abruptly, disheveled and bruised, marching with determination.*

Freddie (*offstage*)   Wait.

Casandra *ignores this.*

Freddie (*offstage*)   Wait! . . . WAIT!

She comes to a halt. **Freddie** *enters, also disheveled, clearly in pain.*

Casandra   I offered to help, it's not my fault you're too proud to let me.

They talk over each other, but without missing a thing the other says.

Freddie   I don't need your help.

Casandra   I know you're hurt or whatever but if you don't want to accept help then that's really on you.

Freddie   You're the one who hurt me!

Casandra   I have somewhere I need to be, so maybe you could just get over this stupid ego thing and let me help you?

Freddie   Oh, it's all about you. You're not even listening.

Casandra   Because I'm trying to get somewhere!

Freddie   WAIT.

I changed my mind. We should turn back, before the storm starts.

Casandra   Don't be stupid.

Freddie   Oh, *I'm* stupid?

Casandra   You're only slowing us down, come on.

Freddie   We can't be caught out here when lightning starts.

Casandra   Lightning isn't coming.

A clap of thunder.

Freddie Let's just go back to the cars.

Casandra And what, sit there? In two broken-down hunks of metal in the middle of a lightning storm?

Freddie Well, we can't be standing out in the middle of the road, surrounded by tall objects.

Casandra What are you talking about?

Freddie The saguaros? I take it you didn't do so great in science class.

Casandra Okay, asshole. What if we try to find, like, a house or a gas station or whatever and get inside where it's safe?

Freddie There's not going to be a "house or a gas station or whatever."

Casandra Yeah there is! I passed something, coming from this direction, just a minute or two before the crash.

Freddie A minute or two? The way you were driving? That could be five miles!

Casandra You're just being a smartass. Let's GO.

She tries to start them again, but **Freddie** *won't budge.*

Freddie There's nothing out here. I've driven this road a thousand times. Why do you think we have no service? It's a dead zone.

Casandra Alright, fine. What's your plan, then?

Freddie We have to get out there. Into the desert.

Casandra Okay, this is why I need to be in charge.

Freddie I'm serious.

Casandra You want us to run out into the desert and, what, burrow into the ground? Crawl under a cactus? Build a yurt?

Freddie Get low to the ground. Lightning wants to strike the tallest object around. So if we get down low, we're less likely to be struck.

Casandra It's going to rain.

Freddie Oh, would that mess up your hair? I'm talking about getting struck by lightning.

Casandra Jesus, are you always like this? What is your problem?

Freddie My problem? I don't know, maybe the fact that you crashed your car into me and stranded both of us in the middle of the fucking desert during a thunderstorm and then proceeded to be a huge pain in the ass about it and not even apologize.

Casandra Oh you wanted me to apologize?

Freddie Yeah!

Casandra   You want me to apologize?

Freddie   Yeah!

Casandra   Well, fuck you, I'm not saying sorry. Wow. Wow. Real mature.

Freddie

Casandra *gives her the finger.*

Freddie   You know what? Fine. I don't care. I don't even know you. Die out here. I don't give a shit.

Casandra   Uh-huh.

Freddie   I'm going to go find a nice ditch to lie in, you keep walking the next ten miles, good luck with your "house or gas station or whatever."

She takes a couple of limping steps away from **Casandra***.*

Casandra *stands her ground.*

Freddie *slows to a stop.*

Casandra *waits her out.*

Freddie *turns back.*

Freddie   Would you just . . . come on. Please? It's not safe.

Casandra   Only if you let me help you.

She reaches out to **Freddie***.* **Freddie** *looks at* **Casandra***'s hand for a moment.*

Casandra   What, are you afraid?

Freddie   Why would I be afraid?

She takes **Casandra***'s hand. A moment of electricity.*

Casandra *pulls* **Freddie***'s arm over her shoulders. They start to walk together, but it's slow going as* **Freddie** *tries to hop on one foot.*

Casandra   Lean on me. I can do it.

Freddie *does.*

They move away from the road, into the desert a bit. She finds a slope in the ground.

Freddie   This seems good. It's lower here.

She lies down. **Casandra** *stays on her feet.*

Freddie   You have to lie down too or there's no point.

Casandra *hesitates.*

Freddie   Fine, stay there. You'll be the lightning rod and I'm in the clear.

Casandra *lies down next to her.*

Casandra Now what?

Lightning flash.

Freddie One one thousand . . . two one thousand . . .

Both Three one thousand . . . four one thousand . . . five one thousand . . .

Thunder.

Casandra A mile.

Freddie (*surprised*) That's right.

Casandra I know. I'm actually not an idiot.

Freddie I didn't say you were an idiot.

Casandra You basically did.

Freddie . . . Sorry.

Casandra I'm sorry for crashing into you.

Freddie What happened? You just swerved into my lane out of nowhere.

Casandra You're really going to think I'm an idiot.

Freddie What, did you sneeze or something? Get stung by a bee?

Casandra I swear, I saw . . . lightning.

Freddie In the road?

Casandra On my car. There's this hood ornament. It's this big, shiny chrome thing. And suddenly it sparked. But it didn't just sparkle and stop, like static. The spark kept going, crackling and glowing like neon. And it moved toward me, like it was going to pass right through the glass into my body. So I kind of reached out to it, toward the windshield, like I thought I could touch it. And it—I swear to God—It reached back. Like it was drawn to my fingertips on the glass. And I almost did touch it, but I guess at the last minute I got scared and I jerked back. Hard, like it burned me. But I never touched it. I guess I must have pulled the steering wheel because suddenly I was in the wrong lane and I slammed on the brakes, but . . . too late.

She sees **Freddie** *staring at her.*

Casandra What?

Freddie Nothing

Casandra Anyway, I'm sorry.

Freddie It's fine, serves me right.

Casandra What do you mean?

Freddie I was ditching work. That's the only reason I was out here.

Casandra   Problem with your boss?

Freddie   You could say that. Where were you going?

Casandra   Uh . . . Home. I guess.

Freddie   You don't know?

Casandra   I've never been there before.

Freddie *waits for her to explain, but she doesn't.*

Casandra   Are they going to miss you? Maybe they'll send someone looking.

Freddie   Nah. They'll just think I'm blowing them off like usual. Is anyone coming for you?

Casandra   No one even knows I'm out here.

They look at each other.

Casandra   Please don't be a serial killer.

Freddie   Excuse me?!

Casandra   I mean. We're all alone in the middle of the desert, no cell service, I just told you no one's looking for me, and you already got me lying down in a ditch. Obviously that's where my mind went.

Freddie   Wow. And here I thought we were having a nice moment.

Casandra   Is that not what you were thinking?

Freddie   No, being alone together did not immediately make me think of murder.

Casandra   Well, we're different.

Freddie   Why would I murder you?

Casandra   Or I could murder you.

Freddie   Yeah, if anything, you're the one who almost killed me.

Casandra   And I said sorry for that.

Freddie   Clearly I'm not a murderer, a few minutes ago I basically saved your life.

Casandra   You did not!

Freddie   You were going to get struck by lightning and I had to practically beg you to come out here.

Casandra   . . . Thank you.

Freddie   You're welcome.

Flash of lightning.

Both   One one thousand . . . two one thousand . . . three one thousand . . .

Clap of thunder. **Freddie** *squeezes her eyes shut.*

Freddie   Fuck.

Casandra   Are you afraid?

Freddie (*yes*)   No.

Casandra   I'm excited.

Freddie   To get electrocuted?

Casandra   I've never seen lightning. Before today.

Freddie   Never? You must have.

Casandra   Only on TV.

Freddie   How's that possible?

Casandra   I used to hide when it happened. When I was a kid I would go into my nana's room and crawl into her bed.

Freddie   And now you're excited.

Casandra   I didn't want to be afraid anymore.

Freddie   You can't just decide not to feel afraid.

Casandra   I did though.

Freddie *considers her.*

Freddie   You're still afraid.

Casandra   Fine. But I'm also excited.

Freddie   Lucky you, we're gonna get a front-row view.

Lightning.

Both   One one thousand . . . two one thousand . . .

Thunder.

Beat.

Casandra   "We were having a nice moment?"

Freddie   What?

Casandra   You said we were having a nice moment. What did you mean by that?

Freddie   Nothing. I was being sarcastic.

Casandra   No you weren't. Why didn't you leave me alone back there, just come out here by yourself?

Freddie   I am a very good person.

Beat.

Casandra You like me.

Freddie *scoffs.*

Casandra That's not a no.

Freddie Wow, someone's pretty sure of herself.

Casandra You like me.

Freddie I didn't say that.

Casandra Because you're too immature. You'd rather be mean to me, like we're in middle school.

Freddie You're an idiot.

Casandra You're an asshole.

They stare at each other: a standoff.

Casandra *leans over and kisses* **Freddie**.

Freddie *kisses her back. Then they're wrapped up in each other, kissing and clinging in the dust.*

Flash of lightning.

One one thousand.

Thunder.

Casandra *suddenly stops, pulls away and sits up.*

Casandra Fuck.

Freddie Don't worry, it's almost passed.

She reaches for **Casandra**, *but* **Casandra** *keeps her at bay.*

Casandra I'm married.

Freddie What?

Casandra I mean. I'm about to get married.

Freddie But you kissed me.

Casandra I just thought you should know.

A moment while they try to gauge each other.

Freddie *reaches out, slowly, like a question.* **Casandra** *responds to her touch. Then suddenly, they're drawn together again.*

Casandra *pulls back.*

Casandra Wait. We're never going to see each other again, okay?

Freddie What if we run into each other?

Casandra You don't know me. Got it?

Freddie I *don't* know you.

Casandra This is so stupid.

Freddie Do you want to stop?

Casandra *kisses her, no.*

Freddie Your skin feels like . . .

Casandra *unbuttons her shirt.*

Freddie Like . . .

Casandra *kisses her chest.*

Freddie Sunlight.

She takes off **Casandra***'s dress.* **Casandra** *goes for the button on* **Freddie***'s pants.*

Freddie Wait wait wait wait. What's your name?

Casandra   . . . Casandra.

Freddie *freezes.*

Freddie Casandra.

The man you're going to marry . . .

Casandra You want to talk about him right now?

Freddie What's his name?

They get to their feet.

Casandra Don't do that.

Freddie Duke.

She freezes. They're staring at each other, holding their clothes, almost naked in the dusk.

Casandra What?

Freddie His name is Duke. But on the radio, they call him the King.

Casandra Who are you?

Freddie I'm his daughter.

Lightning, then thunder. Blackout.

Interlude

Lights up on **Duke**, *in the radio station. He's still live on the air.*

Duke So I say, count your blessings, my friends, because today is going to be a beautiful day. There may be a storm coming, but it's sunny skies on the home front with a big announcement coming from yours truly, Sheriff Duke Howard.

But first. We've got quite a bit of ground to cover, as the mainstream media, the powers that be, the liberal elite, they've been hard at work all week putting out these stories about my policies—about our community. But I know you know better than that, Maricopa County. Those voices might tempt you to doubt, but I am here to restore your faith. Before all that, a few messages.

Dawn *appears, speaking on the phone. [See Note.]*

Dawn Freddie, you have to grow up. This might have been cute when you were sixteen but now it's just sad. I've got enough on my plate, I don't need to be chasing you around town. I'm not your mother, I'm—

Sorry. Poor choice of words. Sorry.

But you need to grow your butt up and come home.

Buzz *appears in uniform, also on the phone.*

Buzz Dawn, tell Duke that I am a law-enforcement officer and it is not my job to drive out to the middle of bum fuck nowhere to pick up chicks for him. Especially when they're not even here! This is just sad. I've been here for forty-five minutes. No one's picking up the phone or coming to the door. She probably just got cold feet.

Dawn Freddie. I love you. Which is why I am telling you. This is a Big Life Moment and you cannot fuck it up by disappearing. You know how pissed he's gonna be. And you're not the only one he's going to take it out on.

Buzz By the way, did you see the picture he gave me? Girl is *fine*. Also, weird question—is she Mexican? She looks kinda Mexican, right? Isn't that funny? 'Cause you know what Duke says.

Dawn I know things are weird, okay? I get it. But just come back home, put on your face for a few hours and then you and I can get margarita drunk at my place and talk bad about everybody.

Buzz Or maybe Asian, she could be some kind of Asian.

Dawn Just please, for the love of God,

Buzz Call me back.   **Dawn** Call me back.

Duke There's no denying that these are hard times. You wake up in the morning and barely recognize the world you're living in. You barely recognize your neighbors. This isn't the Maricopa County it used to be. So we will change; we will adapt as we must. But. I want you to know that my job remains the same as ever. For the past eleven years it's been my mission to keep you safe. And that's what I'll continue to do, you have my word.

On the topic of change—and I don't usually like to talk about myself on the air, but I do wish to be open and honest with you, my neighbors. So stay tuned for that announcement I promised.

He switches the microphone off. A brief knock, then **Dawn** *enters.*

Dawn Duke, got a minute?

Duke For you, sweetheart, I've got two.

Dawn So I've got your tickets all booked, you're set for next week, but you're going to have to fly out of Tucson instead of Phoenix.

Duke Fine. What else?

Dawn There . . . might be a bit of a problem with Casandra.

Duke What?

Dawn Buzz says she's not there.

Duke What do you mean not there?

Dawn He's at the house, but she isn't there. I double-checked the address. He called the number you gave me, but it went straight to voicemail.

She waits while **Duke** *does some mental calculations.*

Dawn He wants to know if he should keep waiting.

I told him she probably just had an emergency of some kind.

And maybe her phone died? And she didn't have a charger?

And couldn't find one to borrow?

. . . I'm sure she's still coming.

Duke Of course she's still coming. Why would she not still be coming? What a stupid thing to say.

Dawn Sorry.

Duke Tell Buzz to stay right where he is. He doesn't come home until she comes home.

Dawn Yes, sir.

He starts to get back to work, but she lingers.

Duke Something else?

Dawn Just Freddie? She's not back yet. She left your office this morning without saying anything and now she's not answering my texts, and none of my calls are going through.

Duke How long has it been?

Dawn A few hours.

Duke This is deliberate. She's punishing me.

Dawn I'm sure she's just confused.

Duke Well, she needs to figure it out. She's too old for this. Well, when she comes back she and I have to have a little sit-down.

Dawn   Of course.

She starts to exit.

Duke   You know what. Better yet, you go find her. Keep calling. And tell me when you find her.

Dawn   Yes, sir.

Duke   And Dawn. We'll hold off on announcing the engagement. Don't post anything yet. Just until we know they're both home safe.

Dawn *exits.* **Duke** *turns the microphone back on.*

Duke   Change of plans, friends. It seems our news will have to wait for another day. But patience is a virtue, and I know you are virtuous. Just one more reason to tune in in the mañana. In the meantime, be good, and stay safe, Maricopa.

Welcome Home

Later that evening, the sound of a doorbell cuts through the dense suburban silence in the dark.

A long pause, then it sounds again.

Duke   It's unlocked.

Duke *flips the lights on in his living room.* **Casandra** *stands in the doorway.*

Casandra   Hi. I'm sorry. I know I'm late.

Duke   Are you alright?

Casandra   I'm fine. Just some bruises.

Duke   What? What happened?

Casandra   I, uh, I met your daughter.

Duke   Freddie did this?

Casandra   No! It was my fault. I was on my way here, driving, and I was rushing, and I was distracted and I hit her. I didn't even know who she was at first. You've only ever shown me baby pictures, I didn't recognize—

Duke   You crashed into her? Where is she? Is she alright?

Casandra   Yes, yes, she's fine.

Duke   And you didn't call?

Casandra   We were in the middle of nowhere, no service.

Duke   Where is she?

Casandra   She's fine. We're both fine. We ended up hitching a ride.

Duke   You what?! From a stranger?

Casandra   It's okay! We made it out. Everything's okay.

Duke   You should never have been driving in the first place!

Casandra   I know, I know you wanted to pick me up. I thought I could make it here before then. So you wouldn't have to worry.

Duke   I sent someone to your house. He waited all day.

Casandra   I just thought it would make more sense this way. So I could have my car down here. I know you said I wouldn't need it, but—

Duke   Someone can give you a ride, if you need to get somewhere.

Casandra   It just doesn't seem practical. Asking you every time I need to go somewhere? What if I want to go on a longer trip? Or go home for a visit?

Duke   This is home.

Beat.

Casandra   I need to be able to see my grandmother.

Duke   I can take you. From time to time.

Casandra   You're so busy. And you'll be out of town for a while anyway.

Duke   Freddie can take you.

Casandra   Or I can just take myself!

Duke   We're about to get married, Casandra.

Casandra   I didn't realize that meant I'd lose my driving privileges.

Beat.

Duke   Don't be silly. I just want you to feel at home here. And we have two cars here already.

Casandra   Not anymore. Freddie's is totaled.

Duke   God damn it, Casandra! Do you realize what could have happened to you? Both of you!

Casandra   It was an accident! . . . I'm sorry. I didn't mean to scare you. I'm sorry.

Duke   . . . You're safe. You're both safe. That's what matters. You're safe now and you'll be more careful.

Casandra   I will.

Duke   Where is it? Your car?

Casandra   I had them bring it here. I figured you'd know a good place to take it.

Duke   I'll have my guy come by to check it out.

Casandra   Thank you.

Duke   This is a compromise, Casandra. I need something from you, too.

Casandra   Like what?

Duke   I need you to make me a promise. I want you to swear you'll never keep another thing from me.

Casandra   You don't trust me?

Duke   All I want is to protect you. That's my job. But I can't do that if I don't know where you are, what's going on with you. I just want to keep you safe, is that so terrible?

Casandra   No.

Duke   So, can you promise? Never to keep anything from me again. If you promise, I'll believe you. But I need you to say it.

Beat.

Casandra   I promise.

He kisses her. She pulls away.

Casandra   . . . I should go get cleaned up.

Duke   Casandra? I'm so glad you're safe.

Lights up on the Starlight, a local dive bar with a jukebox and neon lights. **Freddie** *is already drinking.*

Dawn *enters.*

Dawn   Well, if it isn't the Lost Princess of Maricopa County.

Freddie   Don't.

Dawn   Check your messages.

Freddie   My phone just died.

Dawn   Gee, that sounds like an unsolvable problem.

Dawn *sits, drinks* **Freddie***'s drink.*

Freddie   Back off, Dawn. It's been a bad day.

Dawn (*sarcastically*)   Why, did something happen?

Freddie   What? No, nothing happened. Just everything with my dad, you know, the marriage, that's all I mean. Does there need to be something more than that?

Dawn   . . . Yeah, that's what I meant. I was kidding.

Freddie   Oh.

Dawn   Come on. It's not the end of the world.

Freddie I didn't say it was.

Dawn He said you'd be pouting.

Freddie Whatever.

Dawn *pokes her in the ribs.*

Dawn Freddie. Come on.

Freddie *shrugs her off.*

Dawn What is going on with you?

Freddie She's our age. Did you know that?

Dawn I kind of figured she was young. I mean, you know what your dad's like.

Freddie It's disgusting.

Dawn Well, what did you expect? Your dad gets every girl who passes within fifty feet of him. And none of them is ever over forty.

Freddie It's not the same. She's living with us. Why would he choose her?

Dawn Did you think he was bringing you home a new mommy?

Freddie No! God, don't make this weirder.

Dawn Are you jealous, is that it? Now you're not his "best girl."

Freddie Don't say that.

Dawn That's how he says it.

Freddie It's just embarrassing. You know what it looks like, to people?

Dawn Like the King's finally settling down. Found some exotic new bride from out of town—

Freddie Exotic?

Dawn That's what they're thinking, you know it. He found this girl and he's finally ready to grow up.

Freddie It looks like she's a gold digger.

Dawn So, what, you're worried about his money?

Freddie No, come on.

Dawn He's not like rich, rich. Anyway I'm sure he'll get a prenup, he's not stupid.

Freddie It's not that. Why would he do this? What could he possibly want from her?

Dawn Uh.

She gestures sex somehow.

Freddie Stop. He doesn't need to marry her for that! He doesn't need to have her move into our house and eat breakfast with us every day and be in our Christmas pictures.

Dawn Did you ever think maybe he *wants* people to think he's settling down?

Freddie What?

Dawn Maybe he wants people to take him seriously. Maybe he doesn't want to be just the King of Maricopa County for the rest of his life.

Freddie Do you know something?

Dawn I don't *know* anything.

Freddie Dawn.

Dawn There's an election coming up.

Freddie There's always an election coming up.

Dawn And you know what they've been saying about him. Like in the *New Times*?

Freddie We don't talk about it.

Dawn Right. If you two could actually have a real conversation, I'd be out of a job.

Freddie You're not our therapist.

Dawn What is an assistant but an incredibly underpaid therapist?

Freddie What have they been saying about him in the *New Times*?

Dawn Lately? Use of force violations, profiling, collaborating with ICE.[1]

Freddie He's not a racist. He's just trying to do his job.

Dawn Don't tell me! I wrote that line. Plus there's some new stuff. About his personal life.

Freddie What about it?

Dawn Just some comments about, you know, his dating or whatever.

Freddie *scoffs.*

Freddie So what. That's why he's got the radio show, he can set them straight.

Dawn You know last time his margins were the thinnest they've ever been. If we lose that much ground again, he's out.

Freddie That's crazy. All the real headlines, the major headlines, talk about what a star he is. You know they think he's gonna run for a state office next?

---

[1] US Immigration and Customs Enforcement.

172 The King of Maricopa County

Dawn Well, he better, cause he's not gonna find enough votes in Maricopa County again.

Beat.

Freddie You really think he got married for the sake of his career.

Dawn Well, that and . . .

She does the same sex gesture.

Freddie Gross.

Dawn Maybe he loves her. Who knows. Who cares. Either way, makes my job easier. Speaking of. Have you talked to Buzz lately?

Freddie No. Why?

Dawn He's being weird.

Freddie Weird how?

Dawn Like he never wants to go anywhere together, and he takes forever to get back to me, and he doesn't acknowledge any of the memes I send him!

Freddie That sounds like normal Buzz. That's how he's been since kindergarten.

Dawn Yeah but now we're sleeping together. Like all the time! It's not supposed to be the same.

Freddie I think you probably have to tell him that.

Dawn Why? Why should I have to explain that to him?

Freddie Look, I'm on your side here. I'm just saying I think if you ever want him to step up, you probably have to tell him how.

Dawn I don't know. You know him. If I ask for too much, he'll freak out.

Freddie Maybe just take it slow? Start with just going out on an actual date.

Dawn See, this is why I need you around. Why weren't you picking up all day?

Freddie I didn't have service.

Dawn Why? Where were you?

Freddie *just drinks.*

Dawn Freddie.

Nothing.

Freddie! Are you serious? It can't be that bad.

More nothing.

You're really not going to tell me? I tell you everything.

Freddie I was just driving around.

Dawn   So why is your car not in the parking lot?

Freddie   I, uh, had some car trouble.

Dawn   Like hell.

Freddie *puts some money on the counter before getting up.*

Freddie   I gotta go.

Dawn   Are you okay? Are you limping? What happened to you?

Freddie   I'm not talking about this anymore.

Dawn   Come on. What's the big deal?

Okay, fine. Fine! Wait. Freddie, wait. You can't go home. You want to third wheel their first night together?

Freddie *pauses.* **Dawn** *pats the seat beside her.*

Dawn   Come here. You can stay with me tonight.

Freddie *rejoins her.* **Dawn** *signals for the bartender.*

Prodigal

In the harsh light of the next morning, **Freddie** *tentatively opens the door into their living room. She finds* **Duke** *waiting.*

Duke   Front door, huh?

Freddie   What?

Duke   You used the front door. Figured you'd be sneaking in your bedroom window.

Freddie   I haven't done that since high school.

Duke   You haven't run off in a while either.

Freddie   I didn't "run off." I . . . thought you two might like some time alone together.

Duke   I meant this morning. Dawn was looking for you.

Freddie   She found me.

Duke   I can ground you, if you'd like. If you're feeling nostalgic. We can go back to that. Take away your video games.

Freddie   Okay, I get it, it was immature.

Duke   It was stupid. You know what happens when people go missing, Freddie? They'd find you in a ditch somewhere. I see it all the time.

Freddie   I didn't mean to make you worry.

Duke   I want to count on you. We've come so far, you and me. And I thought we were doing good.

Freddie   We are!

Duke   I know things haven't been easy. But I've always done my best. And lately I thought things were going okay; you're taking on more responsibility, not getting into trouble.

Freddie   If things were so good, why are you getting married?

Beat.

Duke   You are my daughter, I do not have to involve you in decisions about my romantic life.

Freddie   You moved her into our house!

Duke   My house.

Freddie   And if I don't like it, I can get out.

Duke   Stop it. Stop acting like a teenager. I'm getting married, Freddie. It's my right. I'm just doing what men do. And so what? That has nothing to do with you and me. You're still my daughter.

That's paramount. Whatever else is going on, with me, out there—doesn't matter. You're with me.

He reaches for her.

Duke   Come.

She goes to him. He holds her, at first like a restraint, then like an embrace.

Duke   There we go. It's all right.

Freddie   I'm sorry.

Duke   It's okay.

Despite everything, it comforts her deeply.

Are you angry?

Freddie   No! No, I'm not angry. I just . . . it felt like I couldn't come home. I guess I was scared.

Duke   What do I say to that? You have nothing to fear.

Both   If you have nothing to hide.

Duke   You know you're my best girl. Even if there's someone new. This is *your* home. We keep that sacred.

Freddie   I know.

Duke   You know what? I actually think you'll like her. I know she's young. But she's smart. And she's got spirit. And she'll definitely like you. You should try, at least. Nothing would make me happier than to see the two of you friends.

Beat.

Freddie Right.

Duke You're with me, kid. Okay? You with me?

Freddie I'm with you.

Phoenix

That night. **Casandra** *is outside, alone, in the desert, looking at the blank night sky. Suddenly, a flashlight shines in her face.*

She motions to **Freddie**.

Casandra Kill it. God, you really can't see the stars in the suburbs.

Freddie What do you want?

Casandra Just to talk to you.

Freddie What do you want to say?

Beat.

Casandra . . . Are you okay?

Freddie I'm fine.

Casandra What did the doctor say? How's your leg?

Freddie Don't try to take care of me, you're not my mom.

Casandra I realize that.

Freddie Is that it?

Casandra I'm just saying, you should be careful. My cousin got in a car accident once and he thought he was fine and he didn't want to go to the hospital, and then like two weeks later it turned out—

Freddie I don't give a fuck about your cousin! I'm fine.

Casandra Wow. Okay. Great. So this is how you want it to be? Fine. Fuck you, too. That's fine!

Freddie This is so stupid. I shouldn't have come.

She starts to limp off.

Casandra Yeah, that's right. Leave. You got what you wanted from me, I guess, you're done here. One and done, huh?

Freddie Yeah! Maybe when one of us is about to get married, one is enough. One is already too much.

Casandra Don't throw that in my face. I told you about him right from the beginning. And you still wanted me. Is this just how you are? How many other girls around here—If I ask girls in town about you, will they say the same thing?

Freddie (*sharply*) Keep my name out of your mouth.

Casandra I see.

Beat.

No one knows. Don't you have any friends?

Freddie I have friends!

Casandra But they don't know.

Freddie They don't need to.

She is silent.

Casandra Are you going to tell them? About us.

Freddie No! It's . . . There is no "us," it was one—it was just one bad decision. I was upset and I wasn't thinking clearly—I probably had a concussion! I mean, who knows. In the heat of the—It doesn't represent me. It doesn't represent who I am. It was just a stupid mistake.

Casandra I guess you're right.

Freddie Wait. Really?

Casandra What, you think I'm proud of this?

Freddie I don't know what to think.

Casandra I'm not a bad person, Freddie.

Freddie You're marrying a man you don't love!

Casandra Who says I don't love him?

Freddie Well. Do you?

Casandra . . . What has he told you about me?

Freddie Nothing.

Casandra Nothing?

Freddie He said you were a teacher.

He said I'd like you.

Casandra I've known him since I was fourteen. I met him at a county fair, at his campaign booth. It was his first time running, and my nana made me go up and shake his hand. She was like, "My Casandra is gonna be the first woman president." I told him about that later, but he didn't remember. Next time I saw him was years later. In Phoenix, at the teachers' march. He was there for crowd control, and I ended up getting separated from my friends, and we started talking. Afterward, he gave me a ride back to my car, and then he said we should have dinner some time—and I don't know, somehow then it just . . .

You have to understand, at first it was like he was *my* father. It was just . . . safe. And I liked him. He made me laugh, and he's so handsome. And here's this funny, strong, handsome man and everyone knows him and he wants *me*. I was excited.

Freddie   I don't need to hear this.

Casandra   Listen to me. You asked me if I love him. I've been so tired, for such a long time. Doing everything—studying, working, taking care of my nana since high school. Just barely hanging on, always trying to find us a new apartment, get a new job. And she just keeps getting worse, she needs me more and more all the time. Like I know I'm on this treadmill, and I can't fuck up, not even a little bit, or I'm gonna fall off.

And then he showed up. I never asked him for anything, but he took care of it anyway. I kept thinking he was just gonna disappear or get bored or move on, but he kept showing up. People talk a lot—men like to talk a lot about how much they want you, how beautiful you are, everything they're gonna do for you, but not a lot of them know how to show up when you need someone. I know it sounds strange. But it just felt good. Sometimes it was the best thing in my life.

And then our school shut down and I lost my job. Like the whole town was drying up. So I called him, to say goodbye. I told him, we're going to have to move. I didn't even know where. That's when he asked me to marry him.

Sometimes love feels like relief, you know? I think most people would say yes to that.

Beat.

Freddie   So you're still going to marry him.

Casandra   I made a mistake. But this is my home now.

Beat.

Freddie   Good. That's good. That's how it should be.

Beat.

Can I just ask you one more thing?

Casandra   Fine.

Freddie   With you and me. Was it the same kind of thing? A lifeline.

Casandra   No. This is more like drowning.

My turn to ask you something. Why do they call him the King?

Freddie   He's the sheriff.

Casandra   So? It's not like he rules the world.

Freddie   Around here, he might as well.

Casandra So, people love him?

Freddie And they hate him. He's the law. Especially in the unincorporated parts, there's nothing but him. If he doesn't say so, it doesn't happen around here. And if he does say so, just try and stop it. There might be men more powerful than him, but not in Maricopa County.

Casandra Come on. He's not God. How can everyone be so afraid of one man? He still has to answer to someone.

Freddie If you say so.

I should get back. We can't both be missing.

Casandra Wait. What are we going to do?

Freddie Nothing. Just forget this ever happened. I'll stay out of your way, you stay out of mine.

Casandra Alright.

Freddie Also, I wouldn't laugh at him like that if I were you. Not in front of him. He doesn't take it too well.

Casandra I can handle it.

Freddie You don't know him.

Casandra Are *you* afraid of him?

Freddie He's my father.

Breaking Bread

Lights up on the dining room. **Dawn**, **Casandra**, **Freddie**, *and* **Buzz** *appear. As they speak, they set the dinner table. They work together, but speak to us.*

Dawn *appears.*

Dawn You know how people always say play hard to get? Like if you don't give a guy everything he wants, if you're a little unavailable, he'll stay interested longer. Okay, fine. How hard is it to be unavailable? Not hard. But you can't be *too* unavailable or you'll just never see each other. So at some point you're going to have to get to know each other.

So then, what, it's just over, he stops wanting you? Is falling in love just getting more and more used to each other until you get bored and move on? And what's the point of being with someone if you never get to actually *be* with them?

Freddie *appears, sweating, in her running clothes.*

Freddie You know, running isn't as dumb as I thought it was! I used to run track in high school, but that was just because I needed PE credit and I didn't want to be on a team. And since then people would say "Let's go running" and I'd just be like "Why, is someone chasing you?" But you know what? It's not so bad. Great way to relieve, you know, tension!

Buzz *appears.*

Buzz   You know what's weird? Have you ever seen Freddie with a guy? Like literally ever? I mean obviously I've seen her like walking around the store or whatever, and she spends time with her dad and stuff. But not, like, *with* a guy. Like not even a rumor, not even in high school. That's weird, right?
You think she's a virgin?

Freddie   I just mean any kind of tension, really! I've been stressed, okay, just a little stressed. Plus it gets me out of the house, which is, you know. Helpful.

Casandra *appears.*

Casandra   I can't come home yet, the car isn't fixed. But don't worry, I'll get it taken care of. And if you really need me, just call, okay? I'll figure out a way to get there.

Dawn   So really the problem is . . . can you have someone and still want them at the same time?

Buzz   That'd be crazy, if she was a virgin. But, like, who wants to get with the sheriff's daughter?

Casandra   Did you get your pills? Jenna said she was going to drop them off with your groceries. I just want to make sure you got it.

Freddie   I try to keep busy. Stay out of the house.

Buzz   Duke would probably, like, shoot you. Actually, though, he might shoot you.

Freddie   But, you know, I live there. Sometimes . . .

Casandra   I love you, Nana. I swear I'll come home soon.

Freddie   You can't avoid it.

They all sit down to dinner together.

Norman Rockwell

Lights up on the dining room. **Duke** *enters and seats himself at the head of the table. The others sit around him around the dinner table. There's no food.*

Freddie   I think we should just ignore it.

Casandra   You want to ignore it?

Freddie   Yeah. Why not?

Duke   I can't believe I let you talk me into buying dinner from an app.

Buzz   You're *buying* it from a restaurant, you just *order* it on the app.

Duke   I know how it works, thank you very much.

Dawn (*to* **Freddie**)   I love you, but that is the worst possible thing we could do.

Buzz   Delivery?

Dawn   Ignoring it.

Freddie   Worst possible thing how?

Dawn   We always get more listeners when there's some sort of news happening—especially if it's bad news. Listeners turn into supporters. We should take advantage.

Freddie   Yeah but that's just playing into exactly what they want, those *New Times* people. More attention.

Buzz   So what? More attention for them, more for us, right?

Freddie   It's not like he's a YouTuber or an influencer or whatever. He needs *good* news.

Dawn   You can't argue with stats. We've gotten triple the listeners since the *New Times* started hounding you.

Freddie   Yeah, but that's just noise. They're not listening to his ideas.

Dawn   Who cares why they're tuning in, they're tuning in! We just need to boost name recognition. I swear, half this county just votes for the name they recognize.

Casandra   I think people are really upset.

Dawn   Right! A perfect opportunity. Once they know us, then we'll win them over. "We hear you. We feel your pain. Changes are on the way."

Casandra   Like what?

Dawn   Duke getting married, for one.

Casandra   What does that have to do with anything?

Dawn   I'm just saying, it's not a bad look for him to be settling down. Especially with someone like you. You wanna talk about broad appeal?

Casandra   Someone like me.

Duke   Dawn, let's leave my personal life out of it.

Dawn   All I'm saying is, there's a time for hedging our bets, and there's a time for doubling down. People elected him for a reason. They don't want to see him cave now.

And we can avoid specifics. We don't want to commit to any real policy positions yet, especially if we're aiming for a broader electorate. Honestly, we don't even have to answer their accusations, we can just redirect the narrative back to what's working for us. Your values. Family values.

Buzz Listen to you, "the narrative." When did you get so smart?

Dawn I—I mean. Thanks.

Freddie Yeah, but fighting with the media is so risky. You say one wrong thing and you're cancelled. We should just let it go. Rise above it.

Casandra Rising above it would be apologizing, not ignoring the problem.

Dawn That's never been our brand.

Casandra Maybe it should be.

Duke You think we have something to apologize for?

Casandra Look, I know that the media distorts things. Obviously I know they're wrong about you. But people are hurting. Shouldn't we at least see if there's something to be done?

Dawn Duke, to be honest, your people don't give a crap about "rising above." This isn't NPR. No one is checking your sources, they just want to know that you're on their side, and that you're fighting for them. You can't just let these liberals walk all over you. It looks weak.

Duke I appreciate your enthusiasm, Dawn, but we do need to pick our battles. If I'm ever going to branch out beyond this county, I can't have my hands too dirty.

Dawn I hear you, I do, and I'm not trying to step on any toes. But that kind of reach doesn't just come from minding your manners. And honestly, I really believe this is one fight we can win. We're already winning! Have you seen our reports from your last press conference? The comments online? People are listening. Not just locals, the whole country. There's someone commenting from Tasmania! A bunch along the East Coast, California.

Freddie It doesn't matter, that's not our people. Tasmania can't vote for him.

Dawn But maybe one day California can.

Buzz Why would California vote for our sheriff?

Dawn And it's not just randos commenting, it's real big names, too. If you're ever going to get anywhere, we have to catch that wave and ride it.

Freddie We should just weather the storm.

Casandra Why? This is a great opportunity. Why can't we try something new? Put some fire underneath all that smoke.

Freddie Who's that going to help? That's not going to change anyone's mind.

Casandra Why not? People respond when they see you doing good work.

Freddie You want more of this attention? Everything you do will be news. You want to live under that kind of microscope?

Buzz Duke, come on. We need a ruling.

Duke   ... I've never liked being the center of attention.

Freddie   Exactly.

Casandra   So you're just going to ignore it?

Duke   No. I love my girl here, but she's never had a taste for blood. That's why we keep Dawn around.

Things are changing around here, there's no denying that. And we need to do more than just survive, I want us to grow. Truthfully, the *New Times* is a godsend. Those morons have woken me up. We're not done yet; we've got new ground to conquer. And Dawn's right, we need to go much bigger.

Dawn   I really think this is the right decision.

Freddie   What does that mean exactly?

Duke   I'm not running for re-election.

Casandra   What?

Duke   Dawn has already started setting up meetings for me. Phoenix, Tucson, then DC.

Buzz   DC?

Freddie   I thought that was a work trip.

Duke   It is. Gotta make nice with party leadership.

Casandra   You mean ...

Duke   You're looking at your next Arizona senator, folks.

...

Charged silence.

Buzz   Sick.

Casandra   That's ... wow. What's your platform?

Duke   I still stand for the same things that I have always stood for. Folks around here aren't interested in anything too crazy, just old-fashioned common sense.

Casandra   Maybe you could finally do something about healthcare.

Duke   We'll work out the details.

Casandra   Details?

Buzz   Wait. So you won't be the sheriff anymore?

Casandra   That's not details.

Buzz   Who *is* gonna be sheriff then?

Dawn   We'll put out a platform.

Cassandra Okay, what about immigration?

Buzz Maybe I should run for sheriff.

Duke I think you know where I stand on that.

Casandra You just say it's not up to you, you just enforce the law. It's different if you get to make it. What about marriage equality?

Beat.

You have to have a position. People will want to know.

Duke I don't answer to you, Casandra.

Casandra I am a voter, right? And apparently I'm going to be part of your campaign.

Duke What folks do in their own bedrooms is none of my business. But I don't believe we should have to rewrite the rules for them.

Freddie Dad, come on.

Casandra What you mean is, you don't think they deserve rights.

Duke That's enough.

I've got enough to defend against out there, I don't need to be questioned in my own home. We operate together. Especially now. There will be no sign of division. From here on out, we are one creature. One body. With one mind. If we aren't united in here, they'll tear us apart out there. Yes?

Beat.

Casandra *nods.*

Duke Thank you.

On that note. While I'm gone, I can't be worrying about what's going on back here. Freddie, that means you too. I need to know you won't embarrass me. No more running off. No staying out all night, nothing. You cannot give them any more ammunition.

Freddie Yes, Dad.

Duke Good. Where's our damn food?

Freddie *checks her phone.*

Freddie Still says twenty minutes.

Duke I thought technology was supposed to be convenient.

Buzz I'm starving.

Freddie Why don't you cook something, then, Buzz?

Casandra Duke, I was thinking. Maybe while you're out of town, maybe I'll just go visit my nana for a bit. Just while you're gone.

Duke Without your car? Freddie would have to take you up in my truck, and then you'd be stranded.

Casandra I'm sure the repairs will be done soon.

Buzz Nah, they said it's way worse than it looks. Something about the fuel line?

Casandra Oh, yeah, the fuel line? You a mechanic now?

Buzz Don't shoot the messenger! I've been handling it for Duke.

Duke I think it would be best if you stayed. Give you two a chance to get over whatever it is you have going on.

He indicates **Freddie** *and* **Casandra**. *They look to each other.*

Freddie What do you mean?

Casandra We're fine.

Duke Don't tell me you're fine, I see how you two walk around here. You can't get within ten feet of each other. Tonight was the first time I've seen you two even look each other in the eye. While I'm gone, it'll be a chance for you to bury the hatchet.

Buzz Yeah, you two should hang out, people would be, like, "You're her mom? I thought you were her older sister!" You know, people always say that to moms.

Freddie But we don't look alike. People say that when two women look alike because they're related, so—never mind.

Duke You two can start planning the wedding.

Casandra Without you?

Dawn Ooo yes!

Casandra We don't need to do a big thing.

Dawn Nuh-uh! Come on, this is your wedding! Don't tell me you haven't been planning this your whole life.

Casandra I haven't been planning this my whole life.

Freddie*'s phone buzzes.*

Freddie Ugh, it says twenty-five minutes now! How is that possible?

Dawn Well, you better start! Duke, come on, you only get married once. You'll regret it if you don't do it right.

Duke Alright, alright, relent!

(*To* **Casandra**.) She's right though. It *should* be a big thing. You don't want to celebrate?

Casandra No, no, I want to.

Dawn Yes! This is going to be great.

Duke Excellent, it's decided. We'll do something intimate, here at the house, after I get back.

(*To* **Casandra**.) You deserve it.

Casandra . . . Thank you.

Freddie*'s phone buzzes.*

Freddie Aaaaand they cancelled our order.

Duke What did I tell you?

Freddie I can just go pick it up myself.

Duke Send Buzz.

Buzz Why me?

Duke Because frankly, Buzz, you've been eating at my table since you could chew, and I have never once seen you contribute a thing.

Buzz Right back.

He exits.

Duke I know you've been anxious about that. The wedding.

Casandra *nods.*

Duke *looks from* **Casandra** *to* **Freddie***, both silent.*

Duke *extends reaches out to* **Casandra** *on one side and* **Freddie** *on the other.*

Duke I know it won't be overnight. But I have faith that you two will eventually learn to love each other. Maybe not like mother and daughter, I'm not crazy. But you will love each other, as I love you. For now, just tell me you'll try. While I'm away. Just tell me you'll try.

Freddie Of course, Dad.

Duke *moves into the radio station as the rest of the scene clears.*

Duke Friends. Neighbors. You know I hate to leave you, but some urgent business calls, so leave I must. In the meantime, while I'm away, I have just one request: be good. Remember, you have nothing to fear if you have nothing to hide.

Cat's Away

The next day, **Freddie** *is in the backyard, tinkering with a radio. Her phone rings. She ignores it.*

Dawn *appears, on the phone.*

Dawn Freddie, come on, pick up the phone. It's gotta be weird at home with your dad gone. Wanna ditch your stepmom and walk around the mall like in seventh grade? We can get pretzels! Seriously though, I've got a bunch of paperwork for the campaign and you need to come pick it up.

She disappears.

Casandra *enters with her arms full of string lights, carrying a folding chair.*

Freddie   What's that?

Casandra   For the reception. So we're not just out here in the dark. Thought I'd get a head start. I can come back later.

Freddie   No, no, it's fine. He's right, we can't just avoid each other forever. Let me help you.

Together, they start stringing the lights around the yard. **Freddie** *holds the chair as* **Casandra** *stands on it to reach the top of the fence.*

Casandra   Do you think this is what he had in mind when he told us to bond?

Freddie   He'd just be happy that I'm not making you like break into the pool, or, drink forties behind the 7Eleven.

Casandra   Is that what you do for fun?

Freddie   Used to be. He still worries about me. I sort of had a reputation for a while, after my mom left.

Casandra   Why did she leave?

Beat.

I'm sorry. You don't have to talk about it, if you don't want to.

Freddie   He hasn't told you?

Casandra   We don't talk about her.

Freddie   Neither do we. I actually . . . I still don't know.

Casandra   You miss her?

Freddie   I used to.

She stays cold.

Casandra *stops working for a second.*

Casandra   Freddie. You can . . . I'm not trying to seduce you, you know.

I just . . . I can see you don't have a lot of people. I just want to be your friend. You can be real with me. You can say real things to me.

I'm not gonna tell him.

Freddie   Yeah, I missed her. So much I couldn't breathe sometimes.

Casandra   Literally?

Freddie *nods.*

Casandra You panicked.

Freddie More like . . . You know how usually you don't have to think about it, your lungs just do it, automatically, you just breathe. I guess I forgot how to do that. Once that happens, it's like you have to think about it every second. You're constantly reminding yourself just to inhale, exhale. But then, I guess, eventually you don't have to think about it anymore.

Casandra How long did that take?

Freddie A while.

Now I can barely picture her face.

Anyway. Now you know my shit. I don't really know anything about you.

Casandra You never asked.

Freddie I'm sorry. I've been trying so hard to keep my distance. I think I've been mean to you.

Casandra *nods.*

Freddie But I don't want to be that way.

Beat.

Tell me about your grandmother?

Casandra You'd like her. She was a wild child too. Always in trouble. Now, you know, she doesn't get out too much. She lives in a home. But back in the day, I bet she would have been right there with you, with the forties and the donuts.

Freddie No way.

Casandra Crazy lady.

Freddie She raised you?

Casandra Yeah but she never let me do anything like that. She found God before I was born.

Freddie Well, I hope I get to meet her, at the wedding.

Casandra I don't think she's coming. It's hard for her to get around, and it's a long drive.

Freddie So who's going to give you away?

Casandra Give me away?

Freddie Walk you down the aisle.

Casandra So old fashioned!

Freddie You know what I mean.

Casandra I'll walk myself.

Freddie . . . I think you're brave.

Casandra For walking without an escort?

Freddie No, I mean, for moving here, for getting married, for uprooting your life, all alone. Without anyone to hold your hand, you just made your choice and went. I'm still living in my father's house, working for him, in the same place where I grew up. I couldn't do what you did.

Casandra I bet you could. If you really wanted.

Freddie Maybe.

Casandra You're braver than you think. You stood up to him, the other night. At dinner. When we were talking about his campaign platform.

Freddie That's different.

Casandra Why?

Freddie It was just talking. It's not like I did anything.

Casandra Talking is the first step to doing.

Wait!

Freddie *is about to climb onto the chair, but* **Casandra** *stops her.*

Casandra Your leg.

Freddie It's fine, it doesn't hurt anymore.

Casandra Still, be gentle with it. I'll feel better if you stay on the ground. Just help me up.

Freddie *relents. She takes* **Casandra***'s hand, helping her up onto the chair.* **Casandra** *quickly lets it go.*

Freddie Where did you get these?

Casandra Buzz dropped them off earlier. He wanted to stay and help but I told him I had plans.

Freddie Oh, do you need to go?

Casandra *scoffs.*

Casandra What plans could I possibly have? I don't know anyone in town. Except you. And you've been avoiding me.

Freddie You haven't tried to make friends? People are pretty friendly around here.

Casandra Not to me.

Freddie What? I'm sure that's not true. You have to give them a chance. It's a nice neighborhood.

Casandra *scoffs.*

Freddie What?

What?! It is! Isn't it?

Casandra This lady over here—

She gestures at one of their neighbors.

Casandra The one with the bangs? I ran into her in the driveway and she asked what my rate was. For monthly cleanings.

Freddie Okay, yeah, I mean, she's rude, forget her. But don't let her ruin the rest of this place. What about the deputies' wives? Have you thought about hanging out with them? They do, like, book clubs and barbecues and stuff.

Casandra You're not serious.

Freddie What?!

Casandra Can you not see the way those people look at me?

Freddie How do they look at you?

Casandra Like I'm gonna give cocaine to their kids.

Freddie, this place. It's not like the real world. It's like this weird little moon colony where everyone has two cars and three freezers and goes to the same hairdresser. And then I show up—and it's so obvious I don't belong here.

Freddie You mean, because . . .

Casandra Wow, you can't even say it. Say it! Say it, Freddie.

Freddie You're not white.

Casandra And everyone else is. I walk into any of these book clubs and barbecues and it's like an invisible alarm went off. They look at me like they can't really figure out what's going on, like a bunch of robots, glitching out. And then Duke starts introducing me and it becomes this game of, "Oh, you're the new wife," "Where are you from, originally?" And "You're so articulate!" I'm always just counting down the minutes. It's like suffocating.

Silently. In milk. It's so. White. It's whiter than the cast of *Friends*. It's whiter than a turtleneck sale at J. Crew. It's whiter than low-fat mayonnaise on toast.

Freddie Low-fat mayonnaise?

Casandra *laughs in spite of herself.*

Casandra I don't know, I just didn't expect that it would be like this.

Freddie What about Duke. You think he's one of the moon colony people?

Casandra I know what people say about him. But they don't know him. He's not some crazy, redneck racist. He's so normal. I mean, if he was everything they say, why would he be with me?

Freddie I don't know.

Beat.

At least you can see why I don't like to tell people around here about me.

Casandra You mean the fact that you're gay?

Freddie Can we not say gay?

Casandra Legally?

Freddie *scoffs.*

Casandra What would they do? If you told people.

Freddie Try to save me, probably. Send me to some sort of camp.

Casandra Fucking moon colony.

Freddie Well, fuck everyone else. Now we're friends, we don't need them.

Beat.

Casandra Are we friends?

Beat.

Freddie I know I was mean to you. And cold. I'm so embarrassed about the way I talked to you. But all I want now is to make it up to you. I get it if you don't want to. But I'd really like us to be friends. Truce?

She offers **Casandra** *a hand.*

Beat.

Casandra I don't think I can be friends with you.

Freddie Okay. I get it. But just so you know, I'm not like them. I mean, I know everyone says that probably, but I don't think you're—I think you're—

Casandra (*suddenly angry*) You *don't get it.* I'm trying to be your friend, but I can't. I thought I could, but I . . .

She laughs.

Never mind.

She laughs.

I'm gonna . . . Go. Sorry. Forget it.

Beat.

Freddie I want you too.

Casandra *immediately closes the space between them and kisses her.*

Freddie *freezes, then surrenders.*

She clings to **Casandra**. *They breathe each other's breath.*

Casandra   I wish I had waited for you.

Dawn *reappears.*

Dawn   What is the point of having a phone if you literally never answer it? What could you possibly be doing that you never have time for me? Don't worry, I'll save you a trip, I'm coming by to drop everything off. You better be home. We can get tacos after! See you soon.

She disappears.

Casandra   What do we do?

Freddie   Can we . . . just stay here for a minute?

Just stay here, please. Just for a while. Just stay, where I can . . .

Dawn *enters, out of sight.*

Freddie *kisses* **Casandra**.

Dawn *sees them together, freezes, then retreats.*

Starlight Clusterfuck

Two weeks later. **Dawn** *and* **Buzz** *are at the Starlight bar, already halfway through a couple of beers.*

Buzz   It just doesn't make sense. You know you could get a six pack for what you just paid for that one. You could be sitting at home, on your own couch, pounding through six of those.

Dawn   But don't you think it's nicer? To be here, together? With the jukebox, and the lights. Not pounding anything. I think it's nicer here.

Buzz   At home I could play whatever music you want. For free.

Dawn   You just want to have sex.

Buzz   So? You like having sex.

Dawn   I also like being out.

Buzz   No sex. Overpriced beer. Gotta pay a quarter for every song.

Dawn   Lights, atmosphere, conversation.

Buzz   It's just bad economics.

Dawn   Fine, Buzz. Then leave.

Buzz   Sweet. We can stop at 7Eleven on the way.

He downs the rest of his beer.

Coming?

Dawn   . . . Yeah. Yeah, I'm coming.

They start to leave, but immediately run into **Freddie** *as she enters.*

Buzz   Woah. Freddie, what's up? Haven't seen you in a minute.

Freddie   Hi. Dawn.

Dawn   We were just heading out.

Buzz   We don't have to though.

Dawn   What about economics?

Buzz   Don't want to be rude.

(*To* **Freddie**.) Seriously, what has it been, like two weeks? Where have you been? Lemme get you something. What are you drinking?

Freddie   No that's okay, don't let me keep you, go ahead. You two have fun.

Dawn   Okay, see you later.

Buzz   Nah, come on, we can't just leave you here to drink all alone.

Dawn   She likes it that way.   **Freddie**   I like it that way.

Buzz   Thought you grew out of your emo phase, Winifred. No one likes being alone. Come on, what are you having?

Dawn   Buzz, let's go.

Buzz   You can go if you want. No one's stopping you.

Freddie   You know what? I changed my mind. I could get a six pack for what you pay for one beer here. What's the point, right?

Buzz   Word, meet you back at your place?

Freddie   Noooo, thank you. I'll see you later.

She starts to leave and runs into **Casandra** *as she enters.*

Casandra   Hey, sorry. Took me a minute to get him—

She spots **Buzz** *and* **Dawn**.

Casandra   Oh hey. What are you doing here?

Buzz   Oh shit, Mom's here!

Freddie   Shut up, Buzz.

Dawn (*to* **Freddie**)   What are you two doing at a bar?

Freddie   Uh, drinking?

Buzz   Hey, Cas, you're not gonna tell the sheriff about this, are you?

Freddie (*too defensive*)   Tell him what? That we all happened to run into each other? We aren't doing anything.

Buzz Chill, I was just giving her shit.

(*To* **Casandra**.) Guess you must be pretty bored at home, huh? What do you even do all day? I feel like I never see you out. Like I'd never even know the two of you live together, you're both always missing. Like you both just disappear, at the same time—

Freddie (*interrupting*) So what's everyone drinking?

Buzz Yes! There we go. Fun Freddie! Mom, you drinking?

Casandra Can you not call me that?

Buzz It's just a joke, it's cool.

Casandra I'd rather you didn't.

Buzz Come on, when was the last time any of us got to party with our moms? I guess technically you're just Freddie's mom.

Casandra I am NOT her mother.   **Freddie** She's just my step—they're not even married yet, it's completely different!

Buzz Okay, both of you need to fucking chill. I'll get this round, what does everyone want? Just kidding, we're for sure doing shots. Mom party! WOO!

He exits.

Dawn *pulls* **Freddie** *aside.*

Dawn (*to* **Casandra**) Give us a minute?

(*To* **Freddie**.) What's going on?

Freddie What do you mean?

Dawn Did you plan to meet her here?

Freddie No! What? Why would I?

Dawn You tell me.

Buzz *returns with a round of shots.*

Casandra No, I should probably go.

Freddie Okay, cool, see you later!

Buzz You just got here!

Dawn Yeah, don't leave on our account. Were you meeting someone, or . . .?

Casandra Uh, no, I was . . .

Freddie Hey, we doing these, or what?

They do the shot.

Buzz Fuck yeah, Party mom!

Freddie *pulls* **Casandra** *aside while* **Buzz** *and* **Dawn** *talk. We only really need to hear* **Freddie** *and* **Casandra***'s side of this conversation.*

Buzz You're getting the next round then, right?	**Freddie** I told you we should've stayed home.
Dawn What? Why would I get the next round?	**Casandra** How was I supposed to know they'd be here?
Buzz Cause I got the last one.	**Freddie** We shouldn't be going out in public anyway.
Dawn No one asked you to do that.	**Casandra** We're allowed to be seen in public together. They know that we're—friends.
Buzz Come on, Dawnie, don't be a spoil sport.	**Freddie** We're just drawing attention to ourselves.
Dawn I thought you wanted to go home anyway!	**Casandra** I can't live the rest of my life in that house, Freddie, I'll go insane.
Buzz Forget it.	**Freddie** That doesn't mean—

Buzz So. Tell us, what's it like being Mrs. Duke Howard?

Casandra We're not actually married yet.

Buzz Wait, if he's the King, does that make you the Queen?

Casandra Uh . . .

Buzz Totally! Queen Casandra. So where are you from?

Casandra Outside Phoenix.

Buzz What did you do there? Let me guess—

Buzz Waitress.	**Casandra** I'm a teacher.

Buzz Oh! Bet you're glad you don't have to do that anymore.

Casandra What do you mean?

Buzz Well, now you're with Duke, you don't have to teach anymore.

Casandra Who said I don't want to teach anymore?

Freddie Leave her alone, Buzz.

Dawn Why? He's not doing anything. She's fine.

Buzz So how'd you meet Duke?	**Freddie** He's just being . . .
Casandra At a march, actually.	**Dawn** If anyone's being, you're being.
Buzz Duke was at a march? Is that even allowed?	**Freddie** Are you mad at me?
Casandra He was policing it.	**Dawn** I'm just trying to understand you.

Buzz That checks out. So did he, like, save you from the angry mob?

Casandra Have you ever been to a march?

Buzz Pfft. Uh, no. So, what's it like living with Freddie? You ever ground her? Take away her phone privileges?

Casandra It's really not like that.

Freddie What do you mean?

Dawn Would you give it up? I know you're hiding something.

Freddie Why would you say that? That's crazy.

Dawn Don't tell me I'm crazy. Are you even listening?

Buzz Yeah I bet you two are more like friends, or sisters even. That's cool, so you can like hang out a lot, right?

Freddie Buzz, stop it.

Buzz What? We're just talking.

Dawn What are you, her bodyguard?

Freddie No! I'm just—He's interrogating her.

Dawn Fuck this. I'm leaving. Buzz, you need a ride?

Casandra Should you drive right now?

Dawn Get off my back, Mom.

Casandra Sorry.

Dawn Buzz? You don't have your car here.

Buzz Whatever, Freddie will take me home.

Freddie Dawn. Stop. Come here.

She takes **Dawn** *aside.*

Freddie What is wrong with you? You're being a total asshole.

Dawn You obviously came here with her.

Freddie Dawn, I just came here to be alone, like always.

Dawn God damn it, Freddie! Just tell me, or I'm walking out of here. You know what you're doing is wrong. Stop lying!

Freddie It's Buzz.

Dawn What?

Freddie It's Buzz. I've been hooking up with Buzz.

Dawn No.

Freddie I'm sorry.

Dawn Don't do this.

Freddie I didn't want to tell you, I knew you'd be mad.

Dawn I don't believe you.

Freddie I'm sorry. That's what I've been hiding from you.

Dawn You don't even like him! Everyone knows you don't like him.

Freddie It's true.

Dawn No it's fucking not. I'm not as stupid as you think, Freddie. You wanna know how I know you don't want him? You want me to tell you?

Freddie Dawn.

Dawn I know a lot more than you think. Why don't we all just talk about it?

Freddie I'm serious.

Dawn You're lying.

Freddie *goes to* **Buzz** *and kisses him. A clap of thunder. The lights flicker.*

Casandra

Freddie (*to* **Dawn**) What are you doing?

Dawn Happy?

Fuck you.

Generator

Later that evening. The sound of a match striking in the dark.

In the light, we can see **Freddie**'s *face, searching her living room.*

Freddie Cas? Where are you?

Casandra I'm here.

They find each other in the dim light.

Casandra So do you want to tell me what just happened?

Freddie We shouldn't talk about it right now.

Casandra He's not here.

Freddie *avoids her gaze.*

Casandra Why'd you do it?

Freddie I had to. Dawn was saying all this stuff about us—she knew something was up.

Casandra Don't you think maybe we can trust her?

Freddie No.

Casandra Why not?

Freddie I don't want to talk about this right now.

Casandra We're not going to get a better chance.

Freddie We'll figure it out later okay?

Casandra Let's just tell her!

Freddie I don't want her to know, okay? I don't want anyone to know!

Beat.

Casandra Ever?

Freddie *says nothing.*

Casandra You're ashamed.

Beat.

Freddie Of course I'm ashamed. Look at us! Aren't *you* ashamed?

Casandra No! You should never be ashamed of who you love.

Freddie Even when it's your husband's daughter?

Beat.

We can't just hide in this house forever. I can't keep lying to Dawn. I think we're out of time.

Casandra *wrestles with this.* **Freddie** *starts to speak, stops.* **Casandra** *turns away. Turns back.*

Casandra Let's run away.

Freddie What?

Casandra I'm serious. Let's just pack our bags and get in the car.

It's not such a crazy idea. We'll pick someplace on the map and drive there. We could drive all night and wake up somewhere new.

Freddie I—but . . . where would we even go?

Casandra Wherever we want.

California? Or somewhere farther.

We could keep going north. We could drive along the coast. By the water. We could spend a night on the beach.

Freddie I don't want to live by the beach.

Casandra That's okay, we can go wherever you want. Imagine getting out of the desert, seeing the ocean. And then we'd keep going. We'd go until there were lots of trees, someplace where everything is green. Where it really rains.

Beat.

Freddie And the leaves change.

Casandra Exactly!

Freddie I've never even been that far north.

Casandra I'll take you.

Freddie You know it would take us days to get that far.

Casandra Even better. It'll be just us, on a journey. Living on beef jerky and Goldfish crackers and gas station coffee. I'm going to sing along to the radio—

Freddie Please don't.

Casandra The whole time. And you're gonna sing with me. And when you're driving I'll give you neck massages and when I'm driving I'll—

Freddie I think maybe I should be the driver here. Given our history.

Casandra Even better. And we'll stop every so often to get out and look at the sky. And when we get up north we'll find a little motel somewhere to crash and it will feel so good to finally stretch out. You'll fall asleep holding me. And when we wake up in the morning and go outside, everything will be misty and green and smell like Christmas trees. And that will be our new town.

Freddie I've never lived anywhere else.

Casandra Do you want to?

Freddie . . . I do.

Casandra *laughs in excitement.*

Casandra Really? Okay! Okay. Oh my God. I can't believe it. Okay. We have to pack. When do you want to go? Tonight? No, we have to get everything together. Tomorrow? But don't tell anyone, okay? Make sure if you have everything you need, 'cause who knows when we can come back—if we can come back. Who knows what he's going to say, or if he'll—whatever, we'll figure that all out. God I can't believe it. I'm so happy, Freddie.

Outside the house, **Buzz** *approaches, activating the garage light. Before he reaches the door, he runs into* **Duke**.

Duke Buzz?

Buzz Sheriff! I didn't realize you were back.

Duke Thought I'd surprise everyone. What are you doing here? Something wrong?

Buzz No, I just came to talk to Freddie.

Duke Is she expecting you? I can give her a message for you.

Buzz Uh . . . did I say Freddie? I meant Casandra.

Duke About what?

Buzz About . . . her car. I have an update.

Duke It's done?

Buzz Yep! I mean, no. The fuel line is still tanked. Pretty much ready to blow at any time. But it *will* be done. Soon. So just sit tight.

Duke That's the update?

Buzz Yes, sir.

Duke Go home, Buzz.

Buzz Sure thing, sheriff.

He starts to leave.

Freddie Did you hear something?

Casandra Maybe a coyote?

Duke Wait. Buzz. Have you been drinking?

Buzz No. Uh. Yes. But I'll get an Uber.

Duke Alright then. You get home safe now.

They both exit.

Freddie I swear I heard something.

Casandra Do you want to check?

A sound in the dark.

Freddie Someone's here. Go. GO.

Casandra *hides.*

Freddie Hello?

She holds up the light. It finds **Duke**.

Duke It's me.

Freddie Dad! You're back.

Duke Came straight from the airport.

Beat.

Aren't you happy to see me?

Freddie Of course. You just surprised me. I thought you wouldn't be back yet.

Duke You're going to laugh. It turns out being away from home is harder than I thought. I guess I missed you, kid. I had Dawn bring me back a day early.

She hugs him.

Freddie I missed you too, Dad.

Duke Where were you?

Freddie At the Starlight.

Duke With Casandra?

Freddie What? No. I mean, yeah. She came too. But mostly I was there with Dawn. And Buzz.

Duke So she *was* there? With you?

Freddie Yeah. I mean, we shared a ride.

Duke Well, well, guess you two can get along. So where is she?

Freddie We . . . got separated when I went to look for the matches.

Duke Power out at the bar too?

Freddie Yeah.

Duke It is thunder season. I'll head out back and take a look at the generator. You stay and see if you can find her.

Freddie Got it.

Duke Be careful.

He exits.

Freddie He's gone.

Casandra *joins her.*

Casandra Do you think he heard us?

Freddie Doesn't seem like it.

Casandra *nods.*

Casandra Thank God. Okay. Let's start packing. Text me later so we can figure out where we'll meet. And make sure you've got all your papers and stuff, anything important. Okay?

Freddie?

Freddie.

Beat.

Freddie I can't.

Casandra No. Yes you can. We can do this. I love you.

Beat.

Did you hear me? I love you.

Beat.

Freddie   I love you too.

Casandra   So let's go.

Freddie *shakes her head.*

Casandra   Why not? What's stopping you? There's nothing stopping you. No one is stopping you.

Freddie   I love him too.

Duke   There you are, Casandra.

He flips on the circuit breaker. Lights up.

We were wondering where you were.

Casandra   Duke! We weren't expecting you.

Duke   . . . I hope it's a nice surprise.

Casandra   Yes, of course. Sorry, I have to . . . I'm just feeling a little sick.

She exits.

Duke   What did you say to her? Did something happen?

Freddie   Nothing. Just a misunderstanding. It's nothing to worry about, Dad.

Duke   Freddie.

Freddie   It's nothing, I promise.

Glad to have you back.

Duke   I'm not going anywhere.

Love, Cherish, Obey

A week later. **Casandra** *stands in front of the mirror in her bedroom, staring at her reflection in her wedding dress.*

Duke *enters.*

Duke   Beautiful.

Casandra   You think so? Dawn found it.

Duke   Always count on Dawn.

Casandra   Are you supposed to be here? Isn't there a rule that you're not supposed to see me beforehand?

Duke   I'll go if you really want.

Casandra   No, no, it's fine.

He stares at her, long enough that she becomes uncomfortable.

Casandra   Is something wrong?

Duke   I want to ask you something.

Casandra   What is it?

Duke   Do you want to be my wife?

Casandra   . . . We're getting married.

Duke   I know we don't always see eye to eye, but I've always admired you. And I like to think I've brought some balance to your life. We're a good pair.

You know where I've been, this past week?

Casandra   Yes.

Duke   And you know what I've been doing there?

Casandra   Duke, stop playing with me.

Duke   My name is in their mouths now. After today, it'll be your name, too.

It's one thing to make a promise at one in the morning, in a parking lot, when you're scared and upset. That's my fault. I didn't plan it as well as I should have. But marriage is too long for that. You have to choose it every day. And it needs to be worth the sacrifice.

Casandra   The sacrifice?

Duke   I need to know that you stand behind me. Even if you don't always agree with me. Marrying me means joining our ticket. And we plan to win. So if you're with me, there can be no daylight between us. Do you understand what I'm saying?

So I'm asking you again. Can you do this? When you answer, be certain.

Casandra   I need to ask you something first.

Do you love me?

Beat.

Duke   I do.

In a strange way. I do.

Casandra   Why? I know you could have had a hundred other girls. There must be half a dozen women on this block, even, who had a sister or a niece for you. Girls like you. Girls you wouldn't have to ask twice. Why not marry one of them?

Duke   I don't want someone like me. I want someone I don't already understand. You're a mystery to me, it's true. And I'll spend the rest of my life wanting to know more. I don't want something familiar. I'd rather sail uncharted waters.

What do you say? Can you promise me this?

Lights down on them.

Elsewhere in the house, **Dawn** *approaches* **Freddie***, both dressed in their best.*

Dawn   I have something for you.

She hands **Freddie** *a ring box.*

Dawn Duke wants you to hold the rings during the ceremony. You can hand them over when it's time.

Freddie Dawn. Can we talk for a second? About the other night?

Dawn You have something to say to me?

Freddie I'm sorry. I didn't mean to hurt you.

Beat.

Dawn

Freddie Is that it?

Dawn What do you want me to say?

I want you to make it right. I want you to be honest.

Freddie You don't understand. It's not that simple.

Dawn I don't care, I don't need to hear any more excuses.

Freddie Please, Dawn. Come on. It's just some boy, don't let this come between us, it doesn't matter.

Dawn It's not just about some boy! It's about how you treat me. You're supposed to be my best friend. But you have no problem lying to me. Or ignoring me, or using me. As long as I keep your secret.

Freddie What are you talking about?

Dawn You know what I'm talking about.

Freddie I don't have a secret.

Duke You want me to say it? I'll say it.

Freddie I don't know what you—

Dawn I saw you with her.

Freddie

Dawn Say something!

Freddie . . . Have you told anyone?

Dawn That's it? Do you even think about everyone around you? Forget about me, what about your dad?

Freddie Please, Dawn.

Dawn What is wrong with you?

Freddie I'm sorry, I can't explain it, I just . . . I know I shouldn't have done any of it, I just, I—

Please don't tell him.

Dawn You tell him. This is your secret; I'm not keeping it for you.

Freddie I can't. Dawn, I *can't*.

Dawn Freddie you can't keep doing this. Stumbling through your life like someone's pushing you. You know what the right thing is. You just have to fucking do it.

Freddie Please, I just need time.

Dawn If you don't, I will.

Will you?

Freddie.

Will you?

Buzz *approaches them.*

Buzz What are we talking about?

Silence between them.

Dawn I gave you so many chances.

She exits.

Freddie Dawn—

But she's gone.

Buzz She mad?

Freddie She's fine.

Buzz Hey. So that was pretty crazy, huh? The other night? You know, I came by afterward, but—

Freddie It's not a good time, Buzz.

Buzz Are *you* mad?

Freddie I have to go.

In another room, **Duke** *is sipping whiskey.* **Dawn** *approaches.*

Duke Everything all set?

Dawn . . . Yeah. Brad and Karen finally RSVP'd, so I put out a couple of extra chairs for them, and you were right, the caterer was late, but I got them set up in the kitchen so everything should be ready by the cocktail hour, and I told them about the freezer in the garage, so you shouldn't have to worry about that.

Duke Okay . . .

Dawn And then I also just wanted to apologize because some of the flowers aren't the ones you selected, I didn't even know until she got here this afternoon to deliver and by then there was really nothing she could do, so I just wanted to give you a heads-up, and I'll follow up with her next week to try to get some money back.

Duke Dawn. It's fine. Relax. You're making me nervous.

Dawn Sorry.

Duke   Here.

He pours her a glass. She downs it.

Duke   Is something wrong?

Dawn   I have to tell you something. It's about Freddie. And Casandra.

A long moment. However long it takes her to make her choice.

Dawn   I think they're having an affair.

Duke *scoffs.*

Duke   Is that a joke?

Don't be ridiculous.

Dawn   I saw them together.

Duke   They're friends, Dawn.

Dawn   I saw Freddie kiss her.

Beat.

Duke   A kiss can mean a lot of things.

Dawn   What?

Duke   Look, I know you two haven't spent as much time together lately. And the two of them have gotten closer since I've been gone. Is it possible that there might be some jealousy involved here? Seems to me like Freddie's found a new friend, and you've let your imagination get the best of you.

Beat.

Dawn   You can't be serious.

Duke   Why don't you go and greet people as they come in? You can show them where the bathroom is, that kind of thing. Go ahead. I'll tell Freddie to have a talk with you later. It'll all be just fine.

Dawn   Duke. WAKE UP. They're not "friends," they're not "close." I saw them kissing, touching each other, they're—They're sleeping together. And they've been doing it right under your nose, in your house. Who knows how long. It's a joke! You broadcasting to the whole county about love and commitment and your loving wife, and meanwhile she's got her hand down your daughter's pants. They're laughing at you! They're all laughing at you.

Sorry. I—I'm sorry. I didn't mean . . .

Beat.

Duke   Who else have you said this to?

Dawn   No one.

Duke   Thank you.

Beat.

Duke (*a threat*) That's all for now.

Dawn What are you going to do?

Duke Go greet our guests, Dawn. Tell them I'll be down shortly.

Lights down on them.

Lights up on **Casandra** *in the bedroom, where she is packing a bag.*

Freddie *enters.* **Casandra** *freezes for a moment, then resumes, faster than before.*

Freddie What are you doing?

Casandra Stay out of this. It's the least you can do.

Freddie Are you leaving?

Casandra So? What do you care?

Freddie

Casandra

Freddie *strides across the space between them and kisses her.* **Casandra** *pulls away.*

Casandra Don't do this to me. I can't do this again.

Freddie Take me with you.

Beat.

Casandra What?

Freddie Let me come with you. I'm ready now. I know it's late, but I'm here, and I'm ready. I want to drive up north and eat beef jerky and smell the Christmas trees and see the ocean and wake up with you.

Casandra I— . . .

No! You're too late! You—You can't just come here, and—and—

Freddie I know, I know, I fucked up. But I'm sorry and I'm here now I want to do this. Please, Cas. Say yes.

Casandra I wanted to run away. I told you we should go, I begged you. *You* said no—You gave up on me. You chose him. Now it's me again? No. I don't believe you. You're just going to come running back to him tomorrow.

Freddie I know, I know what I said. But this isn't about him.

Casandra *scoffs.*

Freddie It's not even really about you.

Casandra Excuse me?

Freddie I'm done being scared all the time. I can't keep holding my breath and playing it safe and praying no one looks at me too closely. You were right. I have to get out. I have to. So I'm deciding not to be afraid anymore. Even if you tell me to fuck off and never speak to you again, I'm leaving.

I love you. I do. But I am leaving for me.

Casandra . . . Even if I tell you to fuck off?

Freddie But I really, really hope you don't. I'm just asking for one more chance.

Casandra *takes* **Freddie***'s face in her hands and kisses her gently.*

Duke *appears, watching through a door or window, or maybe just listening.*

Casandra Okay. Are you sure?

Freddie I'm sure.

Casandra What are you going to say to him?

Freddie Nothing. He'd just try to stop us.

Casandra Okay, let's go, we don't have much time.

Freddie I'll have to find his keys.

Casandra We can't steal his truck!

Freddie You want to walk out of here?

Casandra Fine, fine, you're right.

Freddie Ten minutes. Okay? Throw your bag out the back window when you're ready, I'll put it in the trunk.

Casandra I can't believe this. Okay, go!

Freddie Wait, one more thing.

Casandra We don't have time!

Freddie *takes her hand.*

Freddie I promise I will not give up again.

She kisses **Casandra***.*

Freddie Ten minutes.

She exits.

Lights shift as **Duke** *shifts into his own mental space.*

Duke What have I done?

What have I done?

What have I *done*?

YOU SHOULD HAVE BEEN GRATEFUL FOR WHAT I GAVE TO YOU.

Lights shift again and he is back in the house.

Enough.

He pulls himself together.

Freddie *appears.*

Freddie Dad.

Duke

Freddie

Duke Going somewhere?

Freddie No. I mean. I was just going to run an errand. I'll be right back.

Duke Don't lie to me, Freddie.

Freddie Okay.

Duke It's my wedding day.

Freddie I know.

Duke Where are you going? Tell me the truth. For once, Freddie, tell me something true.

Freddie *works up the courage.*

Freddie You're right. I'm leaving.

I'm sorry. I never wanted to disappoint you.

Duke Then DON'T. You have *always* taken the easy way out! This is your chance to redeem yourself. This time I need you to stand up and do what is right. For once in your life.

Freddie Dad, I've tried so hard to do things your way. It doesn't work.

Duke You know what this will do to my career.

Freddie Your career? That's what you want to talk about?

Duke It's *wrong,* Freddie. It's that simple. There is right and wrong and this—

Freddie What's wrong about me leaving?

Duke *(frighteningly intense)* You want me to tell you?

I know about you and her.

Freddie

Duke

Freddie It's my fault. Please don't blame her, it was all me. I asked her to—it's my fault.

Duke Oh, I don't blame her. You can't blame a dog for chasing a rabbit. But you. You should know better.

Look at you. So ashamed. That's what it is to live like this. But this isn't who you have to be. Come back to me. You can do better, you will be better.

Don't be a coward.

Freddie I've always been a coward! I've always been terrified! Of you, Dad. I thought I was just going to live the rest of my life without ever feeling right. But she—She wants all those good things for me. Like you were supposed to. You were supposed to teach me to be brave. All I ever learned from you was watch your back.

Duke I gave you everything you have.

Freddie And I don't want it.

Please just let me go.

A frightening silence.

Duke I can't let you go. It's not my decision to make. This is your choice, Freddie. But you have to understand that your choices have consequences. You'll ruin my reputation. More than that, you're ruining your life. This will be the end for you.

Freddie You're right. This is my choice, and I have to live with it. And maybe it'll go horribly wrong. Maybe we won't last a day. But I'd rather have that one day with her than the rest of my life in this house.

We're going to find a new home. We'll go as far as we have to. And if we can't find one, we'll build it.

I'll miss you. I'll think about you every day and I wish you could still love me. But if you can't. She will.

Beat.

Duke How were you planning on going?

Freddie Your truck.

He reaches into his pocket. She flinches. But he holds out an open palm.

Duke The keys.

Freddie Dad—

Duke You can take Casandra's.

Freddie It's fixed?

Duke There's a spare key in the junk drawer.

This will be the last time I see you. Your choices will catch up to you, and by then it will be out of my hands.

Freddie *hands him back his car keys.*

Duke Goodbye, Freddie.

Freddie Wait.

She reaches into her pocket and hands him the ring box.

I love you, Dad.

She exits.

Lights shift. **Duke** *moves into his own mental space once again.*

Duke You try to save your children.

When she was a baby I used to hold my daughter in the middle of the night, in one hand. Just to feel how small she was. I made myself as strong as a man can be. To shelter her. But before I could blink, she changed. She grew. And all the nasty things of life came out to meet her. And now she is different. My girl is gone. She is a woman, and her punishment is her own. She has earned it.

People will send their condolences. They'll offer their prayers, but they won't be surprised. The path she took always seemed to lead this way. Justice is cruel, but it is right. We believe in justice here. And I am only its instrument.

You try, but you can't save your children.

Lights shift. **Duke** *returns to the room. Some time later,* **Dawn** *enters.*

Dawn Sheriff? You haven't spoken to Casandra recently, have you?

Duke Is there a problem?

Dawn I just, I'm not totally sure . . . where she is. I think she must have gone somewhere. I can't find her.

Duke And you've called?

Dawn Yes, sir.

Duke . . . Are the cars in the driveway?

Dawn *goes to look.*

Dawn Hers is gone.

Duke *nods.*

Dawn Wait . . . Did they fix the fuel line?

Duke I don't believe so.

Dawn She's driving it.

She panics. She pulls out her phone and calls **Casandra**.

Dawn She's not picking up. She's not picking up. She—What do we do? Duke?

Duke   I'll find them.

Slowly, he finds his badge and gets ready to leave.

Dawn   Them?

Duke (*calmly*)   Get Buzz, tell him to look around town. I'm sure they're not far.

Dawn   Are you alright? I don't understand, you seem . . .

Duke   Things will turn out right.

Dawn   How long does she have? If she's going fast . . .

Duke *fastens his badge to his belt.*

Duke   I'm sure it won't be long.

Off a Cliff

Casandra *and* **Freddie** *are back on the deserted road, in the dead zone, going fast. It is dusk once again.*

Casandra   How fast are we going?

Freddie   Cas.

Casandra   Sorry.

Freddie   Sixty. Fifty-five. Don't look at me like that.

Casandra   You realize no one actually drives the speed limit.

Freddie   And that's why people die in car accidents.

Casandra   Are you trying to get us caught?

Freddie   I'm trying to be safe.

Casandra   You know he'll send someone.

Freddie   I don't think so.

Casandra   Come on.

Freddie   He gave me the key. Why would he chase us?

Casandra   It doesn't seem right.

Freddie   Can we just—I just want to talk about something else. He's not here anymore.

Casandra   You're right.

Freddie   Where's the first place you want to go?

Casandra   Hmmmmm, surprise me.

Freddie *makes a face, distracted.*

Casandra What's wrong?

Freddie Nothing. I thought I heard something.

Casandra *turns on the radio. Nothing but static.*

Casandra Oh right, of course. The dead zone.

Freddie What about on top of a mountain? For our first stop. I remember you said you wanted to see the stars. What if we find some place high up, where it's clear?

Casandra That's perfect.

Freddie Once we're back in service, can you—

. . . There it is again. Maybe we should pull over.

Casandra It's fine. It just got fixed.

Freddie Right.

Casandra *takes her hand.*

A song starts to play in patches, through the static on the radio.

Freddie I was thinking about something he said.

Casandra I thought we weren't talking about him.

Freddie *nods.*

Beat.

Casandra Go ahead, tell me.

Freddie He said "your choices will catch up to you." What do you think he meant? Do you think he would do something?

Casandra *thinks a while.*

Casandra You told me once not to laugh at him. Cause he was the King, and he wouldn't like that. He's never lost before. I don't think he's ever lost a single fight.

But what about now?

I don't think he could stand to see us without him.

Freddie You're not getting scared, are you?

Casandra *squeezes her hand.*

Casandra Let's get out of here.

She turns up the radio, and music overtakes the static.

END OF PLAY

The Woodingle Puppet Show with Host Mr. C, as Constructed by Mr. Asinine with Calculations and Articulations of the Genius Sort

Julie Taiwo Quarles

The Woodingle Puppet Show with Host Mr. C, as Constructed by Mr. Asinine with Calculations and Articulations of the Genius Sort

Introduction by Robin Alfriend Kello

Like the famous entremés from which it takes inspiration, Cervantes' *El retablo de las maravillas* (*The Marvelous Puppet Show*, 1615), *The Woodingle Puppet Show* blends themes of art and artifice with a cultural commentary on the performance of identity. Where Cervantes ironizes the façade of "Old Christian" blood in early modern Spain, Quarles turns her eye to Los Angeles in the present day, specifically Woodingle, a fictional iteration of the predominantly Black city of Inglewood. Just as Inglewood is currently experiencing a shift in demographics (fewer Black people moving in, and more moving out) as the cost of housing rises, so Quarles' Woodingle becomes an ideal site to explore questions of identity, community, and the reading of race in present-day Los Angeles. If Cervantes skewers the collective bad faith required to perpetuate the myth of "Old Christian" identity in early modern Spain, Quarles examines the ramifications of performing—and being asked to perform—Blackness in the twenty-first-century United States.

Into the petri dish of gentrification and aspirational authenticity that is Woodingle, Quarles introduces Pupita, a pregnant immigrant from Nigeria, and Marionette, a woman of mixed Nigerian and white American parentage, competing for an apartment. To determine who is the more deserving tenant, Mr. C., an American-born Black man, presents them with a puppet show as a test of authentic Blackness: she who sees (or at least says she sees) the puppets, gets the place. The women are thus pitted against each other and forced to present themselves as deserving. While Pupita initially consents to the ruse, describing the invisible puppets in detail, Marionette objects to the manipulation and underscores for Pupita—and the audience—the broader harm in judgments (and opportunities) based on purported cultural authenticity.

The plot develops throughout different variations of the puppet show, while the characters teach us more about their backstories and relation to the fundamental themes of the play—racial identity, authenticity, gentrification, and, ultimately, community. As our trio of protagonists begins to see instead the forms of manipulation and discrimination to which they have all been subjected by powerful forces behind the scenes, they band together in a creative effort that subverts expectations. Competition gives way to collaboration and the complexity of identity becomes a source of cultural solidarity as well as a wellspring for art. The conclusion of the play features "countless gorgeous handcrafted Black puppets of varying shades, shapes, and sizes," in a powerful vision of what could be. As these actual puppets replace the invisible game of Mr. C.'s initial show, the play ends on a note of celebration, and diversity overtakes narrow notions of authenticity.

The Woodingle Puppet Show, written during an upsurge in the Black Lives Matter movement in the United States and widespread protest against police violence, demonstrates the dramaturgical and social opportunities that emerge in the Golden

Tongues project. Transposing the concerns of Cervantes to this moment articulates how categories of identity have functioned across centuries as both restrictive and potentially liberatory, and how art and narrative have always been central to the expression of individual and collective identity. In a metatheatrical mode, the play shows how the performance of the puppet show shifts from a story told *about* a community to a story told *by* that community. As the playwright has said in an interview: "The more that we are able to put our stories out there, the more we voice our experiences, the more progress can be made." Reflecting on the power of stories while simultaneously presenting a narrative of diversity and empowerment, Quarles's drama punctures simplistic narratives about Black identity in America. Mr. C, Pupita, and Marionette transform from competitors to co-conspirators in service of social progress. The cultural context at the beginning of the play has positioned Mr. C as an emcee—and Marionette and Pupita as puppets—in a spectacle designed to perpetuate cultural stereotypes and economic injustice. By the end, they are running the show.

The Woodingle Puppet Show with Host Mr. C, as Constructed by Mr. Asinine with Calculations and Articulations of the Genius Sort

An adaptation of Miguel de Cervantes' *The Marvelous Puppet Show*
by Julie Taiwo Quarles

Characters

Mr. Chirinos (AKA "Mr. C"), *an elderly Black American man*
Pupita Collards, *Nigerian with casual Western style with a British dialect*
Marionette Collards, *mixed Nigerian-American with Afro-centric style*

Time
Now.

Place

The lobby of an upscale housing office in Woodingle, a fictional Black community in LA.

2 women, 1 man.

"The red man was pressed from this part of the west
It's not likely he'll ever return
To the banks of Red River where seldom if ever
His flickering campfires still burn"
 —**"Home on the Range"**

Act One

Interlude One: Mr. C Presents.

A spotlight comes up on **Mr. Chirinos (AKA Mr. C)**, *an old Black American man in a worn-out suit and hat.*

He sits on a wooden chair, rocking. Thinking. Taking his time.

. . .

After several moments, he pulls a harmonica out of his pocket. Plays a tune. Laughs to himself.

Mr. C That sounds about right.

(*Sings "Home on the Range."*)

> Home, home on the range
> Where the deer and the antelope play
> Where seldom is heard
> A discouraging word
> (*Laughs.*)

. . .

After some time, he turns to us.

Mr. C You see: this isn't the business of my generation. In my day, we—well back then we—at least my friends and I, we—we thought we made it if we move up to . . . to them Hollywood Hills. That . . . that Malibu. Somewhere with White folk there. These days, they trying to push against that.

Got Black folk trying to stay in our own neighborhoods. Even got good upstanding citizens in some of these places.

Seems like some young folk seems like they . . . got more pride. Wanna stay connected. It's not like having the dough means . . . you gotta move out.

He grins. Leans in toward us. Whispers.

But that mostly how them youngsters think. My . . . my generation, we . . . we still gotta make do. Find a way keep ourselves in the neighborhood so the young people don't take over. Push us south. I gotta take three buses get to work. Take me two hours on a good day. Cost me five dollars—twenty-five cents with no added stops.

Woodingle. See: it's about Whites movin' in, but it's also about . . . these young . . . "art crowd" types. Now I know I shouldn't be complainin' 'cause at least they Black folk. But they different type of Black folk. I just get the sense there's something about them. Think they . . . think they better. Smarter than us when we ain't had that OPPORTUNITY TO—

Pauses.

Now let me not get started. Well—I was interested in this . . . project . . . when I heard we'd be messin' with these young folk! Didn't know I'd have two sistas on my hands, but it be in God's hands that way! Now let me tell you I'm a good man with morals. But I got pride. I mean—these people keep pushing us further and further south. Ain't much lower I can go!

So in comes this young fella. Calls himself Chanfalla. I know I got some skills with (*holds up harmonica*) showmanship, and I hear he's looking for a showman. I need my dough comin' so I can live, so here I am. Showman at your service. Who won't believe a wise old guy sees puppets?

He returns to his harmonica.

(*Sings.*)

And the skies are not cloudy all day

He laughs mischievously.

Scene One: Surname Sisters

Lights shift to center, revealing a classy Afrocentric housing office lobby, with a couple of leather sofas, a few matching chairs, expensive art, and a large coffee table with a spread of Black magazines.

On one of the sofas sits **Pupita**, *Nigerian, 20s, jeans with Gucci tee and shoes. She holds a magazine but isn't really reading it.*

Instead, she stares off. She wears Beats by Dre headphones and nods her head, moving here and there to the beat. Chewing gum.

. . .

After some time, **Marionette**, *mixed Nigerian and White American, 20s, classy African getup, enters.*

Pupita *pauses briefly when she sees her, then goes back to her distracted reading.*

Marionette *takes a seat on the other sofa. Pulls out a book. Reads intently.*

. . .

Pupita (*without looking up*)   *Americanah*, innit?

Marionette *pauses. Eyes* **Pupita**, *who remains "focused" on her magazine.*

Marionette   Did—I'm sorry, did you ask—were you speaking to—?

Pupita   The book you're reading. Is it *Americanah*?[1]

Marionette   Amer—?

---

1   Nigerian author Chimamanda Ngozi Adichie's 2013 National Book Critics Circle award-winning novel.

Pupita Yes—

Marionette I'm not sure why you—

Pupita Of course—

Marionette I'm sorry—have I—?

Pupita Adichie, innit?

Marionette (*holding up the book*) I know but this has no Ifemelu,[2] right? It's—

Pupita *looks up to face* **Marionette** *directly for the first time. Reads the cover.*

Pupita "*Signs of Life in the USA.*"[3] Heh.

Marionette Prepping—

Pupita I see—

Marionette Research for work—

Pupita Innit.

Pupita *now examines* **Marionette***, looking her up and down without any sign of apology.*

Pupita You have an . . . interesting look.

Marionette *provides a fake smile. Returns to her book.*

Pupita So um . . . why you think you're one of the last two?

Marionette *looks around. Can this woman really not take a hint? Sets the book back down.*

Marionette I'm sorry, I—

Pupita My mistake, innit? I know that's quite private. And you Americans, despite your friendliness, are immensely private—

Marionette What makes you think I'm American—? I mean you thought I was reading Adichie—

Pupita Huh—?

Marionette How do you know that for certain—?

Pupita Well, I—

Marionette You honestly can't really tell these days, right?

Pupita I mean you sound—

---

2 Ifemelu, the protagonist of Adichie's novel, is a young Nigerian woman studying in the United States.
3 Textbook on the semiotics of American pop culture written by Sonia Maasik and Jack Soloman. The text has gone through many editions, the most recent of which was published in 2021.

Marionette I could be an actress.

Pupita Possible, innit—?

Marionette Dialect expert—

Pupita Uh huh—

Marionette They're teaching American English overseas from birth now, right—?

Pupita Innit—?

Marionette Pardon—?

The sound of **Mr. C** *from offstage.*

Mr. C (*offstage*) Collards!

At this, both women rise anxiously.

Pupita That's—

Marionette That's me—take care—

Pupita Me—

Marionette Huh—?

Pupita What—?

Mr. C (*offstage*) Collards—!

Pupita, Marionette (*tripping over each other*) Coming—hey—what are you—?

Pupita He's calling my—

Marionette I heard my—

Mr. C (*offstage*) Collards—final request—

Pupita, Marionette RIGHT HERE—!

At this, both pause. Look at each other.

Pupita Uhh—

Marionette (*to* **Mr. C**) Which—which Collards?

Mr. C (*offstage*) (*annoyed*) Collards, MARIONETTE—

Marionette That's—

Pupita (*to* **Marionette**) Clearly not me, innit—?

Marionette Take care—

She exits. **Pupita**, *still in shock, looks around uncomfortably. Wanders back to her seat. Tries to get into her magazine, but it's pointless by now. She tosses it onto the table.*

Pupita Heh.

She mouths her own last name.

"Collards."

She reaches for the magazine again, then thinks better of it. Stands to head toward the window. Stares off.

. . .

After a long silent moment, she grabs her stomach. Bends over in pain.

Ahhhhhhh—!

She takes several deep breaths. Tries to stand up, but—

AhhhhhhhOwwwwwww—!

Puts her hand against the wall, still leaning down. Breathes.

Suddenly, **Marionette** *storms back in, a pile of papers in hand.*

Marionette   This is nuts, right—?

Pupita (*trying to act cool*)   Innit—?

Marionette   I mean seriously—they— (*noticing* **Pupita**'s *posture*)—oh no! Are you—do you need—?

Pupita   No no I'm fine—

Marionette   Are you sure you don't—?

Mr. C (*offstage*)   Collards, PUPITA—

Marionette   "Pupita"—that's—that's beautiful—let me help you to the—

Pupita   That won't be—

Marionette   It's really no bother—

Pupita (*allowing it*)   If you could just—

Marionette   Absolutely—

Pupita   Thank you . . .

Marionette *helps* **Pupita** *walk to the door and exit. Turns to look back at the lobby. Sits. Skims over the pile of papers in her hands.*

Marionette (*reads*)   "The Woodingle Puppet Show with Host Mr. C, as Constructed by Mr. Asinine with Calculations and Articulations of the Genius Sort. Notice to all current supposed residents of a historically Black community.

Gentrification is upon us, and its fruit is bearing hard. We see people whose families have been residing here for generations being forced to leave and offering up their homes to the highest White bidder—"

A pause. She gasps. Looks around.

Did they seriously write that—(*reads again*)? Yes, they did.

(*Reads.*) "For this reason, our offices are partnering with *The Woodingle Puppet Show with Host Mr. C, as Constructed by Mr. Asinine with Calculations and Articulations of the Genius Sort*—to spread awareness and keep the community beautifully Black as it should be."

Ummm. Okay?

(*Reads.*) "Come to the show tomorrow night, and here's the jig: if you can see the puppets, then you're all about twenty-first-century Blackness and genuinely deserve to reside in the lovely Woodingle neighborhood. If not—you're out, and can go back out to the stifling diversity of this lovely city—"

Marionette (*shocked*)   Hm. Can they even—?

At this moment, **Pupita** *wobbles back into the lobby, paperwork in hand.*

Pupita (*to* **Marionette**)   Nonsense, innit?

Marionette *shrugs. Stands to help* **Pupita**, *who motions that she is okay.*

Both women now sit in waiting, silent.

. . .

Pupita   So . . . what do you do?

Marionette   Adidas feedback loop. We go into the inner city to see what's up, right?—then come up with ideas to market to kids.

Pupita   Ahhh. I've heard of that. Pretty cool gig, innit?

Marionette   . . . I get to travel a lot.

Pupita (*indicating the office/their situation*)   Obviously pays well.

Marionette   I beat out my high school bully Stacy Jones to get this opp. So you're?

Pupita   Oh wow! Five months, innit? I know I'm not showing much yet. They say with the first one—

Marionette   Right—? I've heard that—

Pupita   I don't have a Stacy Jones story, but I am doing it all on my own—

Marionette   She just—always mocked my hair when I tried to braid it, laughed at my lack of soul food knowledge, blah blah—healed wounds! Lookatchu—"We Should All Be Feminists,"[4] right—?

Pupita   Heh—Adichie: the African representative of our times—

---

4   This is the title of a book-length essay by Adichie.

Marionette I loooooove her—

Pupita Innit? But I . . . I got us.

Marionette I hope he's at least helping with (*indicates the lounge*)—

Pupita I didn't put his name down—

Marionette Right. Like that part in the speech when Adichie says "A man is as likely as a woman to be intelligent. To be creative. To—"

Pupita (*nodding*) "To be innovative." (*A pause.*) So we're surname sisters, innit? (*Whispers.*) But my hair braids more easily.

Marionette Seems so. Any relation to the billionaire Byron of Crenshaw?

Pupita (*shaking her head*) African aristocrats. We got Stacy beat.

They share a smile for the first time.

Marionette And what are your thoughts . . . on gentrification?

Pupita . . . well, I'm obviously not from here.

Marionette Right—

Pupita Came for work some years back after years studying in London.

Marionette You do sound more British! So are you a doctor, or—?

Pupita Much more disappointing: Personal stylist. I know—I don't dress the part, but who can in this condition?

Marionette I—I love that. You're in the right town! You must do quite well.

Pupita I love it here—

Marionette That's great—

Pupita Anyways as I was saying: I'm not from here, but I've been here for some time so I kind of am . . . finally getting a sense of how things . . .

Marionette Segregate, right?

Pupita Your word not mine—

Marionette Heh—

Pupita But yes—

Marionette It's the twenty-first century: everything is segregated here.

Pupita And that's progress, innit?

Marionette (*holds up her book*) "How an Angry Mood is Reflected in Pop Culture." Page 531. Fleishman.[5]

---

5 Essay by *Los Angeles Times* writer Jeffrey Fleishman.

Pupita Pardon—?

Marionette This was my old English comp book in college, but I realized a lot of why I was interested in marketing was because of that class. I'm re-reading a newer edition of the book.

Pupita I see—

Marionette And in this article Fleishman is arguing that in the 2010s, right? —the trend became customized content.

Pupita Customized—?

Marionette He's talking about TV and music, mostly, right? Kendrick's "The Blacker the Berry." *Black-ish. Fresh off the Boat.*[6] We don't like universal anymore, right? We like to know our content is being catered toward us.

Pupita Hard for me to find that here—

Marionette But it's not just about entertainment. It's about where we live, too.

Pupita So . . . Woodingle, innit?

Marionette Woodingle. Right.

Pupita Forgive my boldness, but . . . are you not mixed-race?

Marionette (*laughing*) Correct. You following Stacy Jones' lead?

Pupita So should you be in search of a mixed neighborhood—?

Marionette (*still laughing*) I see you, trying to scope out the competition—it's what we do, I guess—

Pupita Girl—

Marionette Right? Bring it!

They laugh, but eye each other.

. . .

Pupita This puppet show . . . you think it's worth it? Sounds quite . . . odd.

Marionette *shrugs.*

Pupita I need to raise my baby in a . . . welcoming neighborhood. A good one, innit?

Marionette I see.

Pupita And I'm sure being single, you find some comfort in—

Marionette Most of my friends are here—

---

6 The references are to a song by Pulitzer Prize-winning American rapper Kendrick Lamar and sitcoms created by Kendra Barris and Nahnatchka Khan, respectively.

Pupita   This building—?

Marionette   Woodingle. But it's nearly impossible these days to—

Marionette, Pupita   Find anything—

Marionette   Right—?

Pupita   Even for a decent price, innit—?

At this, **Mr. C** *comes in enthusiastically.*

Mr. C   Good evening, ladies—

Marionette   Evening—?

Mr. C   Good afternoon—!

Pupita   After—?

Mr. C   Good morning!

An awkward pause.

Mr. C   Have you looked over that there proposal? This comes straight from Mr. Asinine's mouth.

Pupita   Asinine? It was my understanding that your partner was named Chanfalla—

Mr. C   That's correct, miss. Chanfalla is my comrade. Asinine is . . . let's say he's the man up on the ladder. Point is—

Marionette   You do the puppetry, right?

A pause. He grins. Nods.

Marionette   Is it just me, or is this outrageous?

Pupita   Is it even legal—?

Mr. C   Chanfalla brings in the vision from Mr. Asinine—

Marionette   Asinine—

Mr. C   And Mr. Asinine, he—he's quite the storyteller—

Marionette   Chanfalla—how come—how come I've never heard of him—?

Mr. C   Chanfalla, he from out of town.

Pupita   And Asinine?

Mr. C   Um hm.

Marionette   "Um hm" what—?

Mr. C   Um hm visiting. They got a special . . . investment in . . . in us. Black neighborhood development.

Marionette   They Black . . . ?

Mr. C   You won't be dealin' with them. I run the show. I may live south now, but I work here—take me three buses, five dollars-twenty-five-cents—two hours—

Pupita   You haven't answered her—

Mr. C   They real smart and got some good material. I been working with them for some time—

Pupita   I'm unsure how a housing office has anything to do with puppets—

Mr. C   You'll hafta find out, then! Will you come to my show—?

Marionette   Well, it seems we don't really have much of a choice, right—?

Mr. C   Now you two have been chosen from a long list. We think you ought to see that as meanin' somethin'. Chanfalla just wantin' to see if you legit—

Marionette   Chanfalla, huh? Not Asinine?

Mr. C   Ass—? No—Chanfalla—

Pupita   Chanfalla, innit—?

Mr. C   Yes, Chanfalla—

Pupita *leans over in pain.*

Marionette   Let's just get it over with! How hard can it be? I need this place—

Pupita   Me, too—

Mr. C   That's good—I had me a feelin' about you two!

They look at each other.

Mr. C   You all cousins?

Pupita   Can't you hear my accent—?

Marionette (*defensive*)   My dad's Nigerian—

Pupita   Isn't that something—I wouldn't have—

Marionette   Right—

Mr. C   Hold on—so you not American?

Marionette   I am. Just Nigerian, too.

Pupita   Heh.

Mr. C   But are you Black?

They look at him confusedly. Both nod. He rolls his eyes.

Mr. C   Now I don't mean to frighten you ladies. Ya'll both seem decent enough from where I'm standin'. But you gotta be ready to do this tomorrow. I mean I didn't really get a sense that you really got my question I was askin'.

Marionette   We both nodded—

Pupita Innit?

Mr. C Now "innit" to me don't sound no kinda Black, young lady—

Pupita How is it possible—

Mr. C (*to* **Marionette**) And that "Adidas loop" jibber jabber—don't none of us know nothin' about—

Marionette Are you trying to say—?

Mr. C Okay good—I think you get it now. Alright, then.

He smiles.

Marionette (*nervously*) See you tomorrow. The show's here?

He nods, as **Marionette** *exits.*

Pupita Mr. Chirinos—

Mr. C They call me Mr. C—

Pupita Mr. C—

Mr. C Yes, ma'am—

Pupita I . . . I need this. Just let me know what I ought to do—

Mr. C You can't change you overnight. Just show up tomorrow all you can do.

Pupita You see, I'm—

Mr. C I see you gonna be a momma soon. Congratulations to you.

Pupita Thank you.

Mr. C I don't know a lot of Nigerians. Further south you go in the city, there be less and less of ya'll down there. I come up this way by bus. Two hours—five dollars-twenty-five—

Pupita Cents. Two hours if you're lucky. Well, we pride ourselves in our northbound-ness!

Mr. C Uh-huh. But is you Black? We'll find out tomorrow.

Pupita You have some pointers for me, kind sir—?

Mr. C I might have one. Stop in tomorrow before the show.

She exits with a new sense of calmness. He looks to us. Grins apologetically.

Interlude Two: Nat King Cole and Michael Jordan

A spotlight comes up on **Mr. C**, *seated on his wooden chair.*

As he tells his story, he gestures as if performing with puppets, but there are none actually visible.

Mr. C Good evening, and welcome to *The Woodingle Puppet Show with Host Mr. C, as Constructed by Mr. Asinine with Calculations and Articulations of the Genius Sort.*

The story for today called "Nat King Cole and Michael Jordan."

Clears his throat. Begins.

One day, fella named Nat King Cole had a conversation with fella named Michael Jordan.

They was talkin' about—what else? —women.

Now Mr. Cole he approaches things musically, like me. He says

(*Sings.*)

> When I fall in love, it will be forever
> Or I'll never fall in love.

Now Michael Jordan, he—this so beautiful it makes him speechless. He cries. Big ole NBA superstar, he shedding tears. What that verse say? Jesus wept? He wept. Like Jesus. Like that photograph everyone seen everywhere on the Internet.[7]

A pause. He looks to us.

Don't you see?

I known whole bunch of Black folk. Musicians like Cole. Athletes like Jordan.

But can't—can't nobody say them two ain't Black, see? See they from different jobs and all, but they speakin' 'bout love and they speakin' the same language.

(*Indicating the invisible puppets.*) Do you see what I see?

(*Sings.*)

> In a restless world like this is
> Love is ended before it's begun—

So Jordan crying. Maybe 'cause his woman left him. Miss her kisses. All that cheatin'—but don't you go sayin' of course he did, see we not—we not all like that.

Whatchu think it lookin' like?

Tell me—what—what color Cole got on? What color Jordan's suit then?

Ahh—you see. You with us!

He laughs. Grins.

. . .

Chanfalla says go like that. That'll get 'em. Mr. Asinine's orders. Well, I guess it's simple enough for my dough!

Blackout.

Scene Two: Billie Holiday and Ms. Oprah Winfrey

The next day, in the lobby.

Pupita *and* **Marionette** *are seated beside each other, not speaking.*

---

7 The "Crying Jordan" meme became popular in 2015.

Pupita *wears a "Nah. ~Rosa Parks" shirt, and* **Marionette** *is in a dashiki dress.*

After some time, **Pupita** *begins to speak, but then stops herself.*

Pupita   I—I um—

Marionette   What was—?

Pupita   So interesting to have another "Collards."

Marionette   Right—?

Pupita   You said your . . . your dad was Nigerian, innit?

Marionette   Yes—!

Pupita   You might come from the aristocracy—who knows?!

Marionette   Well, I would know, right—?

Pupita   I mean if you were to trace—

Marionette   What do you—?

Pupita   I mean if you were to trace your lineage, innit—?

Marionette   But he told me—

Pupita   And how recently did he—?

Marionette   Right—he's from there.

Pupita   I see. I thought maybe his ancestors. And then you know, after some time—

Marionette   But I told you my dad was Nigerian, right—?

Pupita   I know I know . . . well, it's just that a lot of Americans say that, but—

At this moment, **Mr. C** *enters with a puppet stand on wheels. Pushes it to center to face the ladies.*

Mr. C   Morning, ladies—

Pupita   It's—

Mr. C   Afternoon—

Marionette   Good evening—

Mr. C   Right.

At this, he begins to mime the taking out and setting up of puppets.

This should take an uncomfortably long amount of time, and he should mumble to himself as if he's remembering each item and step.

The women stare at him silently, exchanging looks from time to time.

. . .

Mr. C   Have you sorted out if ya'll two are family yet?

They look to each other, confused.

Marionette How—how did you—?

Mr. C (*laughing*) Puppet-master sees all, young lady. I'm not sure if I see it.

Marionette Is that right?

Mr. C Collards an interesting family name. (*To* **Pupita**.) Will you be passing on the name to your child?

Pupita (*touching her belly*) Well, I . . . I hadn't thought about that too much yet, innit—?

Finally ready, **Mr. C** *holds up his hands to silence the crowd. Both women look around. They're the only ones present.*

He opens up the cart to turn on a small camera inside. Gives it a thumbs-up.

The lights dim, and he speaks out.

Mr. C Good evening, and welcome to *The Woodingle Puppet Show with Host Mr. C, as Constructed by Mr. Asinine with Calculations and Articulations of the Genius Sort.*

Let me remind you that the purpose of this show is to reveal which one of ya'll two sisters is the most . . . what was it . . . the most . . .

Marionette   . . . Black, right?

She looks away, ashamed. So does **Pupita**.

Mr. C That's right. Now the rules are simple. Work hard to see them puppets I'm showin' and tell me what you see. Then I report back to Chanfalla, who report back to Mr. Asinine, who report back to this here housing office who fit to . . . to get this place.

He pauses. Looks to them for agreement. The women look to each other, and then to him. Both nod.

Mr. C The story for today called "Billie Holiday and Ms. Oprah Winfrey."

He begins to act out the story with invisible puppets.

Now these two women, they get together and they talkin' 'bout—what else—? Men.

Now Ms. Holiday, she say—

(*Sings.*)

> Are the stars out tonight?
> I don't know if it's cloudy or bright
> 'Cause I only have eyes for you[8]

---

8   Lyrics from "I Only Have Eyes for You," a love song written in the 1930s and performed by many artists in the decades since then.

The women look to each other, impressed by his singing.

Pupita (*into it*)   Alright now.

Marionette   Mr. C—I should have known you were gonna kill it—

Mr. C   Now hold on—this ain't the—you ain't meant to be participating yet—

Marionette   No call and response—?

Mr. C   I see you . . . you did your research—

Marionette (*offended*)   Research? Come on, now—we all know our slave narrative history—

Pupita (*to* **Marionette**)   Go get 'em—!

Marionette (*to* **Pupita**)   Do you even know whose song that—?

Pupita   Billie Holiday, innit—?

Marionette   Well, that's because he said it, right—?

Mr. C   Ladies we only just now gettin' started—

Marionette   Sorry, Mr. C. It's just your singing—

Pupita   Something so . . . haunting—

Mr. C   Now I hope that's a statement and not a question—

Pupita, Marionette   It is!

He smiles.

Mr. C   Now let's get down to business.

As he gets deeper into the story, his movements with the imaginary puppets become more and more intense. He breaks into a sweat.

Now these two women, good respected Black women, they got men on they minds.

Pupita *and* **Marionette** *share an eye-roll.*

Mr. C   Now they—they meet up and Billie sings her thing, and Ms. Oprah, well—

(*Gesturing.*) She says stop it right there, Billie Holiday. I know you from my past and you my elder and I love your music and wish I could put music in my book club for you, but I can't. Let's get to a story, shall we?

Marionette *holds back a laugh.* **Pupita** *is confused.*

Pupita   Book—?

Mr. C Now Ms. Oprah, she got her thing goin' with her man Mr. Stedman[9] out there in Chicago. Now they been together and treatin' each other real nice for a real long time, but Oprah won't marry the man. Call herself a modern woman. Had too much heart-break make that kinda . . . commitment—

Pupita Now let's just pause, innit?

Frustrated, **Mr. C** *stops.*

Pupita "Modern woman"? "Won't marry"—this is some sort of a joke, innit? Ain't this America?

She starts looking around the room. **Marionette** *laughs.*

Mr. C Now, Miss—

Marionette Hehe—

Mr. C Let me just—

Marionette Looks like my competition don't know that Black Americans traditional as hell—

Pupita I—I do—I wasn't trying to say—

Marionette Just used to seeing single moms in movies, right? The men in jail?

Pupita That's the opposite of what I was insinuating—

Mr. C Insinu—? What kinda (*nonsense*)—?

Pupita The goal here is mockery, innit?

Mr. C I'm not sure that I—

Marionette You think we all reality TV crazy, right?

Pupita "We"? What are you?—*I'm* being mocked!

Mr. C Now, Miss Collards, I'm simply—

Marionette Ahhh okay I do see how you could read it that way—what with the modern woman and your being a single mom and—

Mr. C I meant no harm—

Pupita The older generation, innit? Same everywhere—

Mr. C Now hold on a second—

Marionette I hear you, girl—

Pupita So . . . judgmental, innit?

Mr. C Now please take your seat, Miss Collards!

---

9 Stedman Graham, author, educator, and long-time partner of Oprah Winfrey.

Marionette Which—which Miss Collards? You mocking me, too?

Mr. C Now hold on just a—

Pupita I thought we were helping you out, but now we're hurting your feelings?

Marionette Right?

Mr. C Now I'm here simply trying to make a living and I don't need you calling me old! All ya'll keep doing is pushing me further and further south!

A pause. The women look at each other.

Pupita Okay, Mr. C. I apologize. Perhaps it's—you know—pregnancy brain paranoia—

She looks toward **Mr. C***, who winks knowingly, and then she kneels down as if in pain.*

Mr. C *and* **Marionette** *both reach out a hand toward her, but she motions that she's okay.*

Pupita I'm fine, innit?

Marionette Are you—?

Pupita Yes, just give me a—

Mr. C *now puts his hand somewhat forcefully on* **Pupita***'s shoulder.*

Mr. C (*anxiously*) Now let's get back to the show. Now I worked hard on this.

Marionette (*overwhelmed*) Okay . . . right. But can you tell us more about what's going on here?

Both now have their hands on **Pupita***, who breathes in and out heavily.*

Mr. C Pardon?

Marionette What's—what is going on here? Are we meant to watch an entire invisible production?

A pause. He looks between the two women.

Mr. C Invisible?

Pupita Innit—

Mr. C Now I done worked hard on this and you tryna tell me my work don't mean nothin'?

Marionette That's not what I—

Mr. C Invisible—?

Marionette I didn't mean it like—all I'm saying is you are talking like you got some actual puppets. But there's literally nothing there before you but air.

Mr. C Air?

Marionette *nods. Looks over to* **Pupita**.

Marionette (*to* **Pupita**)   Can you back me up on this?

Pupita *shrugs. Pants.*

Marionette   Right.

Pupita *now sits down fully on the floor. Inhales deeply. As she speaks, she gains a new energy.*

Pupita   The intersectionality between Blackness and female experience places Black women in America into a specific conundrum that doesn't really exist elsewhere. Since current culture is so focused on the female empowerment movement with events such as the Women's March and MeToo, there has been a decreased focus on the specific situation of Black women, whom are amongst the most educated in the country yet receive the lowest salaries—

Marionette   Um—what the—?

Mr. C   Alright, now!—

Pupita   Black women receive about sixty-three cents on the dollar to what White men make, and I'd say that's a best-case scenario—

Marionette   What is this? Your college sociology paper—?

Pupita   Various cultural factors are to blame: the generational American wealth gap tracing all the way back to slavery in which White households currently fork in nearly $135,000 annually yet Black homes an average of $11,000. When we look at education, the White citizen without a college degree makes significantly more than a Black citizen of the same qualifications—

Marionette   I can't believe—so you're fine now?

Pupita *now stands, hands on her belly, overcome by a new fervor.*

Pupita   It just hit me suddenly, innit?

A dumbfounded **Marionette** *just stares at her.*

Mr. C *jumps back enthusiastically.*

Marionette   Um nice speech, but do you honestly think spouting some statistics—?

Pupita   As a Black woman in America, I feel a tremendous pressure to undo the social injustices that women like me face on a daily basis—

Marionette   Who doesn't—?

Pupita   And break the cycle of illiteracy and Black motherhood stigma.

Marionette   Ahhh . . . and there we have it. Riiiight.

Mr. C (*to* **Pupita**)   Miss?

Pupita *looks away for a moment. Rubs her eyes. Shrugs.*

Pupita   Oprah has on a black suit and heels, innit? Billie's wearing a blue sequined dress.

A pause, as **Marionette** *turns to* **Pupita** *in shock.*

Mr. C *grins.*

Mr. C   That be right.

Marionette   Come on—!

Pupita   It's—

Marionette   You can't possibly be into—just a second ago you said you were offended—

Pupita   But something just happened and now I . . . I can see everything!

Marionette   Pfsh—so now you fallin'—

Mr. C   Ain't no fallin' for what's real—

Encouraged, he, returns to his story.

Alright now. So Ms. Oprah say she's learned a lot about love in her years with Stedman as a woman of high society—

Pupita   . . . there they are—blue chairs. Glass coffee table with coffee mugs, innit—

Marionette   Are you—?

Mr. C   And Ms. Holiday, she sings out—

(*Sings.*)

> Maybe millions of people go by
> But they all disappear from view

Pupita   There she is at the microphone—!

Marionette   The micro—? You can't seriously be willing to do this to—

Mr. C (*sings*)

> And I only have eyes for you—

Pupita   Oprah's standing to clap for her—!

Marionette   Now I admit the man has a beautiful voice and is working hard, but he—

Mr. C   Ms. Oprah say she never thought in a million years she'd get a live show from Miss Holiday—

Marionette (*to* **Mr. C**)   Because it's physically impossible—

Pupita (*dancing*)   Go on, Billie—

Marionette (*to* **Pupita**)   You didn't even know who Billie was five minutes ago—

Mr. C   Now maybe Blackness can arrive different time for different people—

Marionette (*to* **Mr. C**)   Oh really? Are you meant to be stopping to talk like this in the middle of your own production—?

Mr. C   This call and response, miss—

Pupita   Oprah's right—if this song were a book, I'd read it, innit—?

Marionette   He's not even singing any—this is so stupid—

Mr. C   Darn right—

Pupita   Love me some Billie Holiday today—!

Mr. C *claps for* **Pupita**'s *"transformation." Returns to his show with a big dramatic spectacle of gestures. At this,* **Pupita** *falls to the floor, all giggles.* **Mr. C** *laughs right along with her.*

Pupita   Oh—oh my! Hahahahahahahahahahahaha—!

Marionette   Oh my—this is sick—

Mr. C (*to* **Pupita**)   That shocked me, too! I know I'm puppet-master, but sometimes they get a mind of they own!

As **Pupita** *continues to laugh,* **Marionette** *stands. Picks up her purse, preparing to leave.*

Marionette   This is—I'm not going to—

Mr. C (*to* **Marionette**)   Where are you off to, miss?

Marionette   Off to call the owners. This is the most ridiculous way to—

Pupita *now notices that her competition is leaving. Goes over to* **Marionette** *to grab her hand, and pull her with her toward the puppet stage.*

Pupita   Come on, surname sister—

Marionette   Get your hands—

Pupita   Open your eyes, innit—?

Mr. C   They're right here—

Marionette   I'm not willing to embarrass myself just to get this place—

Pupita   LOOK AT YOUR PEOPLE!

A pause. **Pupita** *is now in a more focused state.* **Marionette** *glares at her.*

Marionette   You should be ashamed of yourself—

Pupita   How can I be more Black American than you?

At this, **Mr. C** *cringes. Holds back a laugh. Looks out to the audience.*

Marionette   You're pregnant, for goodness sakes.

Pupita   Don't change the subject—

Marionette   About to raise a Black kid, right—?

Pupita   Of your supposed sort, innit—?

Marionette   American, right—?

Pupita   Precisely, innit—?

Marionette   And you're prepared to tell him or her you made a fool of yourself just to get a fancy condo, right—?

Pupita   Just because I see what you cannot doesn't mean you get to judge me, innit—?

Marionette   You make me sick.

A silent stare-down.

Mr. C (*awkwardly*)   Well, Ms. Oprah disagrees.

Marionette   And why Oprah? Why Billie?

Marionette *now approaches the stage, hitting and kicking the empty air surrounding it.* **Mr. C** *tries unsuccessfully to stop her.*

Mr. C   Mr. Asinine—!

Marionette   Ass my ass—!

Mr. C   Miss—would you please—?

Marionette   This is insane! Look at me—hear me! How can you not call me Blacker than her?

A pause.

(*To* **Mr. C.**) Don't you—don't you see? Some white guy's choice of who our icons should be. And you're letting an African win the show. You should be ashamed of yourself.

At this, **Mr. C** *extracts a key from his pocket. Dangles it with a grin.*

As **Marionette** *speaks,* **Mr. C** *begins to move her around as if she were his puppet, and* **Pupita** *starts to cheer him on.*

Marionette *doesn't notice at first, but becomes increasingly agitated.*

Marionette   Why they wanna choose some wealthy billionaire who's so rich her bath tub is molded to her body frame and a well-known drug addict? Why didn't they choose Obama for a respectable American? "Yes we can"—doesn't get more respectable—see, there's a method to their choices, right—stop—

I mean Stacy—Stacy Jones—stop that—Listen, I been through this like a gazillion times already! Stacy Jones . . . I mean back in high school every class had Oprah up on the wall during Black history month. But Stacy Jones got to . . . to calling me Oprah—STOP IT!—Said I was uppity like her 'cause my momma was white and my daddy was from Africa.

And I told her that Oprah's—stop it—Oprah's story and Oprah was Black American, but said Oprah talked like some uppity mixed chick.

So everyone started calling me Uppity Oprah—like she the model of fake Black that White—that White people think of but she ain't really our—ain't really the story. Maaaan—I really don't see why I need to get into this—will you leave me alone?!

All I wanted was a nice place in a nice place, right? Just to feel like I'm part of something, right?

I feel like I've earned that. I've worked hard, I can afford to live here, and I'm an educated and successful Black American woman. I ain't no Uppity Oprah and she the last person they should've been choosing. Give me Barack or Michelle even.

After a moment, **Pupita** *and* **Mr. C** *look to each other. Share a laugh.*

Marionette   Hey—you—are you seriously—what's—? That's what you've gotta say?

Mr. C   All that smarty-pants White girl talk? (*Shakes his head.*) Lord Jesus. "Barack Obama." "Yes we can"—so do you see the puppets or not?

Marionette   Do I—didn't you just hear what I—?

Mr. C   You've said nothing about what you actually see—

Marionette   I see mockery of our own kind by some White puppeteer—

Mr. C   Well, that ain't in my show—

Marionette   I see you dancin' around like you off your rocker just to make some dough—

Mr. C   Well, I—

Marionette   I see an African making herself a fool to fit in as usual—

Pupita   Ouch—

Marionette   But nah: I don't see no stupid puppets—except the two of you.

Mr. C *glares at her. Hands the key to* **Pupita**, *who grabs it and starts off.*

Marionette *glares back at him, speechless.*

Marionette   Right. Just handing our land away.

Mr. C   Your momma is a White woman and your daddy ain't from here. What makes you say it yours more than hers?

She storms away.

Mr. C *hums to himself as he "packs up" his things.*

Mr. C   Now that one went easier than the last. (*Exaggeratedly.*) Innit right?

He laughs. Takes out his harmonica. Plays "Home on the Range."

(*Sings.*)

    The red man was pressed

    from this part of the West

    It's not likely he'll ever return[10]

    . . .

He continues humming as he pushes his cart offstage.

Blackout.

---

10 Lyrics from American cowboy song "Home on the Range," written in the late nineteenth century.

Act Two

Scene One: Scheming

A disheveled **Mr. C**, *half asleep on the bus. Suddenly,* **Marionette** *walks by. Recognizes him. Circles back.*

Marionette   Mr. C, right?

Her voice jolts him out of his sleep.

Mr. C   Who—who you?

He sits up, rubbing his eyes. She takes a seat beside him.

Marionette   I'm Marionette Collards. I . . . participated in the . . . Woodingle Puppet Show a few months back—

Mr. C   Ms. Collards, yes! Cannot forget. How you been?

Marionette   Well, I—I lost, remember—

Mr. C   Seems so, you out of a home now on the bus with us common folk . . . southbound!

Marionette   I'm here for work.

Mr. C   That right?

Marionette   Feedback loop, right? When we head into the city to see what's appealing to young people, I like to take the train. Hoping I'll meet someone interesting, right?

Mr. C   Well, I don't know much about . . . Adidas, was it?

Marionette (*smiling*)   Good memory. Not a problem.

A pause. He looks away awkwardly.

Mr. C   I'm sure I be southbound longer than you still. They movin' me again.

Marionette   Are they?

Mr. C   That be the way it goes with this job. I do somethin' every now and again they ain't find pleasing, and they send me on south.

Marionette   Right. Awful stuff.

He turns toward her.

Mr. C   You . . . you like your job, huh?

Marionette   That's an understatement!

Mr. C   That . . . must be nice. Never had one I really loved.

Marionette You don't like doing the puppet show?

At this, he cracks up laughing.

Mr. C Hell no! I mean . . . I love doing *a* show. But this ain't *my* show. This Asinine's.

Marionette I see.

Mr. C They go on that Wikipedia. They find some facts about some Black people. They make their story and make us pretend we see some Wikipedia page. I make it seem polished best I can but, it ain't. I know there's more to Oprah than her book club and her man.

Marionette If you were in her book club, what would your story be?

Mr. C Well, I ain't done too much reading lately.

Marionette Just humor me.

Mr. C (*ponders*) My—my story—well, nobody ever asks for—well I guess maybe I wanna read *The Autobiography of Malcolm X*. That one always sounded nice.

Marionette No—I mean *your* story. What's Mr. C's story?

Mr. C Not much to it. Born in Woodingle. Lived here my whole life 'til I got old and they started bussing me—

Marionette South—

Mr. C That be it.

Marionette I hope this isn't too forward, but have you—ever traced your genealogy?

Mr. C No need. Slaves on both sides.

Marionette But do you . . . know your African roots?

He shrugs confusedly. She opens up her bag and takes out a card. Hands it to him.

Marionette Info about Africanancestry.com. Find out where you're from.

Mr. C Oh I don't know if I—

Marionette No pressure. I know not everyone is interested. We're giving these out today. Working on a new series called "Africa." Trying to see if the kids are interested in having their history on their kicks.

Mr. C Oh we are into that history—just they don't want us to be.

Marionette Right? We gotta—make things work regardless.

He nods. Eyes the card.

Mr. C Well, thank—thank you, Ms. Collards. That's very kind, considering.

Marionette Considering?

Mr. C Well, I'm ashamed to admit it to you, but they found out anyways. Added another bus to my route—that's another half hour and another dollar sixty-five cents.

Marionette What happened?

Mr. C Well, I seen a lotta mommas on their own in my day. Was raised by one. Saw it fit to give the other Ms. Collards. African one—

Marionette I'm African—

Mr. C One with the accent—

Marionette Right—

Mr. C Give her just a little tip. Told her do her Black women in America research. They eat that up every time.

Marionette I see.

Mr. C Anyway—they givin' her the boot. Say we scheming.

Marionette . . . right.

Mr. C Who knows . . . maybe you can have another shot. Would you like me to—?

Marionette Dance and sing for those White men yet again? Nah—I'm good—

Mr. C Well, alright—

Marionette I mean, no offense. I know you gotta make a living and all—

Mr. C I go on and tell Chanfalla let this . . . Stacy Jones . . . just take it no competition.

Marionette "Stacy"—you know what—actually—let's give it a try. You have Pupita's number?

Mr. C I find it back with my things.

Marionette Great—let's give her a call. I think I have an idea. But what if you end up in Mexico?

Mr. C Well I—*no hablo*—but maybe the real estate better down there anyways!

Marionette I'm gonna put you in touch with my people. I am sure there's something better out there!

Mr. C Well, I suppose we'll see—

Marionette Alright! So you're in—?

Mr. C Well, wait a minute. What you have in mind?

She hugs him. He's taken aback.

Blackout.

Interlude Three: C is for Collards

An anxious **Mr. C** *stares at an envelope. He can't decide if he wants to open it.*

Mr. C (*to us*)   Now look here. I'll tell you why we don't all do these African ancestry tests. 'Cause people say we don't know our history, but we do. Our history begins on them ships. It don't go back further, see? 'Cause that moment before then for us . . . unrecognized. By us and by them—the ones who sold us. We all just erase it. Black Americans just arrived into the air on them ships. We ain't existed nowhere before. Were—was— er —we are invisible. Puppets. That be . . . less painful than the real story.

He starts to open the envelope, and then stops.

That what my momma told me, and she say that what her momma told her. So I stick with that in my mind.

But these Collards . . . they think different. I can't say what's right or what's wrong anymore. Seems interesting enough to give it a shot.

A pause, as he slowly opens the envelope. Takes out his glasses to read a piece of paper.

Heh. Well, I'll be damned. (*Slowly.*) "Thirty-five percent Nigerian."

No shit. Maybe Mr. C be a Collards after all. Chirinos always did sound too European.

(*Hums.*) "Where seldom is heard, a discouraging word . . ."

He laughs. Folds the paper and puts it in his pocket.

Scene Two: Northward Bound

Lights come up on **Pupita**, *seated alone in the lobby. She's visibly much more pregnant. Wears an Adidas sweat suit.*

After several moments, in comes **Marionette**. *She nods when she sees her.*

Takes a seat.

Pupita   Hey, girl. Imagine seeing you here again, innit?

Marionette   I hear you.

A pause.

Pupita   I—I thought of you recently—even before your call. It's been about three months, innit?

Marionette   I see you're about to pop, right?

Pupita   Burst even, innit?

They share a grin.

Marionette Look—no hard feelings. We're grown. We didn't need to be caught up in that game anyways.

Pupita I am in total agreement with you.

An awkward pause.

Where . . . where are you living?

Marionette Oh I . . . I ended up getting a place in West LA.

Pupita I see.

Marionette Not a single Black person in sight!

Pupita *looks off, distracted.*

Marionette Is . . . is everything okay? How's your place?

Pupita It's . . . it's fine, innit?

Marionette Right.

Pupita I . . . I don't know how to say this, but I . . . I've been given the boot, innit?

She pulls a duffle bag out from behind the sofa.

I . . . I've been . . . kicked out. Figured it was still easier to meet here.

Marionette Riiight . . . I ran into Mr. C, actually. What happened?

Pupita I um . . . I'm no longer welcome.

Marionette So it's all because of the scheme?

A pause. **Pupita** *stares off.*

Pupita I got called in by Chanfalla's people. I "wasn't the right fit."

Marionette Heh.

Pupita I guess one of my neighbors called and complained that I wasn't friendly enough and was acting too uppity and too "African" and not "Black enough." So they looked into it and found out that I had met with Mr. C—

Marionette Uppity Oprah. Right.

Pupita I'm sure you've heard the rest. I bet you think I got what I deserved, innit?

Marionette The infamous uppity accusation? Nah—I don't wish that on anybody—

Pupita (*in tears*) Poor Mr. C! He's worried he'll end up in Mexico soon, and he can't speak a word of Spanish, so—

Both women hold back a laugh.

Pupita It's honestly so crazy, innit? I mean "sending him south"? What era are we living?

Marionette I mean . . . you guys messed up. I knew there was something going on, but—

Pupita Are they going to let you compete for your spot?

Marionette Well, yes, but—

An overjoyed **Pupita** *runs over to smother* **Marionette** *with a hug.*

Pupita Oh thank you, Jesus—

Marionette But hold on—

Pupita You got this—

Marionette Okay, but listen: If I do this, it's just for two reasons: to help Mr. C one-up the guys who keep bussing him off, and to beat out Stacy Jones—

Pupita I heard—your eternal bully, innit? I need my Nigerian sister to get it—

Marionette So we're sisters now?

Pupita Don't you see what happened the first time? They wanted two Black women nobody thinks are Black enough to fight to the death. Doesn't that bother you?

Marionette It didn't seem to bother you then.

Pupita I got African blood in my veins. Fool me once, shame on you. Fool me twice—

Marionette So I—I need your help. You're obviously . . . good at . . . imagining puppets.

Pupita I got your back, girl! I will coach you 'til the puppets materialize!

Marionette I hope it's worth it—

Pupita Uppity Oprah—it is!

Marionette It's literally the same old story for me.

Pupita Definitely not what I expected here of all places.

Marionette Right?

Pupita So? Mr. C and I are going to get you prepped and everything?

Marionette Yup—but: isn't this sorta scheming what got him in trouble in the first place?

Pupita He's newly impassioned to "change his story."

Marionette Right—I had him do African ancestry. He found out he's Nigerian like us. Wantstuh help fam—

Pupita I see...

She jumps up to hug **Marionette**, *who is taken aback.*

Pupita The Woodingle Battle of African Ancestry! We're gonna get 'em, sis! Let's move in all the Nigerians! Woodingle becomes "Little Nigeria." Move over, Ethiopians!

Marionette "Little Nigeria." I like the sound of that! So... where do we begin?

Pupita *brings* **Marionette** *closer to her.*

Blackout.

Scene Three: Adichie and Barack Obama

Lights come up on **Pupita** *resting on the couch, as* **Marionette** *stands before* **Mr. C**—*sporting a gorgeous and vibrant African dashiki—at his stand.*

Mr. C Good evening, and welcome to *The Woodingle Puppet Show with Host Mr. C, as Constructed by Mr. Asinine with Calculations and Articulations of the Genius Sort.*

Let me remind you that the purpose of this show is to reveal which one of ya'll two sisters is the most... what was it... the most...

Pupita, Marionette Black!

Mr. C Alright—

Marionette Why is it so hard to remember the most important part, Mr. C?

He looks down in shame.

Marionette No worries! That was good! So. Now tell me: What do I need to do to win Mr. Asinine's good graces by way of winning Chanfalla's good graces?

Mr. C Well, isn't it—isn't it obvious?

Both women look at each other, confused.

Pupita Well, apparently not, innit? And by the way, you are looking sharp, Mr. C!

Mr. C Well, thank you—I work with the best! (*He winks at her.*)

Pupita These guys need to step up their game—they know nothing about styling a host!

Mr. C You... you know what you doin'—

Pupita Innit—

Marionette Okay, soooo—

Mr. C Yes—so you—what you hafta be doin' is you—you have to see the puppets. Before she does. And be better.

The women look at each other, with disappointment.

Marionette   Right. Um—Mr. C—you know you're working with air, right?

Mr. C   I don't believe so, no.

Pupita *sits up slowly.*

Pupita   Mr. C. We've discussed this already.

Mr. C   This ain't the—it ain't the way to do it.

Marionette   What do you—?

Mr. C   You gotta believe it, Miss. (*He points to the stage. Whispers.*) Only way that camera gonna believe it.

Pupita   Jesus—it's not on right now, is it?

Mr. C   No—I mean during the show—

Marionette   Then why were you whispering—?

Mr. C   I only plan for real—

Marionette   Riiiiight—

Pupita   Innit—

Marionette   Riiiight. Yupp—got it. Performance. I hear you—

Pupita   Okay—let's do it. Who we got with us today?

Mr. C *takes a breath. He's now ready.*

Mr. C   Good evening, and welcome to *The Woodingle Puppet Show with Host Mr. C, as Constructed by Mr. Asinine with Calculations and Articulations of the Genius Sort.*

Let me remind you that the purpose of this show is to reveal which one of ya'll two sisters is the most . . . what was it . . . the most . . .

Pupita   Not saying it—

Marionette   Nope—

Mr. C   Now the rules are simple. Work hard to see them puppets I'm showin' and tell me what you see. Then I report back to Chanfalla, who report back to Mr. Asinine, who report back to this here housing office who fit to . . . to get this place.

He pauses. Looks to them for agreement.

Pupita   Don't look at me—I'm not participating—

Marionette   Just imagine—

Pupita   I already got into enough trouble—

Mr. C   Shhhh—

Pupita Innit—

Mr. C The story for today is called (*mispronounces*) "Chimana Aseechie and Barack Obama."

He begins to act out the story with invisible puppets.

Now I gotta say I wrote—I done wrote this script myself for the first time. This just for practice!

Marionette Good work, Mr. C—proud of you—

Pupita Impressive—!

Mr. C Now this African woman and this mixed-race former president, they get together and they talkin' 'bout—what else—? Gentrification.

Now Ms. Aseechie, she say—

Pupita Adichie—

Mr. C That one—

Pupita This is meant to be Black Americans, no—?

Mr. C It meant to be us—we African—

Pupita Innit . . .

Mr. C She say, "We should all be feminists. I'm from Africa and gender roles are tough down over there, so I know what I'm talkin' about and think you all need to listen."

Marionette *and* **Pupita** *both laugh.*

Marionette Riiiiiight—

Pupita Innit—?

Marionette Adichie, really? I'm impressed—

Mr. C Now I been puttin' lotsa practice into this, so please be sure to—

Pupita But you didn't even speak with an accent—

Mr. C Well, they say that you be speaking English over there—

Marionette, Pupita But differently!

Taken aback, he has to pause for a moment to catch his bearing.

Marionette Have you watched Adichie speak?

Mr. C Well, now that's not the way that this works—

Marionette I mean you're asking us to pretend we see fake puppets and make it convincing. It's the least you could do on your end—

Mr. C Now I'll—I'll see what I can—

Pupita Now keep it going before I birth this baby, innit?

He takes a moment, and then continues.

Mr. C So Ms . . . A-deech-E-ay—

Pupita Good—!

As he speaks, he tries to use a Nigerian accent. It's a disaster. He becomes increasingly overwhelmed and unsure.

Mr. C So she explaining how since she thinks even the men should . . . should be feminists . . . so when they go to buy themselves a condo they . . . they get a good one even if they a man or even a woman . . . and should make no difference. And when it comes to gentrification, white women taking places Black women meant to be livin' in.

Marionette . . . okay. We can . . . try to work on that.

Mr. C Now see I just got workin' on this yesterday. Trying to use Asinine's style—

Marionette Forget that ass—!

Mr. C Now just give me a minute—

Pupita Please take a moment to—

He takes a breath. Loses the accent.

Mr. C Now usually I got my athletes and musicians . . . more my cuppa tea—

Marionette Right—

Pupita Innit—

He pauses. Continues with the show.

Mr. C So Ms. Aseechie—

Marionette, Pupita Adichie—

Mr. C She talkin' feminism and tellin' Obama how we should all be feminists, and that includes him. And she tells him there be too much hatin' when a woman tries to get herself some property—especially a Black woman—

Marionette Alright now—

Pupita And Obama—what has he got to say—?

Mr. C Now don't rush me—

Marionette Wow—okay—

Mr. C Now former president Barack Obama, he explain to . . . to—to Ms. Ms. . . . A-deech-E-ay—

Pupita, Marionette Good—!

Mr. C He say listen . . . I'm mixed-race. And I got me a White momma who raised me on her own when my daddy went back home to Africa, so I know a thing or two about strong women—

Marionette Okay . . .

Mr. C And he say "Listen, Ms. A-deech-E-ay, when it comes to property rights in this here Woodingle, all I got to say is Yes We Can."

A pause. He looks to them for approval.

Pupita (*trying to encourage him*) "Yes we can."

Marionette Yes we can—?

Mr. C Yes—"Yes We Can." That been his first campaign slogan—

Marionette I know, but really? That's it? That's from like over a decade ago—

Mr. C Still works, dontcha think. Mr. Asinine—

Marionette Of course he—

Pupita I've always loved that slogan—

Marionette Of course you—

Pupita What's that supposed to—?

Marionette I mean—Mr. C—you're kinda doing the same thing that Asinine and Chanfalla—

Pupita I mean we're being duped. It's kind of meant to be ridiculous. They aren't actually possible to visualize, innit—

Mr. C Now I told you you gotta believe—

Pupita Innit—

Marionette Asinine by way of Chanfalla, man. These—they're still in your head too much—

Pupita Now let's be careful. They hold Mr. C's northward journey in their hands.

Marionette I get that. But this is making me really—I mean look: A Nigerian and a "mixed-race" American talking about housing? What are you doing, Mr. C?

Mr. C I'm supporting my Nigerian sisters—

Marionette Riiiight—

Pupita Innit—

Mr. C Ya'll two talking Ms. Adichie this Barack Obama that, so I figured—

Marionette Okay but let's . . . like show a more complex—

Pupita I think you're on the right track—

Marionette Really? You found nothing simplistic in his telling of Adichie after watching her speech one time—?

Pupita I mean that's all you Americans think of her—

Marionette And all you know is Obama says "Yes We Can"—

Mr. C Alright now—

Marionette I mean—this is not what I—this ain't how feedback loop works! You study the community you enter. You don't show up lazy.

Mr. C Now—

Pupita You guys aren't really African, though. You know nothing about—

Marionette What are you saying?

Pupita No I—I meant no harm, innit?

Marionette Bully number two. And we're supposed to be surname sisters—

Mr. C Now Miss—

Pupita All I was saying was—

Marionette That sounds uppity as hell—

Mr. C Now both ya'll two ain't know nothing about us—this why I chose them two—!

A pause. They look at him.

You can't really see them Black puppets. It's all imaginary to you.

Marionette I was born and raised—!

Mr. C You African—

Pupita Well, not entirely—

Marionette Will you stop—?

Pupita Maybe Stacy does deserve—

Marionette Shipping us off once again—

Pupita You're not a part of that "us"—innit—?

Mr. C Now hold on just a second! Now they gonna want to see this sorta thing, but we ain't gonna let this—

The women glare at each other. He finally steps in between them.

Whew—now look. We all Black. Look at us. But we just gonna keep fighting trying to be Black the same way. Nonsense. We gonna get this Stacy Jones or not?

A pause. Both women ponder. **Pupita** *sits down on the sofa.*

Pupita My . . . my first day in the building, my neighbor asked me where I got my money to live here. I told him I earned it working hard, and he said he knows how it goes with Africans here. Must be from my mum and dad. I hate this model minority bullshit. I worked hard to get here, innit? Everyone just sees people like Adichie and assumes we all educated as hell—

Marionette Oh how offensive mis London—schooled—

Pupita Then he says where's my husband—aren't Nigerians supposed to be more proper—

Marionette No shit—

Pupita I get it. We don't really know much about each other.

Marionette Right?

Pupita *stands up and moves over to* **Marionette**. *Grabs her by the shoulders.*

Pupita I know you can do this. You deserve it just as much as Stacy Jones.

A pause. **Marionette** *looks down, ashamed.*

Marionette I'm sorry, I—

Pupita Nope—we don't need to apologize to anybody—

Marionette Right—

Pupita Now use that energy to see these puppets! I mean Adichie and Obama—hand-picked by our own Mr. C—it won't get any better than that!

A pause. **Marionette** *takes a deep breath.*

Mr. C Miss Collards, if you'd just let me finish—

Marionette Right—

Mr. C We can get something good going—

Marionette And then I mention I've seen my own mirror image?

Mr. C You'll see—things end well—

Marionette Of course they do! I mean "we should all be feminists" and "yes we can"—it doesn't get more optimistic than that, right?

A pause. They all just look at each other with anticipation.

Pupita I think if you give this a try, we can see how it—

Mr. C Now this one suited to us—it's our story—

Pupita Precisely—

Mr. C That means you ain't gotta work too hard to see—that Black American girl she gonna—she gonna struggle to see a Nigerian and a mixed-race man, but you—

Pupita But this is just practice—

Mr. C I convinced them let me make up my indiscretions by writing my own script—

Marionette   And they went for it—?

Mr. C   Mexico if it's schemin'! They ain't know no difference, anyhow—

Marionette   Right—okay—carry on—

Pupita *guides* **Marionette** *back toward the couch with her.*

Pupita   Let's sit you down. See if that helps.

She sits. Closes her eyes. **Pupita** *rubs her shoulders.*

Mr. C   Keeping out the threat of gentrification—!

They all laugh.

Marionette   Right. Okay—hit me.

She closes her eyes, as **Mr. C** *returns to his stand.*

Mr. C   Good evening, and welcome to *The Woodingle Puppet Show*—

Marionette   You can go ahead and jump ahead—

Mr. C   Well, alright. Now the rules are simple. Work hard—

Marionette   Jump—

Mr. C   The story for today called "Chimamanda Adichie and Barack Obama"—

Marionette   Jump—just jump to the next part you haven't shared with us yet.

A pause. He considers, working the story out in his mind.

Pupita   We're ready, Mr. C!

Marionette   Let's go—

Mr. C   Now Ms. Adichie and Mr. Obama happen to be fighting for the same condominium in a Black neighborhood complex.

Marionette   Okay . . . I see them. She's got on a bright red head-wrap, and he's looking dapper as usual in a black suit and tie.

Mr. C   And he says to her, let's talk this over.

Marionette *jumps up from her seat, fully engrossed.*

Marionette   I see her—there she is! Legs crossed. Look at that red lipstick. Somebody bring this woman a glass of water!

Mr. C   So she says she got feminism on her mind, and she deserves the place because her mommy and daddy worked hard in Nigeria to raise her and her siblings right after a terrible war—and he's really only White American so—

Pupita   Jesus—

Marionette   There he goes shifting in his seat! Obama doesn't like what he's hearing!

Mr. C He be mostly White American so he don't know nothing about this place and don't deserve to be getting this place 'cause he knows nothing about the Black struggle in this country—

Marionette Uh-oh he's standing! He's ready to make a speech—go get 'em, President—!

Pupita I'm really trying, but this is—

Mr. C And Barack Obama says he done been president of this country and his daddy was African but everyone forgets, and he knows way more about Black America than some African woman writing her little imaginary books—

Marionette Uh-oh—now she's standing—!

Pupita "Little imaginary books"? Now hold on a second—

Mr. C Shouting feminism this feminism that when her books about wanting a man—

Marionette Go get 'em, Obama! Yes yes I see it. Stare her off the stage—! Yes we can—!

At this, **Pupita** *jumps up from her seat.*

Pupita I've had enough—!

She rushes toward **Mr. C**, *who is now drenched in sweat and panting from exhaustion.*

Marionette Yes we can—!

Pupita Mr. C—

Mr. C Four buses—that's seven dollars—three hours if I makin' no stops—

Marionette Yes we can! Yes we can! Yes we—!

Pupita Please—somebody—!

She stops before the stage box. Waves her hands to get the camera's attention.

Mr. C They pushing me south, but they gotta know I'm a Nigerian—!

Marionette Yes we can! Yes we can! Yes we can—!

Pupita Mr. Chanfalla? Asinine, innit?

Mr. C Next time it be five buses—eight dollars seventy-five cents. Four hours—

Marionette YYYYYYYYYYYYYESSSS!

Pupita Can somebody please come—? Things have—they're getting out of— (*Grabbing her side.*) Ouch!

Marionette WWWWWEEEEE!

Mr. C Then six buses—ten-dollars fifty cents—five hours—ain't make no Nigerian sense—!

Act Two, Scene Three 257

Pupita Somebody, help!

She now moves over to the box and starts hitting it. **Mr. C** *tries to stop her.*

Marionette CCCCAAAANNN!

Mr. C DON'T MOVE ME SOUTH—DON'T MOVE ME SOUTH—LITTLE NIGERIA . . . !

Pupita THIS IS—(*Grabs belly.*) OUCHHHH—!

Marionette *now rushes the box, punching it with her fists. It breaks into pieces.* **Mr. C** *grabs the camera from inside. Tosses it across the room.*

Marionette YES WE CAN—!

Mr. C I CAN'T TAKE NO MORE BUSES—!

Pupita, *overwhelmed and in pain, falls down to her knees.*

The other two rush to kneel beside her.

There is a moment of silence. Increasingly, the sounds of cheers and applause can be heard from outside.

Pupita "A man is as likely as a woman to be intelligent. To be creative. To—"

She passes out, as the crowd sounds cease. **Marionette** *and* **Mr. C** *look down at her helplessly.*

Marionette No we can't—

Mr. C I ain't going south—

They both drop down to comfort her.

Marionette Why is being ourselves so dangerous?

Mr. C *nods in agreement.*

Mr. C You bring up a good point, Miss.

Marionette I mean they shipping you out on six, seven, eight buses out of your own neighborhood, then forcing you back up here for work each day just to be tortured by your own expulsion.

Mr. C You ain't said nothin' wrong.

He goes to the corner to grab a water, as **Marionette** *uses her hand to fan* **Pupita**.

Marionette You think we should call an ambulance?

Mr. C She gonna be fine. They ain't gonna rush. Name like hers, they'll take their time getting over here.

He returns with the water. Hands it to her.

Give her this—

Marionette *grabs the water and tosses it in* **Pupita**'s *face. She jumps up, gasping for air.*

Mr. C   Well, I didn't mean like—

Marionette   Thank God—!

Mr. C   Glad to see you back with us—

Pupita   What—what happened?

Marionette   They tried to push us all back down south. We gotta figure a way out of this.

Pupita *starts to stand slowly, and the other two help her. She looks around in search of something.*

Mr. C   Now take it easy, Miss—

Marionette   What are you looking for—?

Pupita   My bag, innit?

Marionette   I'll find it—you go sit down.

Mr. C *helps* **Pupita** *over to the sofa. After a moment,* **Marionette** *finds the duffle bag and brings it over to* **Pupita**, *who opens it and starts digging around inside, pulling out fabrics of many different colors.*

Mr. C   What's all that?

Pupita   Design ideas.

Marionette   Right.

Pupita (*to* **Marionette**)   They do this at Adidas?

Marionette   I'm only comfortable with the people. I don't have much skill in design—

Pupita   I'm the opposite.

Marionette   Heh—

Mr. C   Well, now I know you a great stylist and all, Ms. Collards, but I think now's not the time to be working. You need to rest for that baby—

Pupita   This is for her, innit?

Marionette   Her? Awww—

Mr. C   That be real nice—

Marionette   So what exactly are you—?

Pupita   We're not invisible, right? I mean they probably on their way over here to kick us out—

Marionette   Of our own neighborhood—

Mr. C   More buses more hours—

Pupita   But we've all got the skills to make this right! Forget about this stupid place! We can do this. Grassroots, innit?

Marionette   I love your enthusiasm, but—

Mr. C   Perhaps she hit her head—

Pupita   I'm fine—listen! We're real. Mr. Asinine and Mr. Chanfalla—they're a scam. At the end of the day, people hear what's real.

Marionette   Right . . .

Pupita   I'm a stylist and designer—that's real. You're a social organizer—that's real. Mr. C is a gifted performer—

Mr. C   Alright—

Marionette   Okay—

Pupita   Forget Asinine and Stacy Jones. What you wanna bet we beat them at their game?

A pause. **Mr. C** *and* **Marionette** *look at each other.*

Mr. C   What exactly you have in mind?

Pupita *pulls together some fabrics and fashions them into a makeshift puppet. Holds it up enthusiastically.*

Pupita   Black visibility!

Blackout.

Epilogue: Mr. C and Ms. Collards and Ms. Collards Present

Lights come up on **Mr. C** *at center. He's in a nice new blue suit, looking very Nat King Cole.*

He smiles at us. Leaves for a moment, and returns with a flashy new puppet stage.

Mr. C   Well, hello there and welcome to *The Woodingle Puppet Show in Celebration of Blackness in All Its Gorgeous Forms with Host Mr. C as Constructed by the Lovely and Talented Ms. Collards and Ms. Collards.*

Boy have we got a show for you tonight! Bring 'em out, ladies!

Enter **Marionette** *in a fabulous kente dress and* **Pupita** *in a fashionable jeans-and-tee number, with a baby strapped to her chest.*

They carry countless gorgeous handcrafted Black puppets of varying shades, shapes, and sizes.

Marionette   Hello, Woodingle feedback loop people, and thank you for coming out to support our show! We're here to share some authentic Black stories and excited to build a new community.

Marionette There's no gimmick: we simply want to make Blackness *visible* in all its beauty.

Pupita We hope you enjoy the show, and remember, there is no charge! This is pure storytelling! None of us live here currently—we don't need the rent money, innit?

Marionette Adidas has generously sponsored this event! Take a shirt designed by the lovely Ms. Pupita Collards after the show!

Pupita A new journey, innit?

Marionette Right? And we'll be back living here when we build Woodingle back up. Stories are a start. Take it away, Mr. C!

Mr. C Now this one called "How Ms. Collards and Ms. Collards Helped Me Sue Mr. Asinine and Get Myself Back Northbound."

Now Ms. Collards, she said—

Marionette Right—

Mr. C And the other one, she said—

Pupita Innit—

Mr. C And they both been Black but in they own way, and me too. Now that be home on our own range.

They all share a smile.

Blackout.

END OF PLAY

Traces of Desire

Lina Patel

Traces of Desire

Introduction by Aina Soley Mateu

Decades ago, in Bombay, Uma Bhatt rejected a suitor: he was Muslim, she was Hindu. Since then, it seems women in her family are cursed to become widows at a young age due to the unfulfilled desire she took to the grave. This tragic preface sets the stage for Lina Patel's comic and hopeful *Traces of Desire*, which explores how women internalize patriarchal norms and tell themselves stories to excuse, suppress, or justify their yearning and sexual passion.

Traces of Desire centers around Preeti Shah, a widow with a daughter, who finds herself caught off-guard when an attractive, well-known actor becomes a visiting instructor at the university where she teaches. What initially seems like a *coup-de-foudre* evolves into a profound process of self-discovery, transcending conventional views—including those of Preeti's vocal mother—in favor of personal and sexual freedom.

Patel takes as her source Lope de Vega's *La viuda valenciana* (*The Widow of Valencia*, 1600), which challenges social norms and expected behaviors for widows in seventeenth-century Spain. Leonarda, the protagonist, employs elaborate schemes to satisfy her sexual desires without compromising her reputation, all while avoiding commitment to any of her suitors. While most married women in seventeenth-century Spain were relegated to domestic roles, widows enjoyed unique autonomy, as they had both economic means and sexual experience. In *The Widow of Valencia*, Leonarda ably makes use of both to satisfy her libido without losing her social status. The play navigates the intersection of the social and the intimate, and the underlying tensions between pursuing sexual desire and maintaining a public image in line with what is expected from women. While Lope's play concludes with the promise of a (second) marriage, Patel diverges, offering a world where women are not defined by their relationships with men but rather by their connection with their own physical needs, their yearnings, and each other.

By delving into the pressures of womanhood, and more particularly of an Indian-American womanhood, in a society where one is constantly labeled, Patel adds multiple layers to Lope's original. The tale of Preeti unfolds without a singular narrator or perspective, which, as author Lina Patel notes, is common in works from communities of color; rather, it is woven together using the voices of her grandmother Uma, her mother Nirmala, her friend Julio, and her daughter Una. Preeti herself becomes a part of this generational choral ensemble, contributing to a finely constructed narrative that fluctuates between the inevitable recurrence of personal tragedy and the delights of building a loving community, one which will ultimately undo the family curse. As Preeti weighs her obligations to her daughter, her mother, and herself, it is her grandmother—a spectral presence throughout the play—who constantly reminds us of the costs of self-denial. The celebration of Holi, a time of release and renewal, serves as a backdrop for many pivotal events, making them equally colorful and bittersweet.

Patel's play emphasizes both the spiritual and material dimensions of personal identity, exploring platonic and familial love, and portraying how sexual desire can manifest beyond conventional romantic relationships. Body and soul play equally significant roles here in the search for one's most intimate self. Across generations, the women in *Traces of Desire* gradually break free from entrenched social norms, embracing their own personhood and ultimately liberating themselves and subsequent generations from traditional and inherited constraints.

Characters (Six Actors Total)

Preeti Shah, *20s–40s, she/her. Mother, wife, widow. Professor of medieval Indian poetry. Indian*

Julio Elliot, *20s–40s, he/she. Her bestie, a professor of biology, gay. Latinx*

Uma Bhatt/Uma's Trace Desire, *forever 50, she/her. Preeti's widowed grandmother. In transit*

Nirmala Shah, *Preeti's widowed mother, 30s–60s, she/her. Worries. Indian*

Aparna/Una, *Preeti's daughter(s), unborn and born, queer. Open ethnicity*

Rizwan/Remo Stone, *younger than Preeti and Uma, he/him, romantic Indian man/ Hot, semi-well-known television actor, capable of deep feeling, humor, fickleness. Open ethnicity. Think hunky, like Idris Elba or Daniel Dae Kim at 28-ish*

Setting

A small college town near a big city today, tomorrow, or any time in which women are not seen as autonomous humans.

Playwright's Notes

Casting is best when it is diverse—race, body type, ability. Dismantle assumed Western standards of beauty. Desire is universal. Female desire is rocket fuel. The actor playing Rizwan/Remo Stone will play an ethnicity different from his own. The diverse cast will deploy Indian accents in one scene. That's okay. It's a play. Play! Punctuation or lack of, words capitalized or not are purposeful. Exclamation marks might express awe, joy, self-love, self-censorship, and might even be whispered, as the actor chooses.

Traces of Desire was first workshopped and presented at UCLA's LA Escena Festival in 2022 with the following cast: Sami Cavestani, Reshma Gajjar, Anna Khaja, Rachna Khatau, Spencer Paez, Ian S. Peterson. The play was directed by Alana Dietze.

About the Play

Inspired by Lope de Vega's sixteenth-century comedia *The Widow of Valencia*, *Traces of Desire* centers female agency and desire in a world of fixed gender norms. In my play, written in the twenty-first century, female agency and desire are still rich territory to explore, even if gender norms are slowly expanding to encompass our full humanity. My play introduces three generations of widows, plus an adopted child—a fourth generation. The adoption of Preeti's daughter embraces continuity different from the typical blood continuity. It is a way to complicate motherhood the way desire complicates womanhood (and wifehood and widowhood). Today, women's full humanity is still being undermined. Where Lope de Vega was interested in how a woman retains her independence while gratifying her sexual desires, I'm interested in exploring what a woman is, in female desire, and in what women do today that is considered transgressive. Whenever today is. My play is dedicated to my daughter Robin, who, like me, is ever finding herself.

Act I

1.

A collective intake of breath and—

Lights! **Preeti** *in a sari or part of a sari. In front of a mirror.*

Preeti (*to herself*)   I am married. It is—

Knocking sounds offstage.

Uma's Trace Desire (*offstage*)   Darn it.

Preeti   I'm married. It's Spring. Happy Holi—

Julio, *t-shirt and long skirt, erupts from a pile of flowers.*

Julio   If someone says "Holi" there's going to be a dance number. It's like Chekhov's gun.

Preeti   I'm married. It's Spring. Happy Holi. If we have a daughter, we'll name her—

Julio   I'm Julio. Julio means "youthful." It can also be a girl's name!

Preeti   We'll name her—

Nirmala *appears with mala beads.*

Nirmala   That's my daughter. Preeti.

Julio   "Preeti" means love!

Nirmala   I am Preeti's mother. Nirmala.

Knocking again.

Julio   "Nirmala" means pure!

Uma's Trace Desire *appears: black hair, white widow's sari, like a black and white film, existing in her own liminal space.*

Uma's Trace Desire (*to audience*)   I'm here! Where? Why? Who knows. Uma. Preeti's grandmother. "Uma" is another name for goddess Parvati—

Julio   That's my line!

Uma's Trace Desire (*to* **Julio**)   If there are any rules here, I'm breaking them.

Nirmala   But rules bring order to chaos.

Uma's Trace Desire (*rolls her eyes—then.*)   Thought I'd be reincarnated already. But that's my daughter. And my granddaughter. Something must be wrong. What's wrong—

Nirmala   Everything is fine. I know what to do. You go.

Uma's Trace Desire Okay, bye, I'll go.

She waits. Nothing happens.

Julio ANYHOO. Uma, or Parvati, wife of the GORGEOUS-God Shiva, is the goddess of harmony, devotion, and motherhood.

Uma's Trace Desire Yes and I felt no pressure to be perfect because of that.

Preeti If we have a daughter, we'll call her . . .

Aparna *appears.* **Uma's Trace Desire** *and* **Aparna** *look at each other.*

Aparna Aparna. I'm a niggling thought—

Uma's Trace Desire It tickles.

Aparna A ticking clock—

Uma's Trace Desire Tickling, niggling.

Aparna A mother's dream.

Preeti We'll call her Aparna!

Julio Aparna is another name for Goddess Parvati.

Uma's Trace Desire (*to* **Aparna**) Did you bring me here?

Aparna I haven't even been born yet.

A **Man** *peeks/enters from offstage. He's eager. Maybe feeling left out.*

Man Hey! I'm just hanging back here? And just wanted to say—hey!

The **Man** *waves. Retreats.*

Uma's Trace Desire Since I'm here I might as well figure out why. Okay! Let's see: Time doesn't matter. Pick a year, any year. That is now.

Preeti Uh. Are we *all* talking to, uh, you know. (*Gestures toward audience.*)

Nirmala You don't have to.

Preeti (*relieved*) Okay.

Julio *I* think you should but I'm just your best friend.

The cast move. A collective intake of breath. Lights!

2.

Preeti *in front of the mirror tentatively touches her body.*

Uma's Trace Desire I can still feel my body under my clothes. Or is it the memory of my body? Do I have a body?!

Preeti (*to herself, excited*) Happy Holi . . . WIFE.

The cast throw rice, flowers, colored powder!

Uma's Trace Desire   We are all just a big clump of tiny molecules.

Nirmala (*to* **Preeti**, *dreaming*)   And soon you will be . . . a *mother*.

Uma's Trace Desire   Little molecules, we are. I find comfort in this but others find it terrifying because we think of molecules as drifting away, as scattering, and we like to be solid and center. It's a fact that's been known for thousands of years but is also being continually discovered. Like desire.

Slaps her own hand.

Similarly centering and scattering. (*Re.* **Preeti**.) She's nervous. (*Wistful.*) She should be.

Uma's Trace Desire   Marriage!

Preeti's *sari pallu¹ slips off.*

Uma's Trace Desire   Widowhood.

Her eyes linger on her breastbone and breasts, through her blouse.

Uma's Trace Desire   "Thousands are my desires . . ."

Nirmala   My mother often spoke in riddles. Especially after.

Preeti (*turns to* **Nirmala**)   After what, Mom?

A collective intake of breath. **Preeti** *exits as the* **Man** *enters.*

Man   Do I know you?

Preeti   No.

Uma's Trace Desire   Molecules passing in the night. (*Then.*) Preeti's story can wait. First: me! Back we go!

She snaps her fingers. **Preeti** *leaves. Lights!*

3.

The **Man** *presses "Play" on an old tape recorder. an old Bollywood love song, like "Aaja teri yaad aaye" (I thought of you today).*

When music happens, the cast dance, swoon, move.

Uma's Trace Desire (*to audience*)   It's before. Before the year you picked.

Nirmala (*sniffs*)   Hmph. Riddles.

Uma's Trace Desire *sticks her tongue out at* **Nirmala**.

---

1   Pallu is the part of a sari that is wrapped over one's shoulder.

The **Man** *dances by himself to the romantic tune. He's good.*

Uma's Trace Desire   What you see now is my trace desire. Apparently, desire is stronger than death.

Daydreams, then slaps her hand.

I think things.

Daydreams, then slap.

I think desire like pain is passed on in the genes.

Man   Shhh. (*Gentle, loving.*)

The **Man** *puts a deep pink flower in* **Uma**'s *hair.* **Uma** *melts.*

Uma   I am a young bride!

The **Man** *turns off the music.*

Aparna *blows a (train) whistle.* **Nirmala** *provides a chair.*

Uma *sits. A collective breath in. Lights!*

4.

Aparna *blows the whistle again.*

Uma   I'm on a train heading from my village to Bombay - it was never called Mumbai - Bombay! The big city! To meet my husband. I'm fifteen he's twenty-one don't look so aghast just listen. Our parents arranged it. He's from our village but studied in Bombay and is now doing business. Selling batteries. Stoves. He worked for a man who took kindly to him and now he's working for himself. Sales. He's so handsome and I know this because when we married I took a peek from under my veil!

Uma *and her new husband, played by* **Julio**, *greet each other.*

Uma   I met my husband at the train station.

Julio   I was waiting for her.

Uma   It was the first time we were alone together.

Julio   Holy shit she's a knockout!

Uma (*serious, to him*)   Hello.

Julio (*grave, to her*)   Allow me.

He takes her suitcase. She blushes. He walks through the crowd. She follows, staring at him, in awe.

Uma   There were hundreds of people about.

The **Man** *does the old wolf whistle.*

Julio I'll kick your ass!

Man (*cowed*) Sorry, very sorry, sir.

Uma He looked so serious. I felt so proud. I was a Married Woman.

The crowd goes slow-mo, heads turning in approval, deference.

Uma People looked at me differently.

Touches red kumkum powder along the part in her hair.

At my *tilak*. With awe and respect. I was in awe of myself. Of my husband. I kept my back straight and my chin high. We walked outside and passed cars and rickshaws and came to a . . . motorcycle. His motorcycle.

Maybe we hear Richard Thompson's "Vincent Black Lightning" as **Nirmala** *gets another chair.* **Uma** *sits behind* **Julio** *on his motorcycle.*

Uma I knew then my parents made the right choice. (*To him.*) A good man.

Julio (*to her*) With a motorcycle.

Uma *wraps her arms around* **Julio**.

Uma I felt his body for the first time. Then we rode.

A collective intake of breath. Lights!

5.

The **Man** *takes the flower from* **Uma**'s *hair and puts it in* **Aparna**'s *hair.* **Aparna** *is now* **Younger Uma**.

Nirmala *carries a small wooden temple and places it down.*

Uma's Trace Desire We were married when I was fifteen but we did not have kids until I was twenty. He waited. I waited. We nearly died waiting. After I turned nineteen we decided enough with waiting and I decided I wouldn't wait again.

Nirmala *places Ganesha, Krishna, Lakshmi in the temple. Photos of dead ancestors. In silhouette,*

Younger Uma *and* **Julio**, *still the husband, pray and grieve.*

Uma's Trace Desire Three children were born and lived. Two miscarriages, then my sixth. My seventh was born but died of fever. Nirmala's little brother.

Nirmala I was the baby, born four years after the others.

Uma's Trace Desire The shape of our hearts changed. My love for my surviving children almost filled up the well of sadness I had dug for my lost ones. So many molecules. I breathed them daily.

Nirmala My brothers and sisters were older, Papa worked, I dreamed of my own house where I gave all my attention to my daughter.

Uma's Trace Desire   I can say that my husband and I had years of happiness. Some fights, of course, this isn't Disneyland, it's marriage and kids and death and love. In India! But it was a good match.

Younger Uma *and* **Julio** *hold each other. Then her husband disappears.*

Uma's Trace Desire   So when he died, I thought, well, that's it, life is over for me after I get Nirmala married. (*Pause.*) She married. But life wasn't over for me.

Nirmala *exits. The* **Man** *psyches himself up in the corner, like a boxer getting ready.*

Uma's Trace Desire   It's 1947. Or 1987. Or 1623. Or yesterday. Time doesn't matter. Some things, like friendship, discrimination, and not knowing yourself, are eternal. I sound wise, don't I? I could say, Yes, I am very wise because I am a feeling and in the whole universe feeling is the only thing that matters . . . but honestly, I am just the same as you. What came first? The molecule or the feeling? Are feelings molecules, too? Do you know because I don't. See, I'm really quite dumb.

Julio   And now! Seven short interludes in Bombay!

Old Bollywood music, as before. **Aparna** *plays young, widowed* **Uma**.

Whoever is available in the cast dance/move to the music as—

Julio *narrates the action and the* **Man** *dons a dapper hat.*

Julio   One. An open window above a busy street. Widowed Uma dreams at the window. A young man walking by stops. He takes off his hat. He waves. Uma blushes.

Nirmala (*offstage*)   Mummy! Baby's got a rash, what should I do?

Uma *reacts, looks at the* **Man**. *Smiles. Runs inside to help.*

Julio   Two. Another day. Uma impatiently waits by the window. The Man, out of breath, arrives. From his pocket, he retrieves chocolate. Throws it up at her. She catches it.

Younger Uma   It's melted.

Man   Like my heart, for you.

Younger Uma   You're young. Maybe Nirmala's age. How old are you?

Man   Does it matter?

Nirmala (*offstage*)   Mummy! Preeti's napping. Could you rub oil in my hair?

Julio   Three. Another day. The Man is waiting with a huge bouquet of pink flowers. Younger Uma comes to the window.

Uma's Trace Desire *mouths the words spoken by* **Younger Uma**.

Man   These are for you but I can't throw them up there.

Younger Uma   They are beautiful. Put them by your window and think of me.

Man   What's wrong?

Younger Uma   Preeti, my granddaughter, kept us awake all night with a cold.

Man   Poor little baby. Can I run to the chemist for you?

Younger Uma   No, Nirmala is making medicine. Thank you.

Man (*big easy smile*)   No problem.

Younger Uma   . . . What's your name?

Man (*dying to know hers*)   Rizwan. Habib.

Younger Uma   I'm Uma. Bhatt.

Rizwan   You're Hindu.

Younger Uma   You're Muslim.

Rizwan   Love can overcome anything.

Younger Uma   Love! Oh, la la.

Rizwan   Love takes many forms.

Younger Uma   What are you talking love for?

Rizwan   In the future we won't have to hide.

Uma's Trace Desire (*to audience*)   Ha.

Nirmala (*offstage*)   Mummy? Can you come? I'm giving Preeti the medicine!

Julio   Four. Another day. Humid. A busy street. Cars honking. Trees. Bright green parrots making a racket.

Uma's Trace Desire (*to* **Younger Uma**)   Can I do this part?

Younger Uma *nods.* **Uma's Trace** *covers her head with her sari pallu. Self-conscious.*

Rizwan, *disguised as a woman, splattered with colors, approaches. Sees* **Uma**. **Uma** *sees him.*

Uma   Where did you get that dress?

Rizwan   My sister's closet. She's very modern.

Rizwan *has a paper bag with chocolates. A bouquet of roses.*

Uma   You celebrate Holi?

Rizwan *raises his arms, moves his shoulders. Dances. Dude can move.*

Rizwan   Doesn't everyone? I was caught in a color fight!

Uma   Nirmala wants to go, but the baby could get sick.

Uma *takes the roses. Inhales. Hands them back.* **Rizwan** *gives her the chocolates.*

Rizwan   Not melted. Nice and cold.

Uma   I thought I'd laugh when I saw you. But you look even more handsome in a dress. How is that possible?

They are burning with desire.

Uma *takes a chocolate from his bag. Feeds it to him. She takes her own. They eat because they can't touch.*

Rizwan *takes a rose from the bouquet and puts it in her hair. His hand touches her hair. They float.*

Uma   I can't wear it, Mr. Habib.

Rizwan   You must wear it, Mrs. Bhatt.

Uma   You are standing in the street with an old Hindu widow.

Rizwan   Think they can tell I'm a young Muslim fellow, in love?

Uma   You don't know what love is and everyone can tell everything.

Rizwan   How is your daughter's pretty little Preeti?

Uma   Better, thank you. Nirmala is tired. She needs more confidence, but she will be a good mother.

Rizwan   She has a good example, Mrs. Bhatt. Uma.

Uma   Don't stand any closer!

Rizwan   I will stand here as long as you like, until you leave me.

Uma   So dramatic.

Uma *laughs and* **Rizwan** *nearly drops dead with delight.*

Uma   You should be a Bollywood actor, Mr. Habib. Rizwan.

Rizwan   Marry me, Mrs. Bhatt!

Uma   Okay!

Rizwan (*stoked*)   Really?!

Nirmala (*offstage*)   That is not what happened.

Aparna *comes back to play* **Younger Uma**. **Uma's Trace Desire** *retreats.*

Younger Uma   You should be a Bollywood actor, Mr. Habib. Rizwan.

Rizwan   Marry me, Mrs. Bhatt! Uma.

Younger Uma Don't be silly.

Rizwan We must be silly until the world catches up to us.

Younger Uma You said Love can take many forms. What do you mean?

Rizwan Maybe in a previous life, you were a doe and I was your hart.

Younger Uma Eh?

Rizwan "H-a-r-t" hart is an old English name for a male deer.

Younger Uma But do you believe in reincarnation?

Rizwan I don't not believe it.

Younger Uma Pssht! Love can't overcome prejudice.

Rizwan Not now, but in the future and we could be that future—now.

Younger Uma Oh God, is that my daughter coming down the street?!

Younger Uma, *panicked, plucks the rose from her hair and runs off.*

Rizwan (*picking up the rose*) Mrs. Bhatt? Wait!

Julio Five. Another day. Rizwan waits under the open window. Younger Uma is hiding under the window. He longs to see her.

Six. Another week. Rizwan waits under the closed window. Younger Uma is just on the other side, biting her hand. She wants to open it. To talk to him. She doesn't make a sound.

Seven. Another month. Rizwan waits. The window is shut. Locked. Younger Uma stands with her back against the window. Sadly, Rizwan walks away.

Julio *is too sad to go on.*

During the following the cast move around **Younger Uma**, *whispering society's judgment, until* **Younger Uma** *is made very small. Very quiet.*

Uma's Trace Desire I told Nirmala about Rizwan. She was upset. Less about the Muslim part than the man part. She never thought her mother could want another man. That her mother could want. She refused to celebrate Holi but she kept my secret. Still, Bombay, like New York City, is a small town and so for three years it was not whispered that I fell in love with a Muslim. (*Slaps her hand.*) It was not whispered that he was half my age. (*Slap.*) And it was not whispered that I went a little mental. (*Slaps her hand.*) Many things were not whispered.

Preeti *appears, at the mirror.*

Preeti "Thousands are my desires and each is good enough to die for . . ."

Uma's Trace Desire What's the rest of it?

A collective intake of breath. Lights!

6.

Uma's Trace Desire *watches.*

Little **Preeti** *(8) and* **Nirmala** *sit in front of the small temple sewing garlands of flowers.*

Little Preeti   Tell me about Nani.

Nirmala   She was a good mother.

Uma's Trace Desire   Translation: "She did her best."

Little Preeti   I wish I remembered her more.

Nirmala   You were very young when she died.

Little Preeti   Of a broken heart, right?

Nirmala   Heart attack. (*Scowls.*) Did your uncle tell you that?

Uma's Trace Desire   Translation: "Your uncle is silly like your Nani."

Little Preeti   Was Nani a romantic?

Nirmala   Romantics exist only in Bollywood movies and America.

Uma's Trace Desire   "When my mother died I lost my sense of humor."

Little Preeti   So you're not a romantic?

Nirmala   I love your daddy.

Uma's Trace Desire   That's not what she asked.

Little Preeti   Why do we have to move?

Nirmala   Daddy's work is there now.

Little Preeti   It's so far away.

Nirmala   Los Angeles is warm. Like Bombay.

Little Preeti   And full of romantics?

Nirmala   You just focus on your studies.

Uma's Trace Desire   It's tempting to say I died of heartbreak but I didn't love Rizwan. I was only forty-four when my husband, the only man I had ever known, was in a boating accident. Forty-seven when I met Rizwan, and the world became so bright and Forty-seven and a half when Nirmala saw us in the street. After three years of squinting against the bright world at fifty I—

Plays dead. Opens her eyes.

It really does no good to suppress things, does it?

Uma's Trace Desire *sits up.*

Uma's Trace Desire   *Chalo, chalo!* Fast forward!

Lights!

7.

Nirmala Years passed. Preeti got into graduate school. I was proud but I wanted to see her settled—she was already twenty-one and America is no place for a girl. Alone.

Beat.

Believe me, I know. It's been eleven years.

Preeti *sits by her mom.*

Preeti There's a South Asian poetry class I want to take—

Nirmala (*tending* **Preeti***'s hair*) Poetry? Focus on science. You're good at math.

Uma's Trace Desire I never finished school but I kept our household accounts.

Nirmala There's a boy. Doctor. He's in Philadelphia but has an interview in Los Angeles. You'll meet him?

Preeti But Mummy, I'm just starting graduate school!

Nirmala His father and Daddy were at college together.

Preeti . . . They knew Daddy?

Nirmala (*nods*) He's very handsome and his mother is kind.

Uma's Trace Desire A good sign.

Preeti What's his name?

Nirmala Dilip. Just meet, no rush, but if you like him, tell me.

Preeti You like him, don't you?

Nirmala It's not about me.

Uma's Trace Desire Ha.

Nirmala I've done your charts and it's a good match. I know you think it's old fashioned, but Nani never did mine and, well.

Uma's Trace Desire Nirmala met the man she wanted to marry in college. He came from a good family so I said yes.

Preeti Would you have married someone else?

Nirmala No! But it would have helped us make different choices.

Uma's Trace Desire When Preeti was ten, two years after they moved to Los Angeles, her father was hiking and got his first bee sting.

Preeti Choices like what?

Nirmala Like not coming to this country!

Uma's Trace Desire He had a bad reaction.

Nirmala There are no bees in Bombay!

Uma's Trace Desire That's not true.

Nirmala Stupid hiking.

Uma's Trace Desire But there was a possibility of a different life here.

Nirmala Stupid Los Angeles.

Preeti (*soothing her*) I'm glad you did our charts, Mom.

Uma's Trace Desire Away from the big sad eyes of everyone in Mumbai.

Nirmala He's older, but strong, intelligent, and has a lovely laugh.

Uma's Trace Desire Away from the whispers that we were cursed.

Preeti Okay, Mummy. I'll meet him.

Uma's Trace Desire And that our men would die until our past *karmas* were paid.

Preeti How old is he?

The cast moves. A collective intake of breath. Lights!

8.

A bus stop. **Julio** *whips off his long skirt to reveal pants. He and* **Preeti** *stand together, mid-convo.*

Julio I am obsessed with India!

Preeti (*laughing*) Why?

Julio Why not? The honking, the Himalayas, the Hee-jras!

Preeti The—?

Julio Hee-jras?

Preeti Oh. *Hijras*.

Julio Yeah, a four-thousand year history of a third gender!

Preeti We don't talk to them.

Uma's Trace Desire I spoke to Hijras. Gave them money before each of my children's weddings. For luck.

Julio *holds out his hand.*

Julio Julio Elliot. Bio-chem.

Preeti *shakes his hand.*

Preeti Me, too! Preeti Shah. Nice to meet you, Julio.

Julio I want to be the head of my own lab.

Preeti I will marry Dilip Shah, son of my late father's friend. I don't even have to change my name.

Uma's Trace Desire Nirmala fell in love at school and *with* school but then she had Preeti and forgot about her studies and doted on her.

Preeti Can I confide in you about something?

Julio I love confiding—and I keep things to myself. Always.

Preeti There's a poetry class. Old Indian poetry. My mother doesn't know, but I am taking it—a night, once a week, a seminar.

Julio Does your mother not like poetry?

Preeti My mother disapproves of romantics. But I want to recite one of the poems for my husband, after we are married.

She looks at **Julio** *shyly.*

Julio Okay, let me hear it. Come on.

Preeti "Thousands are my desires and each/ Is good enough to die for/ The more my desires are fulfilled/ The more I crave and long for."

Julio Ooof, I am swooning! (*Wistful.*) Look at you! First love. I envy. I'd love to find The One. But . . . it's complicated.

Preeti My mother says don't overthink. It's all quite simple.

Julio Got a picture of your lucky fiancé?

Preeti No. But Dilip is thirty-two and his mother is very nice.

Julio Thirty-two?! What are you, twenty-two?

Preeti Twenty-one. He's a surgeon doing his second fellowship—

Julio If he's marrying you, he better have a degree in the Kama Sutra!

Uma's Trace Desire (*delighted*) Shameless!

Preeti Julio, the Kama Sutra is an ancient philosophy about emotional fulfillment and—

Julio Sex!

Preeti —the nature of love and—

Julio Sexual positions?

She thinks he's flirting.

Preeti (*stern*) Julio. We are in school together but we can *only* be friends.

He is flirting. He is also gay.

Julio (*winks*) We're the only gals in bio-chem so we better be friends.

Preeti *smiles, confused.*

Uma's Trace Desire   I never had a Julio in my life. Maybe things would have been different if I had.

Julio *wheels in a second mirror—with see-through or no glass.*

Uma's Trace Desire   It seems to me they've known each other over many lifetimes.

During the following **Preeti** *stands in front of the transparent mirror.* **Aparna** *stands on the other side.*

Julio   We were fish in the same tank. I was the sloth and Preeti was the saber-tooth cat who ate me.

Nirmala *stands where* **Preeti** *was. The* **Man** *stands where* **Aparna** *was.*

Julio   I was the bear and she was the wolf and we hunted together. I was an elephant and she was my baby.

Nirmala *leaves.* **Uma's Trace Desire** *stands where the* **Man** *was. Sees the audience.*

Julio   We were humans a few times. Then dogs. Then—

As **Julio** *stands at the mirror, it is whisked away.*

Julio *(facing* **Uma's Trace Desire***)*   Maybe I was once you.

Uma's Trace Desire   Who is Rizwan now? Who will I be next? When? I feel lighter but I am not yet free. How annoying! And why?

A collective intake of breath. Lights!

9.

Uma's Trace Desire   It's 1973. Or 2016. Or 2025. In this man's world, women always try to find solid ground in shifting sands.

Uma's Trace Desire *rings a bell.*

Nirmala   Preeti and Dilip are married.

Dilip *(played by the* **Man***) and* **Preeti** *garland each other.*

Uma's Trace Desire   Does he have a motorcycle?

Dilip *and* **Preeti** *get in a car. He drives. They hold hands.*

Nirmala   I am a mother. Worry is love and it is what we do.

Dilip *and* **Preeti** *get out of the car.* **Dilip** *exchanges his garland for a stethoscope. He's at work.*

Preeti *takes their garlands and puts them around a statue of Krishna. She's at home.*

Nirmala *turns to* **Preeti**, *now buried in books and papers.*

Nirmala   But why take a job with the county when he could go anywhere!

Dilip (*from work, patiently*)   I became a doctor to help people, Mom.

Preeti (*at home*)   And I love that about him.

Uma's Trace Desire   A good marriage, despite no motorcycle. Bully for astrology.

Nirmala   But it's so far east!

Dilip   Thirty miles—

Preeti   Mom, please, I have a deadline—

Nirmala   You might as well be in India!

Uma's Trace Desire   Fast forward!

Lights!

10.

Nirmala *holds* **Preeti** *who is doubled over in pain, holding her stomach.*

Preeti   Mom, it hurts—

Nirmala   Dilip's rushing back—we'll get you to the doctor—

Preeti   I can't go through this again—

Nirmala   Shh, just pray to God—

Preeti   Owwwww . . .

Nirmala   My poor girl, it's my fault—

Uma's Trace Desire   Not helpful.

Preeti   Mom, I'm afraid . . .

Nirmala   Preeti. You are strong. I am here.

Preeti   What if he doesn't love me anymore?

Nirmala   How can you say such things! Dilip loves you so much—

Preeti   But if I can't have children—

Nirmala   Shh! Preeti, don't talk this way—

Preeti *moans.*

Nirmala   Please, God, give me her pain!

Uma's Trace Desire   This is too hard. Fast forward.

11.

Nirmala *cooks.* **Preeti** *enters, tired, with her book bag.*

Nirmala Two hours it took me to get here.

Preeti Hey, Mom, thought you were coming Saturday . . .

Nirmala I wanted to make you and Dilip some *handvo* and *khamman*—

Preeti That's nice of you .

Nirmala And *dal dhokli* and I've frozen twenty-four *rotis* and *dal*—

Preeti Thanks. Smells good.

Uma's Trace Desire She's sad. Poor girl. Poor Mom.

Preeti I need to change.

Nirmala Preeti, are you okay?

Preeti Fine.

Nirmala You're too thin. Both of you.

Preeti Okay, Mom—

Nirmala He works hard—

Preeti We both work—I'm Professor Singh's research assistant—

Nirmala Ya, left a good job at the lab, for what? Another PhD? And in poetry!

Preeti Mom, you loved school—

Nirmala Forget about school! I am talking about having children! A woman does not really become a woman until she is a mother.

Preeti (*cold*) I hope you stay and eat with us. But we are not discussing kids, Mom.

Nirmala Preeti, please—

Preeti No. That's between Dilip and me.

Preeti *leaves.* **Nirmala** *slumps.*

Uma's Trace Desire *Chalo*, let's fast forward again!

Lights!

12.

Julio *and* **Preeti** *in mid-conversation.*

Julio Four years? How—?

Uma's Trace Desire Because we're hurtling on a rock through space!

Preeti   Four years of trying, Julio.

Julio   I know. Preeti . . .? What is it?

Preeti   No, I just. Can we. Can we talk about dumb things?

Julio   Yes! Do I look puffy? I tried cucumber, tea bags, ugh.

Uma's Trace Desire   His molecules are flitting about.

Preeti *really looks at her friend.*

Preeti   Have you been crying?

Julio   No—

Preeti   You miss him! Oh, Julio, I'm sorry—

Julio   No, I'm pathetic, I mean it's been six months—

Preeti   You guys were together for three years.

She takes his hand.

Julio   You know what? I just need to get back out there.

Preeti   You will when you're ready.

Julio (*chokes up*)   Will I ever be?! I want a Dilip damnit!

Preeti (*checks her cell phone*)   He's running behind on a procedure, sorry.

Julio (*looks for a server*)   I need another mimosa. Maybe that'll make me puffier though?

Preeti   I should wait for him but. Argh. Okay—we—we're thinking about adopting? And. I just really need your, I just—

Julio (*hearing her*)   Oh my gosh!

Uma's Trace Desire   I had a friend who adopted her niece after the mother died.

Preeti   We're more than thinking about it. Domestic. We thought India but we want to know the birth mother and be there when—

Julio   Oh my gosh!

Preeti   So, yeah I just need to tell my best friend because—

Julio *jumps up and hugs* **Preeti**.

Preeti   We need your help to create the album? For the birth mother—

Julio   OH MY GOD SO ON IT.

Preeti   We need good pictures, friends, family, our pictures are old—

Julio   Parties! Photos! Gatherings! Students! I got you.

Preeti   And the house—there's a social worker who visits and—

Julio First things first: I want to be her godfather.

Preeti We won't know if it's a girl or boy—we don't care—

Julio GODFATHER OF YOUR CHILD.

Preeti (*smiles*) Julio. Who else would we ask?

They hug again. Then—

Julio Wait. Have you told Nirmala?

Lights!

12.

Nirmala *sits with her friends, the* **Aunties** *(played by the* **Man, Julio,** **Aparna***).* **Uma's Trace Desire** *watches.*

Auntie 1 It's very noble. Very open-minded, truly.

Auntie 2 Truly. Kids today don't have our hang-ups.

Uma's Trace Desire These three stooges. Ugh.

Auntie 3 But there is something very special . . .

Auntie 1 True! The bond . . .

Auntie 2 My first—the labor was so hard—but you forget all the pain when you see their eyes—

Uma's Trace Desire You remember all the pain when they look at you like you betrayed them.

Auntie 3 And your own eyes reflected back—

Auntie 1 And you can't know the complications with adoption—

Auntie 2 And what if the woman changes her mind last minute?

Uma's Trace Desire What if, what if, what if tonight you go home and your heart explodes!

Auntie 3 And why not India at least? Get an Indian baby—

Uma's Trace Desire Nirmala came all the way to America to surround herself with the same type of Indian ladies she ran away from at home.

Nirmala They want to know the birth mother. To bond with the baby. They want the child to know the birth mother if the child chooses. They don't want any secrets. It's all very open.

Auntie 1 Very noble. But . . .

Uma's Trace Desire No buts. Secrets lead to swollen organs.

Auntie 2   Won't the child be confused meeting the mother?

Nirmala   Birth mother. Or first mother. Preeti says.

Auntie 3   It's expensive, no?

Auntie 1   But Dilip's a doctor, darling!

Auntie 2   Of course, I know that, darling!

Nirmala   So is Preeti.

Auntie 2   Of course, I know that, two PhDs, smart girl—

Auntie 3   Bio-chem and literature, so . . . *unusual*—

Auntie 1   Anyway money is not the issue - they can choose as they like—

Auntie 2   Too many choices leads to chaos—but I'm old fashioned!

The **Aunties** *laugh.*

Auntie 3   At least tell them they should try one more time—

Auntie 2   Don't give up!

Uma's Trace Desire   Phhft. Easy for you to say.

Nirmala *stands. The* **Aunties** *leave. Lights!*

13.

Nirmala *suddenly hugs* **Preeti**. **Preeti** *is startled.*

Nirmala   I'm so sorry. It's my fault.

Preeti   Mom, is this about the curse—

Nirmala (*knocking on wood, etc.*)   Shh! Don't say that!

Preeti   Mom? I will be a mother. Just not the way we thought.

Nirmala   I know. I know. I'm sorry. I love you so much, Preeti.

Everyone except **Aparna** *and* **Uma's Trace Desire** *retreat into shadow.*

A liminal space. **Aparna** *and* **Uma's Trace Desire** *inhabit it. Move within it and around each other.*

Uma's Trace Desire   Something's happening.

Aparna   I feel it, too.

Uma's Trace Desire   Am I going to be—

Aparna   Me?

Aparna *starts to fall, is caught/carried by the cast. Spun around. Set gently down.*

Uma's Trace Desire (*bummed*) Nope. Still here.

A wee cry. A baby is born.

The cast stands in a circle. **Preeti** *holds a tiny bundle. She passes it to* **Julio**.

Julio Their birth mother had an emergency C-section and she was born three weeks early and Preeti was stuck in traffic—

Nirmala Stupid traffic!

Julio Dilip was already at the hospital so he was in the O.R. with their birthmother. Oooh, look at her nose! Her toes!

Julio *passes the baby to the* **Man** *(***Dilip***)*.

Dilip Hello, little love. Welcome. I'm your daddy.

Dilip *passes the baby to* **Preeti**.

Preeti Mom? Meet your granddaughter . . .

(*Gives* **Nirmala** *her baby.*) Una.

Uma's Trace Desire Eh?

Nirmala But it sounds just like Uma.

Preeti She smiled at you!

Nirmala No. That's just gas.

Uma's Trace Desire Tiny little molecules, very bunchy and warm.

Nirmala But why not Aparna?

Preeti She's not Indian.

Nirmala But you are!

Preeti "Una" means "remember your journey." We like it.

Nirmala *examines the baby.*

Uma's Trace Desire Remember your journey. I can't forget mine.

Preeti You can pick her middle name.

Nirmala Her middle name should be her father's name.

Preeti Would you mind if I lie down? Dilip will be home soon.

Preeti *exits.* **Nirmala** *talks to* **Una**.

Nirmala Pffht! No *Jatakarma*[2] to properly welcome you, with God's name whispered in your ear. No naming ceremony.

---

2 Hindu sacrament (*samskaras*) that celebrates the birth of a child.

Uma's Trace Desire   No fuss!

Nirmala *sings an Indian lullaby. Stops. Sings an American lullaby.*

Nirmala   I will tell you stories about Ganesha and Krishna. Teach you our values like I did with your mom. Your mom is still my baby! She's a good girl and you must be like her, okay? And Dilip. Your dad. A good man. We are your family. Una.

Lights!

14.

Uma's Trace Desire   Let's keep this brief.

Preeti *sits by* **Dilip**'s *covered body.* **Nirmala**, *elsewhere, prays.*

Nirmala   We are cursed! This is payment for our past karma!

Dilip (*lifts head up*)   I was operating on one of my favorite patients, a sixty-year-old woman with a wonderful laugh wonderful family very diligent a model patient when I had a massive heart attack. My patient was fine. I only got eight years of being a dad. I love that goofy kid. Preeti got the news while Una was at school.

Offstage, a guttural wail.

Uma's Trace Desire   Okay, that's enough. Fast forward.

Lights!

15.

A bed. **Preeti** *with* **Una**, *age nine.*

Preeti   Can't sleep?

Preeti *holds her.*

Una   Is your heart going to get sick?

Uma's Trace Desire   I hope she doesn't burst, too.

Una (*hearing something*)   What?

Uma's Trace Desire (*startled*)   Can you hear me?

Preeti (*to* **Una** *about her heart*)   My heart is fine, honey.

Una   How do you know?

Preeti   I exercise and eat well and see the doctor regularly and she says my heart is strong.

Uma's Trace Desire   Strong is good but open is better.

Una   Daddy was strong and he's gone.

Preeti   Mommy's not going anywhere. In fact, I'm going to glue myself to you—

Una (*small smile*)   Mooomm—

Preeti   Because you're my favorite nine-year-old—

Una   I'm your only nine-year-old—

Preeti   I'll be going to school with you and later on dates—

Una   Ew!

Preeti   We'll have to use the bathroom and shower together—

Una   Ha!

Preeti   We'll need a bigger toilet with two seats side by—

Una   Mommy is loopy-de-loo -

Preeti   About you!

Preeti *smothers her in kisses.*

Una   Mom?

Preeti   Yes?

Una   You can't get stuck.

Uma's Trace Desire *reacts.*

Preeti   What do you mean?

Una   Maybe that we can't stay only sad? Even though we are.

Preeti (*awed by* **Una**)   I love you so much.

Lights!

16.

Preeti, *alone, cries. Her cell phone rings. And dings.* **Preeti** *keeps crying while—*

Lights up on **Julio***.*

Julio   Preeti I had the best date! Let me take you out and bore you to death with all the details. Una's eleven, order pizza and tell her to put on a movie. She'll be thrilled to have you out of her hair! I'm her godfather, she tells me things.

Lights on **Nirmala***.*

Nirmala   Preeti, I'm leaving now, so I should be there in three days. That was a joke. Are you eating? I am bringing *kichdi* and *puris* and *shirkand* for Una, she's twelve but still loves the same food she loved as a little girl!

Lights on the **Man** *as* **Random Dude**.

Random Dude Uh—I think I have the wrong number. Is this "My Huppah Your Huppah Party Rentals"? If so, please call me back.

Preeti *cries.*

Uma's Trace Desire *rings a bell. Lights!*

Act II

1.

As at the top, **Preeti**. *In front of a mirror. In a plain white sari.*

Preeti (*to herself*)   I was married. Once. It is Spring. Again.

Uma's Trace Desire   The fifth Spring since Dilip's molecules scattered.

Preeti *takes off the plain sari. She is in a bright top and jeans. She sits to grade papers.*

Nirmala *enters with a bouquet of flowers. A card sticks out. She also has a box of Indian sweets.*

Nirmala   Happy birthday!

Nirmala *puts her stuff down and quickly snaps a photo of* **Preeti**. **Preeti** *reacts.*

Uma's Trace Desire   Oooh, parties!

Preeti   It's not my birthday yet and why are you taking my picture?

Nirmala (*opens box*)   Two days. *Prasad* from the temple—eat.

Preeti   I will later—Mom—mehffaghldge—

Nirmala *puts a piece of cashew mithai in* **Preeti**'*s mouth.*

Nirmala (*exits to kitchen*)   Just wait.

Preeti (*chewing*)   Mom—

Nirmala *brings out a glass of milk.*

Nirmala   Your birthday falls on Holi this year. I went to a special *pooja* and paid the priest to recite a special prayer for you.

Preeti   Hope it was about getting this grading done.

Nirmala   Very funny, but I'm serious—

Preeti   It's Holi and I've spent a month planning the color fight, a dinner, a Bollywood double-feature, which has nothing to do with—

Uma's Trace Desire   Let us take a dip in colors of love on the occasion of Holi!

Nirmala   Forget all that—I'm talking about your fortieth birthday! It's a very auspicious week. A sign of good things!

Preeti   Everyone has spring fever. Even you.

Uma's Trace Desire   Holi is very HOLY because it is the time to wash off all the hard feelings from your life, ha ha ha.

Nirmala Easter is also on Holi this year.

Preeti (*surprised*) How did you know that?

Uma's Trace Desire Jesus would have loved Holi.

Nirmala I saw Julio at Trader Joe's buying things for your student parties—I hope the college is paying—

Preeti Beer pong and electro-fusion blasting all night—can't wait till they all go away for a week—

Nirmala Drink your milk. (**Preeti** *does.*) What will you do for the rest of your life—beside work?

Uma's Trace Desire There were no other choices for widows when I became one.

Preeti (*wipes her mouth*) Be Una's mom. Like you were mine—

Nirmala I came from India—how could I marry some American! And your grandmother was old when my father died—

Preeti Grandma was only fifty—

Uma's Trace Desire Ya!

Nirmala —which you will be in ten years, and then what?

Preeti I like being on my own.

Nirmala What nonsense. You need companionship.

Uma's Trace Desire Rizwan was a man, but the last thing on my mind was help.

Preeti Phhft! Not this again, Mom—

Nirmala It's been too long—you don't go out, never have fun—

Preeti Una and I have fun, I'm fine—

Nirmala Una is a child and I know you're fine, but you must remarry.

Preeti Why?

Nirmala Why not? In America there are no rules about anything!

Uma's Trace Desire No rules!

Preeti When Dad died, you were my north star. That's what I want to be for Una -

Nirmala But what about you—what about love—

Preeti Una and my work—and you—are all I need—

Nirmala What about when you're eighty and I'm dead?

Preeti Una's about to start high school—

Nirmala And tomorrow she will be in college and you'll be alone!

Preeti (*gathers her work*) I'm going to my office—

Nirmala Wait! Little early but open your card.

Nirmala *hands it to* **Preeti**.

Uma's Trace Desire Presents!

Preeti *opens the card, and a folded sheet of paper falls out. Reacts, annoyed,* **Nirmala** *rushes on*—

Nirmala Just look at him—

Preeti Mom.

Nirmala His bio-data is there, picture—photocopy, but— (*Retrieves her cell.*) His mother sent me these also—

Nirmala *tries to show* **Preeti** *pictures.* **Preeti** *grabs her bag.*

Uma's Trace Desire Little chubby, nice face.

Preeti *tries to get out the door.*

Nirmala Divorced. Two boys in college, one studying computer science—

Preeti (*re grading*) I have to finish—

Nirmala Like Dilip, he is a doctor, but your age—

Uma's Trace Desire She was right about Dilip, after all.

Nirmala I was right about Dilip, after all! You have to trust me—I know what's best!

Preeti No, thanks—

Nirmala It's not my fault Dilip died!

Preeti (*stops*) Mom! I know that.

Nirmala Just have coffee. Be friends. I spoke to him and—

Preeti You talked to him?!

Nirmala You know, he touched my feet when we met?

Preeti You *met* with him?!

Uma's Trace Desire Uh-oh.

Nirmala His parents are members of the temple, he has a beach house very near me—only son, he will inherit all—

Preeti You are impossible!

Nirmala Just see his kids' photos—Una can have big brothers—

Preeti No, no, no!

Nirmala   You're cranky because you're not getting any—

Uma's Trace Desire   *Hare Ram.*

Preeti   MOM.

Preeti *slams the front door.*

Nirmala   Affection! So stubborn! You'll be a cranky old maid!

Uma's Trace Desire *rings a bell. Lights!*

2.

Preeti *and* **Una** *have pie.*

Una   Giselle says you're a young mom.

Preeti (*grabbing a piece*)   Can I have a bite?

Una   Giselle thinks it's sad you don't have a man in your life.

Preeti *tucks hair behind* **Una**'s *ear.*

Uma's Trace Desire   I remember how it felt when Rizwan touched my hair.

Una   Me, too.

Uma's Trace Desire (*startled*)   What?

Preeti   You think so, too?

Una   Huh?

Preeti   Anyway, are you excited about Holi? My freshmen seminar can't wait to meet you—

Una   Were you a virgin when you married Dad?

Preeti *chokes on pie.*

Uma's Trace Desire   It's expected. Assumed. Demanded.

Preeti   What's with all the—has Nani been talking to you?

Una   Like, you say I can ask you anything and when I do you—

Preeti (*breathes, then*)   No, I'm sorry—let's start over. Yes I was—a virgin and honestly? I have no desire to get married again—

Una   Uh, okay, but I was just talking about sex.

Uma's Trace Desire *giggles.*

Preeti   Why are you talking about sex?!

Una   Why, is that WRONG?

Preeti Una, listen to me—

Una I'm fourteen!

Preeti I'm not lecturing, okay, but sex is, it's—

Una Special.

Preeti Yes, and when you have sex it means, it means that—

Una You love someone.

Preeti Yes—look, I'm just saying. All I mean is. Don't have sex.

Una What, like EVER?

Preeti Very funny. But please. Just say no. NO SEX. NO SEX. Books before boys. Until you graduate—from grad school.

Uma's Trace Desire Some things never change.

Una Forget it.

Preeti Sexting, too—you know what that is, right—

Una MOM.

Preeti It's hard—so much freedom, technology, and you're my one and only—

Una Ugh—

Preeti I'm not pressuring you and I want you to know yourself—

Uma's Trace Desire Ha, look who's talking!

Una (*agreeing*) Seriously.

Uma's Trace Desire *looks at* **Una**—*are they talking to each other?*

Preeti Sex is a way of showing love. With someone you trust. Who loves you. Who has your best interest at heart. Who will never hurt you. The right someone. The right someone who I get to know very well first. Whose family I get to know.

Una Like Dad?

Preeti Exactly.

They eat pie.

Una But how do you know who the right person is if you've never even been in love before?

Uma's Trace Desire *rings the bell. Lights!*

3.

Preeti *and* **Julio** *mix colored powder with water and fill up balloons.*

Preeti I'm not ready for—

Uma's Trace Desire Holi!

Julio Your daughter to be a sexual creature?

Preeti (*stops her ears*) Ahhhhh!

Julio You can't react that way—she'll never talk to you again—

Preeti Thanks, Julio, really helpful—

Julio Una's fine—

Uma's Trace Desire A strange but interesting girl—

Preeti There's something in the air.

Julio Can Nirmala set *me* up with a hot Indian man?

Preeti More powder.

Julio *lobs over a bottle and exits.*

Preeti (*planning mode*)—After the color fight—

Julio (*offstage*) It should be called a color PARADE or rainbow STORM—

Uma's Trace Desire Molecule-explosion!

Preeti (*checks a list*) The dance, dinner, the double-feature. The Indian Student Association is going to move the chairs after dinner—

Julio *enters, with a bottle of bubbly and glasses.*

Julio Drink. Happy birthday, pretty-Preeti. I love you.

Preeti I love you more.

Julio I am going to make sure you get plastered—with color!

Uma's Trace Desire Wonderful.

Julio Isn't it the more color, the more likely you are to fall in love?

Preeti That's henna for a wedding—the more henna you have the more your husband will fall in love with you.

Uma's Trace Desire No, he has to find your name hidden in the henna on your wedding night or no fun in the bed!

Julio I want a big Indian wedding someday. Here.

Julio *hands her an envelope.*

Preeti Ohhh! Thanks, Julio . . . (*Opens it.*) What is—a plane ticket?!

Julio (*excited*) And . . .

Preeti (*she brings out small card*) Oh!

Julio Before you say it's too much—I'm a single, child-less, tenured professor who inherited his house. And you only turn forty once.

Preeti Thank you so much—I—I mean, I—but Una—

Julio Is fourteen—

Preeti I can't just traipse off to New York—

Julio It's work-related! You'll see the exhibit on medieval Indian art you've been talking about plus . . .

(*Indicating the small card.*) You're staying at the most adorable boutique hotel. It's a new decade! It's Holi! And, girl, Christ has risen! Can't you feel it?

Uma's Trace Desire I can.

Preeti Holi is not about going crazy.

Julio A little cray is okay!

Uma's Trace Desire If I could go back I would not have run away.

Preeti Holi is about—

Uma's Trace Desire Maybe if I had broken the rules, I wouldn't be here now . . .

Julio New beginnings.

Uma's Trace Desire And she would listen to Julio . . .

Preeti It's about the triumph of good over evil—

Julio Sex!

Preeti Duty. Devotion.

Julio Here. (**Preeti**'s *about to object.*) Last one. Promise. (*Can't remember.*) I think.

Preeti Julio, this is too much—

Julio Open it before Una gets home.

Preeti (*opens gift*) Oh my—what is . . .? Really, Julio?

Preeti *holds up a rather incredible-looking vibrator.*

Uma's Trace Desire New phone?

Julio It was not cheap—

Julio *reads the instructions.*

Preeti (*puts it down*) I hope you kept the receipt.

Uma's Trace Desire Maybe for cooking.

Julio (*reading*) You have to try it! It's flexible, ergonomic—

He turns it on.

At the store she said *toe-curling orgasms*—hold it—

Preeti No!

Julio PREETI, HOLD YOUR NEW VIBRATOR—

Preeti No, thanks.

Julio *looks at her with the buzzing vibrator.*

Julio Preeti, you masturbate, right?

Uma's Trace Desire Oh. Not for cooking.

Preeti Yes.

Uma's Trace Desire At least not food.

Giggles.

Preeti Doesn't everyone?

Julio Preeti, don't lie to Julio.

Preeti (*defensive*) What?

Julio Can I ask you something?

Preeti Could I ever stop you?!

Julio Did you and Dilip, you know—do it regularly?

Uma's Trace Desire (*simultaneous with* **Preeti**, *below*) How often is regularly?

Preeti How often is regularly?

Julio Okay. Honey. I'm just saying—if you stop doing it, you stop wanting to do it—

Preeti Oh yeah, well, same to you!

Uma's Trace Desire Ouch.

Julio What are we, twelve?

Preeti Julio, look—uh—thanks for this, but I just want to—

Julio Live like a nun for the rest of your life?

Preeti Yes. No! But—I love my daughter and my work—

Julio No, no. Shh!

Julio *puts the vibrator in* **Preeti***'s hand. He flips it on again.*

Una (*offstage*) Oh my God we ran like ten miles *in the sun*!

Preeti Oh crap, crap—

Preeti *tries to turn it off.*

Preeti Hide it! Hide it—

Una *enters.* **Preeti** *panics, tossing the vibrating vibrator behind her.*

Preeti Sweetheart!

Julio *catches it in the gift box.*

Una Oh, hey Julio—

Julio (*closing box*) It's "God-papa"!

Una Uh I stopped calling you that when I was seven.

It's still vibrating.

Una What's that?

Preeti Oh, uh, Julio got me a, uh—

Julio *extravagantly embraces* **Una**.

Preeti *opens the box, turns it off.*

Julio (*still hugging*) Have you gotten taller?

Una Since this morning?

Preeti *tucks the gift box out of sight. Maybe sits on it.*

Julio You need a shower, goddaughter.

Una Later—PB&J's, anyone?

Preeti Now?

Julio Yes, please.

Una We need energy for the color fight—

Una *exits.* **Preeti** *looks at him.*

Julio (*so proud*) Look at her, all grown-up, making us food. (*Then.*) Get a life, Preeti.

Preeti My life is perfect just the way it is.

Julio Happy birthday, Preeti. I hope you find yourself.

Preeti I haven't lost myself and I'm perfectly content—life is quiet, secure, and Una's happy. What more could I want?

Uma's Trace Desire *rings the bell. Lights!*

4.

Holi. Everyone throwing "colors"—lights will do the trick. Chasing. Ducking. A Bollywood dance. Joy.

Uma's Trace Desire *dances among everyone, in her own world.*

Thunder! Rain! Everyone scatters.

Uma's Trace Desire   It's a sign!

Uma's Trace Desire *snaps her fingers.*

Uma's Trace Desire   To the next life!

Nothing happens.

Uma's Trace Desire   Bollocks.

The rain stops! The sun shines.

Preeti *and* **Uma's Trace Desire** *turn . . .*

. . . to see: **the Most Handsome Man**. *On his back.*

On a bench.

His arm hanging, fingers stroking the ground, daydreaming.

Preeti *is riveted. So is* **Uma's Trace Desire**.

Preeti (*mouth hangs open*)   Uh.

Uma's Trace Desire   Rizwan?

Most Handsome Man (*did he hear someone?*)   Huh?

Uma's Trace Desire (*to* **Preeti**)   Don't—

Preeti (*jumps*)   Oh crap—

Preeti *runs. The* **Most Handsome Man** *looks to where* **Preeti** *just was.*

Uma's Trace Desire   Run.

Most Handsome Man (*wondering who was there*)   Hm.

Lights!

5.

Julio   Why didn't you talk to him?

Preeti   Do you think I had a stroke?

Julio   Yes.

Preeti   It's that special *pooja*—that priest cast a spell on me!

Julio   Maybe you saw an Indian Spring god—is there one?

Uma's Trace Desire   Saraswati gets a festival each spring.

Preeti (*swooning*)   His shirt was pushed up . . . I could see his stomach . . .

Julio   Who just lies in the rain and doesn't even get wet?

Uma's Trace Desire   Handsome men.

Preeti (*woozy*)   His profile. His chin. He looked like . . . a poet.

Julio   Maybe you have a fever.

She smacks his hand on her head.

Preeti   Do I?

Julio   Hot flash?

Preeti (*affronted*)   How dare you.

Julio   Have some tea and you'll be your dear, old, single, I'm not using a vibrator, self again—

Preeti   Julio, can't you see I'm dying?!

Julio   Okay, let's pretend that this dashing hallucination born of your ascetic lifestyle is actual flesh and blood—

Preeti   Pinch me. (*He does.*) Ow.

Julio (*an idea*)   I know!

Preeti   What?

Julio   Forget about him.

Preeti   We have to find out who he is!

Uma's Trace Desire   And where he is!

Julio   Oh, now it's "we."

Preeti (*horrified*)   What if he's a student?!

Julio   Ooh, he's *young*? You didn't mention *that*—

Preeti   I'm frantic! Help me! What do I do?

Julio   Use my birthday gift. It'll help you think.

Preeti   Julio, be serious.

Julio   Darling, I am.

Preeti   My skin is tingling. I'm dizzy. And a little nauseous—

Julio   Sit.

Uma's Trace Desire   Float.

Preeti   Why is everything so bright?

Uma's Trace Desire   Loneliness is a curtain.

Preeti   I'm here but I'm not here . . .

Julio (*wistful*)   I know that feeling . . .

Uma's Trace Desire   I *am* that feeling.

Preeti I can't get his face out of my mind, images of him and me—it's like I'm floating or scattering into a void—

Uma's Trace Desire Molecules! A dark movie theater. A walk by the sea.

Julio (*teasing*) You're fine. You're good and focused.

Preeti I'm molecules!

Julio You're Preeti. Mother of Una.

Preeti Who?

Julio Scholar of Indian medieval poetry.

Preeti What?

Julio Daughter of Nirmala, wife of the late Dilip Shah—

Preeti (*electrified*) OH MY GOD THERE HE IS.

Julio (*a ghost?!*) DILIP?!

The **Most Handsome Man** *walks with air pods on, book bag slung.*

Preeti It's a sign! Go talk to him. Find out his name!

Julio *runs over to the* **Most Handsome Man**.

Julio Hi, uh, excuse me—I, uh—

The **Most Handsome Man** *turns.* **Julio** *is struck dumb. The* **Most Handsome Man** *is used to this. He smiles.*

Most Handsome Man Hey.

Julio Hi.

Uma's Trace Desire Fast forward.

Uma's Trace Desire *rings the bell. Lights!*

6.

Julio *runs back to* **Preeti**.

Julio You're in love with an actor! (*A gleeful cackle.*) Hahahahaha!

Uma's Trace Desire (*claps*) A movie star?

Preeti What are you talking about—

Julio *puts his phone in her face.*

Julio It's Dr. Jones. *Jaques Jones?*

Uma's Trace Desire Ooh la la, a doctor?

Preeti Is he French?

Julio Oh my God! He's the hot new star of *Officer Doctor Jones*! He plays *Dr. Jaques Jones*? Only son of a firefighter and biologist? Oh my God, okay, they love him but worry—he works too hard—he's a cop who moonlights as an ER doctor, plays the flute, he's haunted by the little kid he couldn't save when he was a resident, and he's hunting the nasty drug dealer who shot his best friend.

Preeti (*clueless*) Uhmm—

Uma's Trace Desire Sounds good.

Julio (*scolding*) Stop only watching anime and Norwegian stuff!

Preeti Are they filming on campus?

Julio He's on hiatus! Guest teaching! Okay, now he didn't *say* this but I think he's here because he and Bianca McKenna broke up but she's kinda been stalking him on the socials? And IRL, too. He needed to shake things up, get away from LA—

Preeti But we're only thirty miles away.

Julio Traffic. You *do* know who Bianca McKenna is?

Preeti (*no*) Uhmm—

Julio Only the hottest hip-hop-country-soul singer Scotland ever produced! She had a recurring on *Jaques Jones* and they fell in love! Then she died—

Preeti What?!

Julio On the *show*. Anyway, he's single! And hon, he *is* young—

Preeti Don't tell me—

Julio *shriek-laughs, delighted.*

Preeti (*head in hands*) It's hopeless.

Julio You're right, give up.

Preeti (*grabbing him*) How would we even meet? Where? How? Why would he even want to?

Julio Stop thinking, keep plotting! You need an Instagram account—

Preeti Huh?

Julio You'll follow him . . . we'll see what he's into . . .

Uma's Trace Desire (*to someone in the audience*) What's he talking about?

Julio Then we get his attention.

Preeti Isn't that—stalking?

Julio IT'S SOCIAL MEDIA.

Uma's Trace Desire Like a Bombay ladies' tea party.

Julio   He has to notice YOU.

Uma's Trace Desire   Like at a cousin's wedding—

Preeti   Julio, I could kiss you.

Julio   I could kiss him.

Preeti   GOD that man has pierced me through with desire, like Radha for Krishna, Rosalind for Orlando, Shakuntala for Dushyanta, feel my hands! I'm trembling for this—for . . . Jaques!

Julio   Oh and his real name's Remo Stone.

Beat.

Uma's Trace Desire   Remo Stone . . .?

Preeti   I like Jaques better.

Lights!

7.

Una *plops down next to her mom.* **Preeti**, *eyes glazed, scrolls through her new Instagram account, a first-time addict.*

Una   Isn't Nani here yet?

Preeti   I don't understand hashtags . . .

Una   You're on Instagram?

Una *taps on her cell.* **Uma's Trace Desire** *watches, with interest.*

Una   Mom your *book cover* is your profile pic? So lame.

Preeti   Huh?

Una   And you need a bio—it looks so rando.

Uma's Trace Desire   Bio-data. Like putting an ad in the paper.

Nirmala (*offstage*)   Bloody traffic!

Una (*to* **Preeti**)   You rejected my follow request?!

Nirmala   Hello! Food! Una, have a snack before we take off—

Una   Hi Nani!

Una's *cell phone pings.*

Mom, you rejected Giselle's request!

Offstage, a microwave beeps.

Preeti   You kids don't follow me. Adults only.

Una   Rude.

Nirmala (*enters*)   Hurry! Everything's getting cold. Hi, Preeti, eat something.

Preeti   Mmmhmmm . . .

Una *gets up and hugs* **Nirmala**.

Una   Smells good, Nani!

Uma's Trace Desire (*about herself*)   Tummy's growling.

Nirmala (*about* **Una**)   Too thin! Why you make her swim every night, I don't understand—

Uma's Trace Desire   Do I still have a tummy?

Preeti   She's on the swim team, Mom.

Una   Mom's on Instagram? But she won't let me follow her!

Nirmala (*excited*)   Is she?

Uma's Trace Desire   Or just the memory of a tummy?

Ping! **Una** *looks at her cell.*

Una   Oooh, but you want to follow me?

Preeti (*focusing*)   ACCEPT.

Una *does, annoyed.* **Preeti** *goes back to scrolling.*

Uma's Trace Desire   Phantom tummy.

Nirmala   Why don't you join us, Preeti, get some new clothes—

Preeti   I'm busy.

Una   You're just staring at Instagram. Like you say I shouldn't.

Preeti (*staring at her phone*)   Mmhmm.

Una   Ugh!

Una *exits to the kitchen.*

Nirmala (*hands* **Preeti** *a photo*)   Here. Look. He's a widow. Only fifty years old and—

Una (*offstage*)   Aloo Parathas!

Preeti   Mmmhmmm.

She lets the photo fall. **Una** *re-enters, parathas in hand, puts half of one in* **Preeti***'s mouth and eats the other one.* **Preeti** *starts to get annoyed at all the interruptions.*

Nirmala   His wife passed away three years ago.

Una (*picks up photo*)   Aw, he has a dog!

Nirmala (*grabs photo*)   Ay! Your hands have *ghee* on them.

Uma's Trace Desire   Mmm, *ghee* . . .

Nirmala   He has two PhDs, like you! One in engineering and—

Preeti (*mouth full*)   Unbelievable.

Nirmala (*pleased*)   Like it? I put extra chili—

Preeti   No. YOU are. But yes, I like the *paratha*. Thanks.

Una   Mom, you could just like meet the dude.

Preeti   *Et tu*, Una?

Nirmala (*to* **Una**)   Your mom would cook Indian food more with a husband around!

Uma's Trace Desire   Hard to go through all that trouble for just two.

Preeti   If you want to beat traffic coming home, you guys should go—

Nirmala   Didn't want to meet anyone, but when I showed your picture—

Preeti   Stop showing my picture to everyone—

Nirmala (*on her cell phone*)   Who's everyone? Just the divorcee and now the widow—

Una   Well—

Nirmala   Shhh. (*To* **Preeti**, *smiles.*) What's your Instagram handle?

Preeti (*surprised*)   You're on Instagram?

Found you.

Nirmala (*ping!*)

Preeti (*scrolling* **Nirmala**'s *feed*)   You post pictures of me?

Nirmala   Why not? You're my daughter—

Preeti (*to* **Una**)   Did you know about this?

Una   Nani and I follow each other.

Preeti (*scrolling*)   Mom, I was doing laundry—

Nirmala   You look nice with your hair up—

Preeti   #beautifulkindeffecient . . . #doublephdbeauty. Awww. Me and Una at Universal—#bestmotherbestfriends. This was two days ago, I was cooking—

Nirmala   That top brings out your color. Plus you cook so rarely—

Preeti   #bringshomebaconandcooksit . . . #mostlyveg—oh my God—

Una   Nani knows how to hashtag—

Preeti (*exits to bedroom*)   You are *not* allowed to post any more pictures of me.

Nirmala   Did you reject my request?!

Una   Let's just go, Nani.

They gather their stuff and begin to exit out the door.

Uma's Trace Desire Her molecules are all over the place.

Nirmala She just needs to get married. Have a man in her life—

Una She won't even talk about sex—

Nirmala *You* don't talk about sex!

Una Here we go.

And they're out. Lights!

8.

Preeti *and* **Julio** *with her cell.* **Uma's Trace Desire** *dances, alone.*

Uma's Trace Desire If I keep dancing, perhaps I'll scatter completely . . .

Julio "Badass poetry scholar. Indian Goddess."

Uma's Trace Desire Move, like the wind . . . go with the wind . . .

Julio "Graphic novelist."

Preeti It's not published yet.

Julio So? Just write it—you need followers—old students—

Ping! Ping! Ping!

Julio Look—they're finding you already—

Preeti (*not cool*) Oh no, these are my current students—

Julio Your profile pic—how about this one?

Preeti (*unsure*) Mmmmm—

Julio This one?

Preeti (*anxiety*) My hair looks weird—

Julio (*takes her in*) Wait. Oh. Yes.

Uma's Trace Desire *is dancing behind* **Preeti**. **Julio** *takes a photo.*

Julio There's a glow around you. This is the one.

Preeti Oh, fine—if you like it.

Julio *creates* **Preeti***'s profile.* **Preeti***'s cell keeps pinging.*

Julio Ooh. Ooooh. (*Then*). Who's this guy?

Preeti Mom's eldest cousin in England—

Julio Reject. Switching to private. NO FAMILY. I'll block Nirmala.

Preeti I don't know about any of this—

Julio And here is our guy!

They and **Uma's Trace Desire** *look.*

Preeti (*views posts, lusting*) God.

Julio Wow.

Uma's Trace Desire Muscular.

Preeti /Uma's Trace Desire/Julio (*sigh*) . . . .

Julio Now he needs to follow you back. We'll DM at the appropriate time . . . for a specific reason . . .

(*Shrieks.*) Your publisher just requested to follow you! Accept!

Lights!

9.

On his bench. Sexily lying down as he was when we met him.

Remo Life's weird. Oh, Bianca, you pain in the ass. What did we think we were doing? We swore we wouldn't be tabloid fodder. Yet, here we are. I thought going away would help. I guess thirty miles isn't that far. With traffic though, it can take days. And I can't go to—Iceland! I have the commercial to shoot, the *Late Show* interview, acting class, next season's scripts are coming in, and my publicist says I should focus on dating a normal person. No more actors or singers or directors. But like—an engineer? Or. There's an actual professor following me. Professors make the same as fry cooks or something, right? This prof-lady makes cool comments on my posts about mental health—I am super pro-mental health. I followed her—she's super popular on campus. She posted a pic of this sexy Indian dancer and a poem about how dancing for God is a metaphor for desire. I always dreamed of being an actor. Of being a lead in a series that says something about the human condition. I'm living my dream! People notice me. They say I make them cry. And turn them on. I'm scared of people. But I want them to notice me. That turns *me* on. Sometimes I think I was a better carpenter than I am an actor. At least I always have that to fall back on. (*Sits up.*) I can fix shit! That is hot! Bianca, I bought you clothes and candles and your Bichon. I am over your drama! (*Gets a notification.*)

The prof DM'd me! My publicist says the public has to see me as a smokin' everyman who can do normal things like go to the grocery with my normal girlfriend who does a normal job. Are professors normal? How would I find someone in marketing or dentistry? (*Gets a notification.*) "Do I like poetry?" She's adorable. (*Another notification.*) Whoa. That's a hot poem. She write that? (*Scrolling.*) She wrote a graphic novel. Maybe it'll be adapted for television. I should let my agent know.

(*Typing on his cell phone.*) I mean, having a thing with a sexy prof is kinda . . . sexy. But what if she's not hot? Her picture is cute. Understated.

Definitely older than me but I'm down with that. But what if she has dry hands? And smells like books? And wears cardigans? (*He shudders.*)

Lights!

10.

Preeti *shows up at* **Remo***'s door.*

Remo Oh—hi?

Uma's Trace Desire What are we doing?

Preeti I've liked all your posts on Instagram and you liked a poem I posted and then I posted about the talk I'm giving, "Kisses and Sidelong Glances: Desire and the Medieval Indian Woman," and you liked that, then I DM'd you a link to my book, and you responded with a heart. And you followed me.

Remo Uh. How'd you know where I live?

Uma's Trace Desire If she doesn't run, I'm free.

Preeti It's a small town. You're a big star. Julio told me. You both talked? I'm Preeti Shah.

Remo Remo Stone.

They shake hands and . . . keep shaking hands for a few beats.

Uma's Trace Desire Don't run.

Preeti Can I call you Jaques?

Remo That would be weird.

Preeti Yeah, I guess—like if you called me professor. Because I'm not your professor.

Remo (*bummed*) So I can't call you professor?

Preeti Definitely not.

Uma's Trace Desire So far, so good.

Remo (*smiling at* **Preeti**) So . . . this is not like you, I gather? Just showing up at a dude's place?

Preeti How did you know?

Remo I study human nature for a living.

Preeti Why are you in faculty housing? Don't you live in Hollywood?

Remo Yeah but with traffic.

Preeti It wasn't me.

Remo   What?

Preeti   My friend Julio—who you met—kinda runs my Instagram account?

Remo   Oh—my agent's assistant, Skylar, mostly runs mine.

Preeti   So *she* liked my poem?

Remo   Well—see, she texts me when I should look at something in particular? And she thought I'd like it—and I did. So it was me who actually *liked* it.

Preeti   I'm so glad.

Remo   I write a little poetry.

Preeti   I mostly translate. That one was my translation of Kalidasa.

Remo (*hopeful*)   My poetry is kinda lame.

Preeti   . . . I could read some if you want?

Remo   Really?

Preeti   I mean I'm a professor of medieval poetry and literature of ancient India but sure.

Remo   Pioneer Boulevard.

Preeti   What?

Remo   Cerritos.

Preeti   Artesia?

Uma's Trace Desire   Modern-day courtship is strange, no?

Remo   We used to go there for Indian food. Me and my . . . ex.

Preeti   Bianca McKenna!

Remo (*dismay*)   Are you a fan?

Preeti (*honest*)   I don't really know who she is.

Remo   You wanna come in?

Uma's Trace Desire   Ah-ha!

Uma's Trace Desire *snaps her fingers. Closes her eyes. Then opens them: still here.*

Uma's Trace Desire   Okay, fine. Fast forward!

Lights!

11.

Preeti *and* **Remo** *sit on a bench.*

Preeti This is where I first saw you.

Remo Everything about you is mysterious and there's no mystery in the world anymore, you know what I mean.

Preeti (*running hands along the bench, distracted*) Deeply.

Remo (*earnest*) I feel like I'm on the edge of a precipice and this is the first time I can see. My dad is a painter.

Preeti That's perfect.

Remo Give me your hand. (**Preeti** *does.*) You have the hand of a pianist. I'm a flautist.

Preeti How remarkable.

Remo I'm not really a flautist but I play one on the show. I had to tell you the truth. What is wrong with me?!

Preeti This is the first time a man who wasn't my husband has held my hand the way you're holding my hand.

Remo How am I holding your hand?

Preeti Like you want to rip my clothes off.

Remo I'm sorry—but I'm not sorry if you—

Preeti (*jumps up*) Oh—crap! Hide!

Uma's Trace Desire Uh-oh.

Preeti *is crawling behind the bench.* **Remo** *follows. Someone strolls by.*

Remo What's going on?

Preeti Did she see us?

Remo Oooh. I get it. Ex-girlfriend? You're bi, right?

Preeti Ew—not the bi part—no, that's our department chair. She's awful—

Remo I hate her!

Preeti *pulls him down.*

Preeti Okay. We need to set some rules. We can only meet at night. At your place. Or we can drive to the Inland Empire. Like deep into it where no one knows me.

Remo How deep? Riverside? You don't mean Redlands—

Preeti Remo, you're here for a minute. I live here. It's home. This stays between us. And Julio. But you can't tell anyone.

Remo That's not fair!

Uma's Trace Desire It really isn't.

Preeti I know.

Remo I accept your terms.

Preeti Oh God my students!

They crawl further away, behind some bushes.

Remo I want to know everything about you. I want to come to your house! Meet your kid! I want to see your office!

Preeti Absolutely not, Remo.

Remo Say my name again.

Uma's Trace Desire Oh boy. Fast forward!

Lights!

12.

Remo's *bedroom. Lit by candles.* **Preeti** *unbuttons his shirt.*

Uma's Trace Desire *He Ram* not here! Fast forward! Fast Forward!

She snaps her fingers frantically.

Remo Are you trembling?

Uma's Trace Desire I really should go. I'm going!

She claps. Knocks. Nothing.

Preeti *unties* **Remo**'s *drawstring pants . . . which knot. She fumbles.*

Uma's Trace Desire *closes her eyes.*

Remo *seizes* **Preeti**'s *hands. Kisses her wrists.*

Preeti *guides him to the bed.* **Uma's Trace Desire** *covers her ears.*

Remo (*points to his neck*) . . . .

Preeti *kisses* **Remo**. *He takes her face in his hands. Kisses her face.* **Preeti** *can't stand it.*

Preeti Oh boy oh boy oh boy—

Remo Do you want to wait?

Preeti *looks at him. She blows out the candles.*

Uma's Trace Desire (*in the dark*) Thank God.

Lights!

13.

Preeti *sits in her living room.* **Julio** *knocks then enters.*

Julio   Hi...

Preeti   ...

Julio   Are you crying?

Uma's Trace Desire   Yes.

Preeti   No.

Julio   Is he as wonderful as—

Uma's Trace Desire   It isn't him—

Preeti   It's me. It's. This—

Preeti *and* **Uma's Trace Desire***'s hands go to their hearts.*

Preeti   I'm here. All of me.

Uma's Trace Desire (*closes her eyes, ready*)   Yes. I feel it. Now I can go.

Preeti   Mom would never get it.

Uma's Trace Desire *opens her eyes.*

Uma's Trace Desire   Darn it.

Lights!

14.

Preeti *and* **Una**.

Una   Mom.

Preeti *is in her own world.*

Una   MOM.

Preeti   Hm? Hungry?

Una   Ugh, why do you always think I'm hungry?

Preeti   Because you usually are—

Una   I need tampons!

Preeti   I have pads—

Una   I have swim!

Preeti   You can bike to the store—

Una   I woke up last night and Julio was watching *Golden Girls.*

Uma's Trace Desire   Sophia is too funny.

Preeti   Yes?

Una   Where were you?

Preeti (*guilty*)   Oh. I.

I was at the office.

Una   I kissed Giselle.

Preeti *blinks at* **Una.**

Una   Hellooo? I kissed Giselle?

Uma's Trace Desire   I kissed my second cousin once.

Preeti   I heard you.

Uma's Trace Desire   She studied in London and wore a men's cologne. Aramis.

Una   And I couldn't sleep and I woke up to tell you.

Uma's Trace Desire   She was glamorous.

Una   And you weren't here.

Preeti   So . . . Okay. Are you gay, honey?

Una   I mean! I don't know!

Preeti   Are you attracted to boys? Have you kissed a—

Una   Why does that matter!

Preeti   Are you and Giselle—like, are you—what? Dating now?

Una   Are you going to freak?

Preeti   No, honey, I'm just asking—

Una (*defensive*)   Don't get mad!

Preeti   Una, I'm not—

Una (*walking out*)   I can never talk to you!

Preeti   You want some *roti* and honey and warm milk?

Una (*offstage*)   Fine!

15.

Preeti *and* **Julio. Uma's Trace Desire** *watches. Quiet.*

Julio   You're handling this well.

Preeti She says she's queer.

Julio You know queer is not about who you're having sex with right?

Preeti She's not having sex, Julio, she's fourteen.

Julio Queer is about being at odds with the world—about creating the space you can thrive in. bell hooks.

Preeti I can't tell her about Remo. Right?

Julio Well, what would you tell her?

Preeti I am not committing adultery so why does it feel like I am?

Julio Because you're married to your daughter?

Preeti I just don't want her to get hurt.

Julio Broken hearts make us better lovers.

Preeti *leans her head on his shoulder.* **Uma's Trace Desire** *leans her head on his other shoulder.*

Lights!

16.

Preeti *and* **Remo**. **Uma's Trace Desire** *meditates.*

Preeti Did you always know you wanted to be an actor?

Remo I think so?

Preeti When did you know?

Remo Maybe junior high?

Preeti How did you know?

Remo I did this play and when I heard the audience laugh—and the end, when everyone was clapping, and my parents were there, and my baby sister—it was like . . .

Preeti What?

Remo Getting kissed. Lots of kisses.

Preeti You liked the attention.

Remo I liked the kisses. I miss the kisses.

Uma's Trace Desire *opens one eye.*

Preeti What do you mean?

Remo With TV there's no applause. I can't hear what the audience is saying or if they're laughing or crying.

Preeti When's the last time you did a play?

Remo New York, after I dropped out of school. I was a serial killer.

Preeti Sounds intense.

Remo It was a new musical.

Preeti Do you sing?

Remo Not really.

Uma's Trace Desire *meditates again.*

Preeti (*confused*) Oh.

Remo It's how I got my agent! She was visiting the New York office and had a client in the show—who I was dating.

Preeti Were you in love?

Remo No. It was just fun.

Preeti It's how you got your agent?

Remo Huh? Oh! Yeah. And my new agent knew the casting director of *Doctor Jaques*—he wanted me for a recurring but then the show got canceled. Moved to LA anyway. Started doing commercials, small stuff here and there. Then it was picked up again! And I got cast as the lead!

Preeti (*sighs happily*) I don't understand your business.

Remo No one does.

Lights!

17.

Remo *watches* **Preeti**.

Uma's Trace Desire, *at the same time as* **Preeti** *below, recites the poem in Sanskrit.*

Preeti "I see your body in the sinuous creeper; your gaze in the startled eyes of deer . . . Your cheek in the moon, your hair in the plumage of peacocks . . . And in the tiny ripples of the river, I see your sidelong glances. But alas, my dearest, nowhere do I find your whole likeness."

Remo That's from the fourth century?

Preeti I know!

Remo It's so—now.

Preeti Yes.

Remo No. Like NOW. Like how I feel. Now. It's about you. And me!

Preeti Remo.

Remo Like every poem ever written is about us!

Preeti That's sweet.

Remo It's not sweet! It's the truth, damn it!

He grabs her and kisses her. Lights!

18.

Uma's Trace Desire *watches* **Remo** *and* **Preeti**.

Remo It's a small part in a really cool film with this incredible Iranian director.

Preeti What's important is how excited you are.

Remo Why won't you come?

Uma's Trace Desire Yeah, go, so I can go.

Preeti To New Zealand?

Remo Yeah! To New Zealand! With me!

Preeti My life is here.

Remo Bring Una.

Preeti She doesn't even know about us.

Remo I like when you say us.

Preeti We should talk.

Remo I have a better idea.

He kisses her. Her knees go weak. Lights!

19.

Uma's Trace Desire *watches* **Preeti** *and* **Remo**.

Remo You're breaking up with me?

Preeti Technically we weren't dating.

Remo Do you think I'm—not smart?

Preeti (*startled*) What?

Remo That I'm not—I'm—

Preeti You are enough.

Remo Don't say it's not me.

Preeti People who don't understand love become dictators. You understand love.

Remo That's what I'm saying!

Preeti Remo—

Remo Say my name again.

Uma's Trace Desire (*covering eyes*) Oh no—

He grabs her, kisses her, her knees go weak. Lights!

Lights! A few minutes later.

Remo (*re. their quickie*) Whoa.

Uma's Trace Desire Hare Ram.

Remo What if I asked you to marry me?

Preeti Once you're in New Zealand, this will all seem silly.

Uma's Trace Desire That was a "no."

Preeti I don't want to get married.

Remo To me?

Preeti To anyone. I just want to be. Free. I want you to be free.

Remo *seizes* **Preeti**. *Plants a kiss.*

Uma's Trace Desire If only I knew how to say these words then.

Remo Can I ask you something?

Preeti What?

Remo Is there someone else?

Beat. For the first time **Preeti** *turns to the audience. Scans us.*

Preeti Not yet . . .

Preeti *lips curling upward.*

Lights!

20.

Uma's Trace Desire *watches as* **Julio** *and* **Preeti** *look at* **Dilip**'s *picture in her temple. She removes it. Places it on her dresser.*

Preeti You were here.

Here.

She touches her breasts. Her stomach.

I will always love you, Dilip.

Julio *opens a drawer and puts the picture in it.* **Preeti** *shuts it. Lights!*

21.

As at the top of the play, **Preeti** *is in front of a mirror.*

Nirmala, **Una**, *and* **Julio** *stand behind her.* **Uma's Trace Desire** *in her own liminal space.*

Remo *watches them.*

Nirmala, **Una**, *and* **Julio** *throw rice, flowers, colored powder!*

Preeti I was married during Holi.

Uma's Trace Desire A beautiful man and I ate chocolates on Holi.

Remo I met this cool chick one Holi.

Nirmala I think I accidentally broke my mother's heart one Holi.

Preeti I remember looking at myself one last time as a virgin.

Nirmala I remember that, too.

Uma's Trace Desire Can a girl ever forget?

Una TMI, people!

Preeti *locates parts of her body. The body she knows so well.*

Preeti This mole is from you, Dad. My chin, from you, Mom. Dilip, your caresses shaped me. This dent here is from you, Una.

Una Oof.

Preeti From when we were fencing. I love it.

Una She's weird.

Julio I know, honey.

Remo What about me? Any trace left?

Preeti Oh, yes . . . (*Taps her head, delicious memories*)

Nirmala My good girl. You never judged me.

Preeti Mom, if you forgive yourself?

Julio For every mistake you think you made?

Uma's Trace Desire It was a different time.

Preeti That's a gift.

Uma's Trace Desire I could not have been with Rizwan.

Nirmala I didn't even try.

Julio Forgive yourself.

Nirmala What about you?

Julio But I'm really quite flawless.

Uma's Trace Desire So much is the same. But so much is different. Una! A new element. A healthy breaking of the DNA trail? When two very different things collide, what can happen?

Nirmala Love?

Preeti Yes!

Julio Love is . . .

Uma's Trace Desire Love is . . .?

Una Gross?

Nirmala Unexpected?

Preeti Yes!

Uma's Trace Desire Love is Time.

Una *turns to* **Uma's Trace Desire**.

Una What is Time?

Uma's Trace Desire *looks at* **Una**.

Uma's Trace Desire Time doesn't matter the moment you begin to love yourself. But . . . a definition? Your Nani's *parathas*.

Nirmala Your child's stray sandal in the stairwell.

Preeti The sun on your eyelids. The feel of breath against your neck. The lips on your thigh.

Julio A true and lasting friendship.

Uma's Trace Desire (*to* **Una**) The chocolate in . . . our mouth on a humid summer day.

Una (*to* **Uma's Trace Desire**) And the roses in our hair.

Uma's Trace Desire's *eyes grow wide.* **Una** *puts out her hand.* **Uma's Trace Desire** *puts out hers. Just before they touch,* **Uma's Trace Desire** *vanishes.*

Lights!

Florence and Normandie

June Carryl

Florence and Normandie

Introduction by Robin Alfriend Kello

Named for a Los Angeles intersection, *Florence and Normandie* reimagines the Christian–Islamic religious conflict in Calderón's *Amar después de la muerte* (*To Love Beyond Death*, 1677) within the racial tension and looming violence of Los Angeles in 1992. Like Quarles's *The Woodingle Puppet Show*, the play emerges from a specific area, here the neighborhoods of Koreatown and South-Central Los Angeles, in which Black Americans, Korean Americans, and Korean immigrants—including proprietors of corner stores—lived and worked within the same predominantly nonwhite urban enclaves. Florence and Normandie Avenues, from which the play takes its name, intersect in this neighborhood, center of the uprising following the not-guilty verdict of the LAPD officers who brutally assaulted Rodney King.

In Carryl's adaptation, first-generation Korean American Sydney Jeong works at her family's corner grocery alongside Toony Berry, a young Black man who lives in the same neighborhood. While their flirtatious friendship begins to bend toward romance, Toony's sister Iz is growing impatient with the privileged naiveté of her boyfriend Danny, an educated white man, who fails to acknowledge the racial injustice before them. The dramatic narrative hinges on the historical events surrounding the trial of the LAPD officers and the tensions in the community following the acquittal of Soon Ja Du, a Korean immigrant and grocery clerk who had shot and killed the fifteen-year-old Latasha Harlins, whom she had accused of attempting to steal orange juice. The play thus examines how we live history within the context of our identities, generational as well as cultural. Yet those identities to do not predetermine our reactions to history: Sydney finds herself at odds with both Toony and her parents; Toony and Iz disagree about how to respond to both political and social conflicts; Danny, in love with Iz but with his perspective conditioned by white privilege, is baffled and frustrated by those around him.

As the protests following the King verdict threaten Koreatown—and Jeong's Market in particular—with fire and destruction, the divisions within the city become increasingly personal, and Sydney and Toony find themselves struggling not only to grow up but just to survive. While recreating the details of 1991–2 Los Angeles, including memorable television and radio reports from journalists Tom Snyder and Dan Rather, *Florence and Normandie* speaks to our current moment in its invocation of police violence, racial conflict, and the ongoing legacies of economic disenfranchisement in American communities. A powerful evocation of social struggle and racial trauma, the play dramatizes a flashpoint in American history while also itself offering a vital dramatic text in our present movements for social justice.

Calderón's *To Love Beyond Death*, set amid a minority uprising and its brutal repression in the Alpujarras, in southern Spain in the 1560s, provides a dramaturgical frame for a story that unfolds simultaneously on the level of character and of history. Set in the recent past rather than the loose present in which many Golden Tongues adaptations take place, *Florence and Normandie* dramatizes a flashpoint of violence that insistently repeats throughout American history. Like its source text, the play has a violently tragic arc; yet in illustrating how larger political and social decisions filter into individual lives—here precluding possibilities for love, life, and peace—the drama makes history immediate for the audience. Following the riots of 1992, much of south Los Angeles received investment to rebuild, but the area around Florence and Normandie did not, and the poverty rate remains comparable now to what it was during the early 1990s. The play suggests ultimately that in the embers of destruction, facing loss with honesty, perhaps we can begin anew. It also illustrates, with a dramatic narrative as intricate as it is direct, the consequences of failing to address structural racism, economic disadvantage, and state-sanctioned violence.

An adaptation of *To Love Beyond Death* by Pedro Calderón de la Barca.

Commissioned by "Golden Tongues," a festival of Golden Age adaptations at the UCLA Clark Library in conjunction with Playwrights' Arena.

Characters (in Order of Appearance)

Sydney Jeong, *17*	*First-generation Korean American*
Toony Berry, *17*	*At Rise, African American*
Jeong Chung-Hee, *51*	*Korean, Sydney's father*
Yoo Heejin, *48*	*Korean, Sydney's mother*
Izzy (Iz) Berry, *24*	*African American, Toony's sister*
Danny Brown, *24*	*White American*
Gabe, *26*	*African American*

Time

March 7, 1991–May 8, 1992.

Place

Jeong's Market and an alley; Iz and Danny's apartment, Koreatown, Los Angeles.

I.1

Jeong's Market, March 7, 1991: small, packed to the gills. **Sydney Jeong** *enters from the back, 1990s-era cell phone to her ear. She is in baggy jeans, Doc Martens and a plaid shirt.*

Sydney   I told him you can't call it Sydney's. . . Yeah, but then how will people know it's Korean?

Toony Berry *enters from the street. He, too, wears baggy jeans, but with a basketball jersey and t-shirt underneath, and a red baseball cap. He holds a small chain with a heart pendant, shoves it in his pocket. He tries to get* **Sydney**'s *attention.*

Sydney   I care. . . Because I'm gonna be the one stuck with it.

She waves, raises the box. He takes it off her hands, unloads items onto a shelf.

Sydney   I gotta go. . . I gotta go, Nancy! (*Hanging up.*) Bye. . . Bye!

Toony   Does Nancy ever stop talking?

Sydney   She's cute—cool. She's cool.

He makes the talking gesture with his hand. She smacks it. She rounds the counter to the register. He watches her. Looks away.

What? What?

Toony   Who're you taking to Prom?

Sydney   It's three months away. I don't know.

Toony   Syd.

Sydney   What?

Toony   Syd!

Sydney   What? You're such a dude.

Toony   I'm a dude?

Sydney   You're a dude.

He chuckles, hops up onto the counter.

Toony   Naaancy?

Sydney   Don't be stupid.

Toony   It's cool//

Sydney   //Shut up. You're being a dick//

Toony   //I'm just saying it's cool//

Sydney   //Why are you being such a dick?

Toony   How am I being a dick//

Sydney   //Shut up!

Pause.

Toony   I was gawn say I could go with you, but . . .

Sydney   Total dick.

Pause.

Toony   What do you like about her?

Sydney   Jesus!

Toony   I mean, she's cute. Don't get me wrong.

She shoots him a look.

So?

Sydney   I'll let you know in two months.

Jeong Chung-Hee *enters in a huff followed by his wife,* **Yoo Heejin**. **Toony** *hops down from the counter.*

Toony   Hey, Mr. Jeong. Mrs. Jeong.

Heejin   Hi, Toony.

Chung-Hee   I don't pay you to sit on your ass.

Toony   Wasn't sitting on my ass.

Heejin   Never mind//

Mr. Jeong *points at the counter.*

Chung-Hee   //That: what's that? Ass prints. I don't pay you to sit. I pay you to work.

Sydney   You okay, Dad?

Chung-Hee *(Korean)*   Deoleoun don-i changnyeoleul galg-ameogneunda!

Heejin   Never mind, Chung-hee! Time for your medicine.

Sydney   *Appa*?

Chung-Hee   Go and count something!

Sydney *heads for the back of the shop.*

Chung-Hee   Sydney.

He beckons her back. They tap foreheads. She exits.

Heejin   We had a visit today. Developer. Wants to buy the block.

Sydney   The whole block?

Heejin   They want Koreans out. Pay arm and a leg to get it.

Toony   He said no?

Heejin   Of course, he said no.

Jeong Chung-Hee *marches in from the back.*

Chung-Hee   And if they think for a second, I am giving up an inch//

Heejin   Go and take your heart medication. Nobody coming for us this afternoon.

Chung-Hee   Every day another one. Twenty-one years I've been here, he talks to me like I'm fresh off the boat//

Heejin   //Go and take your pills!

Chung-Hee   Heejin!

She stares daggers at him, taking the wind out of him. He exits to the back.

Chung-Hee   Whoever said a man is king of his//

Heejin   //

Chung-Hee (*to himself as he exits*)   *Jiog-ui chuun nal, naneun dangsin-ege geugeos-eul malhal geos-ibnida!*

Heejin *watches him exit, turns to the inventory.*

Heejin   Man his age taking heart pills—where's the topokki?

Toony *roots around in the box, as* **Sydney** *returns. He hands* **Heejin** *a package.*

Toony   This it?

Heejin   One box?

Sydney   Mom, it's, like, a thousand calories.

Heejin   What's the difference? You don't eat! Skinny like a chicken!

Toony *reads the box.*

Toony   Five hundred eighty-five to be precise.

Sydney   Not helping.

Heejin   Your father will give himself a heart attack.

Sydney   Would it be so bad to sell? I mean, they don't want us here.

Stung, **Toony** *buries himself in counting cans.*

Heejin   Don't talk like that! What about college? Future? You think we come all this way to give up everything? Stupid child.

Sydney   I'm not stupid! *Eoma!*

Heejin *waves her away.*

Toony   Y'all need green beans.

Heejin   You stupid, too! I go and see to your father.

Heejin *storms out to the back.* **Sydney** *and* **Toony** *work in silence.*

Toony   Wanna come by after?

Sydney   I got homework.

Toony   You never have homework.

They work again in silence.

What you get in math?

Sydney   Toony!

Toony   What? I'm asking a question.

Sydney   But what you really wanna know is am I studying with Nancy.

Toony   I ain't said shit about//

Sydney   //I'm not seeing Nancy!

Toony   I didn't//

Sydney   //

Pause.

You talk too fucking much.

Toony   What'd y'all break up or something?

Sydney   Toony!

They stare at each other. He realizes.

Toony   Oh, shit.

Sydney   . . .

He comes over. Starts arranging items for her.

Toony   I got it.

She watches him.

Sydney   She thinks I'm not Korean enough. I'm too American, whatever the fuck . . .

Toony   You curse too much.

Sydney   Fuck you.

He grins.

Don't say anything. Just//

Toony   //'bout what?

He smiles. Goes back to arranging items on the shelf. She pecks him on the cheek.

Toony   What's that for?

She shrugs. They work.

Sydney   The tape was awful. I thought it was awful.

Toony   . . .

Sydney   Are you okay? I mean//

Toony   I'm always okay.

Sydney   Toony//

Toony   //Y'all gawn need more green beans.

He works. She watches him. She works.

Sydney   Ask me in three months.

He looks at her. She smiles. He smiles. They work.

I.2

Iz *and* **Danny**'s *living room later that day: small but roomy somehow.* **Iz** *is on the phone in leggings and Loyola sweatshirt, curled up on the couch with* **Danny** *in jeans and matching sweatshirt. The TV is on. They watch rapt.*

Iz   . . . Yes, Mrs. Gorham. I—Yes. Always lock the door, yes . . .

A knock at the door.

Sorry, I have to. . . Sorry. Yes. . . Bye. Bye.

She hangs up.

That woman. Jesus.

Iz *goes to answer, not taking her eyes off the screen.* **Toony** *brushes in.*

Toony   Fuckin' white folks, man! They got—

Sees **Danny**.

Oh.

Danny   Hey, Toony.

Iz   What'd the white folks do now, Toony?

He settles in front of the TV, puts his feet up.

Toony   They keep tryin' to buy Jeong's.

Iz   Feet. I smell a bargain.

Toony   Mrs. Jeong said they might give them a good price.

Iz   They're not going to give them a good price.

Danny   Fun fact: redlining? Korean, Chinese all of them were lumped in as

Japanese, considered "subversive racial elements."

They stare at him.

Toony Do he have to be here?

Iz Why do you know things like that? And yes, he does. He lives here. Feet!

Toony *takes his feet off the coffee table.*

Toony Man! Niggas can't have nothin'.

Iz The Jeongs aren't//

Danny The Jeongs aren't exactly//

Toony //"The Jeongs aren't exactly." Who talkin' to you?//

Iz Have we met? I was speaking.

Danny Sorry.

Toony With yo' Loyola ass.

Iz Baby boy!

He gives her the finger.

Toony I got yo' baby boy ri' cheah.

Danny Are we still watching this?

Toony/Iz YES.

Danny *shrugs.*

Danny Anybody want anything?

Iz I'm good.

Toony Me, too.

Danny *exits.* **Toony**'s *eyes are on the TV.*

Toony You seen this shit? Like a damn dog.

Iz *settles next to him. They watch.*

Whachu think they give that muhafucka for the tape? Gave the nigga five hundred.[1]

Iz Can you not use that word?

Toony Guy who got Kennedy got a hundred thousand. One mo' nigga. Beat a muthafucka between fifty-three and fifty-six times. *Between* fifty-three and fifty-six. Don't even know how many. Fuckin' lost count.

Iz D'you take the bus here?

---

1 George Holliday, who filmed the brutal beating of Rodney King by the Los Angeles Police Department, sold the videotape to the TV station KTLA for $500.

Toony Naw, I ain't take no bus. It's fifteen minutes.

Iz From now on, you take the bus.

Toony I ain't takin' no damn bus! Dare one of these muhafuckas step to me.

Iz Just, please.

His eyes are on the TV.

Toony Niggas is up though. Caught that shit on camera.

Danny *enters with a beer, hands raised.*

Danny Is it safe? White boy coming through.

Toony Nigga, don't joke.

Iz Toony.

Danny Just . . . lightening the mood.

Toony How 'bout you shut up, Sweden? Every time I look around you here. With yo' neutral ass.

Danny You mean Switzerland?

Toony Yeah, one o' them white places.

Iz He's just//

Danny //I'm just//

Toony What kinda sense that make? Muhafucka gettin' beat like a dog and this fool talking about light!

Danny I'm just//

Toony //Just shut the fuck up! Dang!

Iz Don't you have homework?

Toony's *on his feet.*

Toony You know what? You right.

Iz Toony//

Toony //I don't need this shit.

Iz Toony, sit down. Sit!

Toony *sits.*

Toony Fucking fifty-three times! Straight up racist muthafuckas! Give that dude five hundred dollars.

Danny Okay, it was excessive, but I mean, technically, from a legal standpoint it may not necessarily be//

Toony   Please don't do this shit right now//

Iz   //Babe//

Danny   //It's just, it's a high bar in terms of intent//

Iz   BABE.

Toony   What the fuck you sayin'?

Danny   I'm just—from a technical, legal standpoint//

Toony   //What legal//

Danny   //Racist. I mean excessive force, maybe, but//

Iz   //Maybe?

Danny   He's a big guy. I mean, he looks//

Iz   By a reasonable//person

Danny   Normal reason, normal, not a policeman//There's leeway

Toony   //Oh, I feel better now.

Danny   He could have had a gun, or//the shit they go through?

Toony   Thank you. That ain't the point!

Danny   I'm just saying is it racist.

Toony/Iz   . . .

Danny   It's just an interesting proposition!

Toony   Niggas getting beat to shit every damn day. Getting beat like it's they damn job and that ain't racist? Only reason Gates[2] talking 'bout it now is they got the shit on tape and the shit got out. How many muthafuckas walkin' around got the same story, but ain't got no damn tape? That's fucked! Y'all's shit is fucked.

Iz   Clearly there is evidence of misconduct.

Danny   And the men involved will face the consequences.//

Toony   //And that's enough for you.

Iz   //Remains to be seen.

Danny   I am just talking about//intent.

Toony   //That's fucked, man. That is fucked.

Iz   Okay, just—everybody breathe.

Toony   You wid' him?

---

2   Daryl Gates, chief of Los Angeles Police from 1978 to 1992.

Iz Toony, would you please//Where are you//

Toony You gotta make up your mind, Iz, who you for. All this "we are the world" shit. Who you for?

Iz Toony//

Toony Ts! Right.

Toony *stomps to the front door, exits. Silence.*

Danny You okay? You//

Iz What was that?

Danny Iz//

Iz //What was it?

Danny I meant as thought experiment. Purely academic.

Iz I'm not talking about that.

Danny Okay. Then, I am—confused.

Iz Confused. You're—can you turn that off, please?

Danny I'm//

Iz //Turn it off!

He turns off the TV. She sits. Silence

Danny Okay . . . ?

Iz This hurts.

Danny Okay.

Iz This hurts. I hurt.

Danny I'm sorry.

Iz No. I don't—I don't need you to be sorry.

Danny So, then—

Iz . . .

Danny . . .

Iz . . . Two days.

Danny What did I do?

Iz Two days//

Danny //

Iz Since the tape.

He stares, mystified, then:

Danny   Okay. I'm sorry.

Iz   Again, don't need you to be sorry. Not a peep. Until today.

Danny   I was just . . . What did you want me to say?

Iz   Something. Anything!

Danny   I just said//

Off her look.

//Iz, I//

Iz   . . .

Danny   Okay. I'm . . .//

Iz   . . .

Danny   So . . . no makeup sex.

Iz   . . .

Danny   Sorry—I mean . . .

They sit in silence.

Danny   I just . . .

Iz   //

Danny   I mean . . . Shit.

Iz   . . .

Danny   What can I do?

Iz   I just, I//

She breaks a little. He moves to her. Holds her.

Danny   Hey, sh, sh . . .

Iz   I think sometimes I . . . I'm on this island, and I'm just . . . I'm waving and saying help and you just . . ., I mean everybody's just . . . Okay. Done. Okay.

She recovers.

Danny   You know, I, um, okay, I'm not, the guy was obviously drunk, and I'm not saying . . . I just: why didn't he stay down?

Iz   Why didn't he//

Danny   //Just//

Iz   That's your question? That . . . that's your takeaway?

Danny   Just . . . maybe he should have stayed down.

Iz I don't//

Danny //I'm just saying//

Iz //Just lay down.

Danny No. Okay, you know, I don't//

Iz //Lay there and//what?

Danny //I'm just asking the question//

Iz //Would you?

Danny No, Iz. I just//

Iz //Of course you wouldn't. Because it would never happen to you.

Danny Iz, come on.

Iz No. It wouldn't. It wouldn't happen to you.

Danny You don't know that. You don't know. I have had my share of//

Iz //When? When did you//

Danny I'm just//

Iz Ever? EVER?//

Danny //It's not like it would happen to you either. Iz, seriously: top of your class, fuckin' Brown University, fuckin' Loyola School of Law. Four-point-oh.

She stares at him like he's from another planet.

Okay. No. Just. You know, I'm gonna go for a walk.

Iz You should do that.

He puts on his shoes. Is out the door.

Danny I'm... Yeah.

He starts to put on his shoes.

Iz Is that how you see me?

Danny Shit. Okay, Iz.

Iz No. I'm serious. How do you see me?

Danny Okay, you're being incredibly emotional right now//

Iz Don't fucking tell me tell me I'm being emotional. How dare you!

Danny ...

Iz How do you see me? I'm like one of your thought experiments?

Danny That//Where is this coming from?

Iz You just said//

Danny //

Iz I am proving myself every fucking minute of my life. That I have a right to be here. To exist. That I deserve to be here. This is not an intellectual exercise for me.

Danny You know what I mean.

Iz No, I don't. I honestly don't.

Danny ...

Iz That day at the library. That fucking day. What made you decide to talk to me?

Danny You're asking//

Iz //I didn't know you from Adam. Why did you talk to me?

Danny Four years, fifty-three days in you want to know//

Iz //Did you think you were gonna get laid?

Danny Pretty! I thought you were pretty!

Iz For a Black girl.

Danny What? No!//

Iz //Fuckable then? Thought experiment?//

Danny NO!//

Iz On Saturdays, or when it pisses off your parents?

Danny It was a question. I can't ask a//

Iz No, I am asking//

Danny Wait, you're calling me a racist?

Iz I am asking//

Danny //You're calling me a racist?

Iz I didn't say//

Danny //I'm gonna marry you! I'm gonna fucking marry you and you're calling me a fucking racist?

Iz I am asking why you spoke to me//

Danny //No, you're accusing me//

Iz A guy with his face in the pavement and you don't know if it's intent? Do you love me?

Danny Do I—you know what? You're right. I don't. You've met my family. We live together. Picked out baby names, so obviously, I don't, I'm a terrible human being, and fuck you.

Iz Yeah, well fuck you, too.

Pause.

Danny   This is about something else.

Iz   What? What else?

Danny   This . . . you really think. . .

Pause.

Your mom lives in fucking Brentwood, okay? So, this thing you do, this thing, whatever it is? It isn't you. It's not Toony either. He's a fucking stock boy.

Iz   You should go for a walk.

Danny   Yeah. Yeah. Fucking unbelievable.

He exits. She stands there.

I.3

1 a.m. Keys in the door. **Iz** *wakes on the couch—as* **Danny** *enters. The TV is still on. He crosses to the bedroom, offstage without so much as a word.* **Iz** *watches TV. Finally, she can't stand it anymore. She crosses to the bedroom where* **Danny** *has already climbed into bed.*

Iz   So, what, are you just never going to speak to me again?

Danny   . . .

Brief pause.

Iz   I didn't call you a racist.

He rolls over.

Oh, my God!

She storms to the bathroom. She reemerges, stomps over to the bed and climbs in. They lie there in silence. Suddenly **Danny** *is out of bed and stomps out.* **Iz** *lays there a beat, follows.*

I did not call you a racist!

Danny   Well, what do you call it?

Iz   Is that what's actually bothering you?

Danny   What's actually bothering me is you called me a racist.

Iz   You hurt me! Remember? *You* hurt *me*! How am I the one being punished?

Danny   And so to get me back, you call me a racist.

Iz   I didn't call you a//

Danny   Yeah, you did! You kinda did.

Iz   Okay.

Danny   There. Always gotta have the last word.

Iz   . . .

Danny   I mean, if that is honestly what you think of me, then maybe we shouldn't talk anymore.

She stares at him.

Iz   Maybe we shouldn't.

Danny   Wow.

Pause.

Are you unhappy or//

Iz   //I don't know.

This hits.

When we first . . . that first night out, karaoke, and I said I didn't want to sing and you promised, "When you go, I go." And you wouldn't stop looking at me. Every time I looked up there you were looking at me, and you had that little smile. And you sat so still. I was singing—you finally got me to sing—and you were so still. And I thought, okay. I'm not supposed to—you're you: you complicate things, you fold up sometimes, just—and I mean, we'd only been hanging out a couple months. But that night I told you how my godmother was super religious and when I told her about my dad she told me get down on my knees and pray, and you said you broke a window in the school chapel once because you were angry at God, which I thought was romantic and scary and . . . And somehow I ended up saying I think I love you. It just sort of slipped out. I didn't even think I'd said it out loud. And your mouth sort of went flat for just a second. And I thought, Oh, God.

Danny   . . .

Iz   But you didn't leave. You kept coming back. I don't remember half of what I said to you most of the time because I kept waiting for you to leave, or for things to get "complicated." You didn't leave, just kept filling up more and more space in me. And I thought, "Why do I have to choose?" Who I am versus . . . loving you. And then, one day you kissed me and I thought, okay. Just, Okay. And then this happened. And I waited for you to say something.

Danny   I did//

Iz   //No. You didn't//

Danny   //Signed petitions, fucking phone calls to City Hall//

Iz   Not. To me. Intellectualized, theorized, sure. But not to me.

Danny   . . .

Iz   Two fucking days. Walking around on egg shells, like nothing happened. It's like one minute you want so much of me I feel like I'm disappearing into you and the next things get messy and it's like you're watching me drown. You are watching me drown, and I am waiting, and praying. Just . . . You watched me drown.

Pause.

And now I can't get it out of my head. That frown. The way you just fold up, close up whenever I'm in danger of saying I'm sad, or I need. You punched God, I mean . . .!

Danny I didn't know what to say.

Iz When you go, I go.

Danny I didn't know what to say! That I *had* to say anything. I'd have thought . . .

Iz . . .

Danny You can't just let things be.

Iz Things?

Danny Things between people. Things.

Iz You have to name things.

Danny Why? Why do things need names? Maybe some things don't need names!

Iz You have to name them.

Danny No! You don't!

Iz Then why the fuck are you here? Why are you here? Why did you talk to me?

Danny So you are calling me a racist.

Iz . . .

Danny I was nice to you! I was being nice!

Iz Nice? Oh. Wow. Gosh! Thanks! Thank you!

Danny I didn't mean it like that.

Iz Just doing me a favor.

Danny I didn't mean it like that. I didn't//

Iz //Then how exactly did you mean it? You know every rap song. You know all about South Africa. You never cease talking about South Africa. How exactly did you mean it?

Danny . . .

Iz *starts for the bedroom.*

Danny You want to know why I talked to you? Because I liked you. You have this smile. Like, like you know something the rest of us don't, like there's some secret deep, deep down inside you that nobody can touch. Nobody else knows. And I wanted to lay claim to that part of you, yeah. To know every part of you. So I could be the one to make you smile like that. And there you were walking to the elevator in the Sci-Li. I heard somebody say your name, and I ran after you and I said, are you Izzy. And your mouth kinda crinkled like how the fuck does he know my name? And then you smiled anyway. And I got scared. Because I'd never been so happy. And then. . . You said those three little worlds and. . . I didn't know what to say. I was scared. So scared I couldn't breathe.

Long pause.

I didn't know what to say.

Iz   How about, "Are you okay?" How about, "I love you."

Danny   . . .

Iz   . . .

They stare at one another.

Okay, well.

They stand there looking at one another, the divide between them growing.

I.4

April 21, 1992. A TV is on.

Voice of Newscaster   . . . The merchant, Soon Ja Du,[3] was convicted of voluntary manslaughter. Her sentence: five years' probation, no jail time . . .

Danny *is on the couch. He rises when he hears keys in the door.* **Iz** *enters. She stops. Pause.*

Danny   Hi.

Iz   Hi.

Danny   Sorry. Um, Toony let me in.

Iz *nods. She crosses to the table with her books.*

Danny   Haven't seen you around//campus

Iz   How's your place? Sorry I didn't get you a gift.

Danny   Hate living with guys.

Iz   Yeah, well.

---

3   Soon Ja Du is a Korean immigrant and convenience store clerk who shot and killed fourteen-year-old Latasha Harlins, a young Black woman who had placed a bottle of orange juice in her pocket while walking to the counter to pay. The incident, which occurred in 1991, and the light sentence she received, outraged the Black community in LA and played a role in the riots following the Rodney King verdict.

They look at the television.

Danny I mean, I just, with everything, I just thought I'd check on you.

Iz I'm fine. I bought Weird Al Yankovic's new album: *Off the Deep End*. Sounds just like Nirvana. Guy's gonna get sued.

Danny . . .

Iz One of the songs, his girlfriend's trying to kill him. It's a ballad, believe it or not.

Danny Did you declare a JD?

Iz Is that what you came over to ask?

Danny . . .

Iz I dropped out.

Danny Iz//

Iz You remember how I was going to be a Supreme Court Justice? I mean, I think about it now, it's just . . . I used to think that there are truths. That there are facts and there are truths. And now, I think I don't even believe in the law anymore. Toony was right. I do have to choose.

Danny It's one case!

Iz No. It's not. It's all of it: the words, the buildings, the people. I mean, if you can look at a thing and say it's not what it is. And I'm looking at it with my own two eyes. I see it. No. I'm . . . I started subbing. Get certified. Gonna teach high school.

Off his look:

What?

Danny It's just I thought you were braver.

She laughs.

Iz Wow. You came here for a pep talk.

Danny You're smart, Iz!

Iz Yes. I am. And so I'm doing what a smart person does. Finding another way.

Danny I guess that's everything then: boyfriend nixed, law school. What next? Join the Peace Corps?

Iz That's not why you came here, is it?

Danny I came here because I'm worried about you.

Iz No! No. You came here because you wanted to know if I was broken yet.

Danny Is that really what you think?

Iz Tell me I'm wrong.

Danny Wow. You know, your mom's worried about you.

Iz Thank you both for your concern, but I don't need you right now. I don't. Not now. Maybe I never did.

He starts to go.

Danny Okay, well, when you get back to reality, give me a call.

Iz This is reality.

Danny No. This is bullshit.

Iz Lock the door behind you.

Danny Whatever.

He goes. Jeong's Market. **Sydney** *is seated on the counter on the phone.* **Toony** *mans the register but mostly watches the TV.*

Sydney . . . It's cool. It's like, I'm Sid Vicious and you're Nancy Spungen[4] . . . It's not a stupid name. It's cool. German or something. Well, not that Germans are cool. I mean, fuckin' dorks . . . How is that racist? They tuck their shirts into their underwear. Come on!

She catches **Toony** *looking at her.*

Better go . . . No . . . No. (*Hanging up.*) Goodbye.

Toony How's Nancy?

She flips him off.

Toony So, like, when you get married, you'll be like, it'll be like in a church or like//

Sydney If I were getting married. And I'm not. It'd be like a wedding hall.

Toony How you know you not gon' get married?

Sydney Because I'm not.

Toony Yeah, but just say//

Sydney I'm not getting married.

Toony . . .

Sydney . . .

Toony But say, like, somebody wanted to marry you.

Sydney I'd say tough shit.

Heejin *bustles in. They go back to work. She exits.*

Toony Even Nancy?

Sydney You're being weird.

---

4 Sid Vicious, member of the punk rock band Sex Pistols, and his girlfriend Nancy Spungeon, whose destructive relationship served as the basis for a 1986 film.

Toony I'm not being weird.

Sydney You're so being weird.

Toony I'm not being weird. Fuck you!

She laughs.

So who you takin' this year?

Sydney Oh my God. This is like a yearly thing with you!

Toony I'm just saying like maybe we could double date?

Sydney Yeah? You and who?

Toony Asshole.

Pause.

Sydney Why do you want to get married anyway? The world sucks.

Toony I don't know. I just do. Think I see myself as a dad.

Sydney *stares at the television.*

Toony Could get married in South Korea.

Sydney What for? Anyway, I don't think you could come visit me.

Toony Why not?

Off her look:

Oh. Yeah.

Sydney My cousin got arrested in South Korea. I didn't know her. I wasn't even born yet. And then that student got killed by the government. They packed my mom up and sent her here. Never even met my grandpa. I mean, he's dead now, so.

Chung-Hee *and* **Heejin** *enter.*

Chung-Hee Toony.

Beckons him over.

Toony Mr. Jeong?

He hands **Toony** *several bills.*

Chung-Hee I think it's best you take a couple days.

Toony Couple days?

Sydney Dad//

Chung-Hee Take couple days.

Toony Yeah, but you gawn need the extra help.

Chung-Hee You get straight As. You study. You take a couple days.

Toony   I can study here. You gawn need the extra help.

Chung-Hee   Toony.

Toony   Yo, Mr. Jeong is this cause of the trial//

Chung-Hee   //No trial, just//

Toony   It won't be trouble. And if it is, you might need//

Chung-Hee   Just . . . You finish. Couple days. Please.

He pats **Toony** *on the back, exits. Silence.* **Toony** *gathers his bag. He goes.* **Heejin** *pats* **Sydney** *on the elbow.* **Chung-Hee** *crosses to an aisle, stacks items.*

Chung-Hee   Not one word.

Heejin   Nobody say anything.

Chung-Hee   Long faces. Everywhere, long faces. Dark clouds hanging over this place. It's no wonder everyone stays away.

Sydney   It's just it's not fair.

Chung-Hee   I don't make fair. I'm not in the business of make things fair. Your boyfriend will be back soon enough.

Sydney   He's not my boyfriend!

Chung-Hee   Oh, no? Aha! There! I see it.

Sydney   He's not my boyfriend.

Chung-Hee   Mn.

Heejin   Never mind. Toony is a good boy.

Chung-Hee   Well, I have a shop to run. What good does it do me if it burns to the ground?

Sydney   We need the help.

Chung-Hee   Look around you! Does it look like we need help? Two weeks nobody. This rate we'll be lucky to make it through June.

Sydney   And what happens when the neighbors hear we let him go?

Chung-Hee   How do you think it looks to have him here? A black boy. And you running around after him? Who do you think they'll arrest when the police come?

Sydney   Great. Now I'm fucking him.

Heejin *slaps her.*

Heejin   You are an embarrassment.

Sydney *stares at her mother, then the ground.* **Heejin** *exits.*

I.5

Toony *and* **Sydney** *lie in bed. They share a joint.*

Toony So.

Sydney So.

Toony So . . .

They break into giggles. **Sydney** *swings out of bed.* **Toony** *watches her dress. He rifles through his jeans, for the pendant. She turns. He holds it out to her.*

Toony I think we should get married.

Sydney Oh, God.

Toony Seriously

Sydney Grow up.

Toony I'm grown.

Sydney You're not grown.

Toony I'm—I'm saying I love you.

Sydney . . .

Toony . . .

Sydney Toony.

Toony You don't have to say it back.

Sydney That's not//

Toony //

Sydney You know what the word for wife is in Korean? *Waipeu*. It's basically saying wife but like with an accent.

Pause.

It was supposed to be better.

He holds her hands. She touches the pendant.

What are you going to do after school's over?

Toony Get the fuck outta LA.

Sydney *(funny voice)* "You're gonna be rich and famous."

Toony Shit yeah. Be a mogul.

Sydney You're gonna be a seventeenth-century Indian prince?

Toony I'm—ts!

Sydney Racist.

She gets off the bed.

Toony   I'ma own the Knicks.

Sydney   Knicks suck.

Toony   Knicks don't suck.

Sydney   Knicks suck!

Toony   Orlando, Milwaukee, Miami//

Sydney   //Bulls, muthafucka! You don't even like basketball!

Toony   No, but see, I'ma own the Knicks, and then I'ma start a sports network like ESPN and they only gawn play there. If you want to see 'em, you gotta pay.

Sydney   Nobody's gonna pay to watch the Knicks suck.

Toony   Girl!

A door somewhere. They freeze.

Oh, shit! My sister!

Sydney   What do I do?

He motions for her to hide. She dives behind the bed.

Ow! Fuck!

He shushes her as:

Iz (*off*)   Toony?

Toony   Yeah?

Iz enters with a stack of books.

Iz   You left your bag in the hall. What are you doing? Why are the lights off?

Toony   Sleep. I was 'sleep.

Iz   In my room? It's four in the afternoon.

Toony   Sorry.

Iz   Well, call Mom. She was worried.

He nods.

You okay?

He nods. She comes over, sits.

Iz   You'll find another job.

Toony   I don't need another job. Mr. Jeong just needs me to lay low a minute.

Iz   He cut you loose.

Toony   He a'aight.

Iz   Toony//

Toony   //Don't you have, like, substitute teacher-ing to//

Iz   Okay.

She taps his chest.

Little bird chest.

She gets up.

Hey, Syd!

Toony   Shiiiit.

Sydney *slowly comes out of hiding.*

Sydney   Hey, Iz.

Iz   My bed? Really?

Sydney   Sorry.

Toony   You're not gawn tell Ma.

Iz   Just do me a favor and wash the sheets, please. Iew.

She's gone. **Sydney** *sits next to* **Toony**. *Pause.*

Sydney   So, like, are we . . . like, about my dad?

Toony   Well, this was a revenge fuck, so I think we good.

Sydney   Fuck you!

Toony   You got to marry me now. We done did the deed!

He grins. Pause.

Sydney   He's such an asshole.

Toony   He's not an asshole. He's your dad.

Sid   He's my dad, and he's an asshole.

Toony   Scared don't make him a asshole.

Sydney   He wasn't scared.

Toony   You the one talking about nobody wants you here.

Sydney   He wasn't scared.

Toony   . . .

Sydney   He didn't like how it looked: you and me.

Toony   So why he hired me then?

Sydney   My mom made him. Thing with the trial is just an excuse.

Toony ...

Sydney Told you. He's an asshole.

Toony So this was a pity fuck.

Sydney You can be so stupid.

Toony Don't call me stupid.

Sydney Well, you're being stupid.

Toony I'm not!

Sydney You are!

Toony I don't need you coming over here feeling sorry for me.

Sydney Toony, shut up and just kiss me!

Toony What if I don't want to kiss you?

Sydney You don't want to kiss me?

Toony I don't want to kiss you.

Sydney ...

She gets up, moves to the door, marches back, snatches the pendant.

You're so stupid.

Toony I told you//

Sydney //Right.

Toony Go kiss Nancy.

She gathers her things.

Sydney Fuck you. Fuck you!

Toony No, fuck you.

Sydney Fuck you!

She gets to the door, stops.

We fucking broke up.

Toony ... How come//

Sydney You know how come!

Toony ...

Sydney I can't be. Just ... You know what? Fuck you.

She storms out past **Iz** *on the couch reading.* **Sydney** *gets to the door, opens it, but doesn't leave.* **Iz** *watches a moment, goes back to reading.*

Iz You're letting in the cold air.

Sydney   What is wrong with boys?

Iz   Pity fuck?

Sydney   Oh my God!

Iz   So: revenge fuck.

Sydney *shuts her eyes. She drags herself back to the couch and capsizes.*

Iz   I mean, I love my brother. I think he's cute, but . . .

Sydney   He's nice. He's—I'm more me than I am with anybody, but then I get scared that maybe I'm not. And . . . Shit.

Iz *watches her.*

Sydney   My dad's a racist.

Iz   Technically, he can't be since he's//

Sydney   //Oh, he is so racist. He's like, "you better not bring home any babies" racist.

Iz *chuckles.*

Sydney   Do you miss it? Law school. It's so. . .! I mean, kids suck.

Iz   The world sucks. (*Then:*) I think for the first time I feel useful. Like the lightbulb goes off in a kid's head and I know I did that. And that's something.

Pause.

Sydney   Toony said you were at the trial.

Iz *nods.*

Sydney   Do you think . . . Maybe she was scared or . . . I don't know. I just have a bad feeling.

Iz   Maybe. Maybe she was, too.

Pause.

Sydney   We are so fucked-up.

Iz   We are fucked-up.

Toony *appears in the doorway.* **Iz** *looks from one to the other. She's on her feet.*

Iz   I'm gonna order a pizza. You staying?

Sydney   I don't know. Am I staying?

Toony *shrugs.*

Iz   Oh, you kids.

She exits.

I.6

April 29, 1992,[5] 3:07 p.m. The TV is on, sound down. **Sydney** *does her homework at the counter.* **Chung-Hee** *stacks items.* **Heejin** *enters, watches her daughter who ignores her, settles at the other end of the counter.* **Gabe**, *Black, 25, enters. He wears combat boots and all black. He scans aisle after aisle.*

Sydney   Can I help you?

Gabe   I like your boots.

Sydney   . . .

Gabe *chuckles half to himself.*

Sydney   You gonna buy something or//

Gabe   //You're Syd, right?

Off her look, points to her name tag.

Name tag. It's a nice touch. Very friendly.

Chung-Hee   Is there something you want?

Gabe   He your watchdog?

Chung-Hee   What did you say?

Gabe   Arf! Arf!

Heejin *enters from the back.* **Chung-Hee** *steps around the counter.*

Gabe   Used to play around here. The lot. It's changed.

Chung-Hee   If you're not going to buy something, I suggest you leave.

Heejin   Mr. Jeong.

Gabe *throws his hands up.*

Gabe   Just saying there's history here, man. You should know the history before you just take shit . . . Kidding, dude. Kidding.

He extends a hand.

Don't leave me hanging, dude.

Chung-Hee *stays put.*

Gabe   Wow. Sense of humor.

Pause.

Smokes?

Sydney   What brand?

---

5 On this date, the four LAPD officers accused of using excessive force on Rodney King were all acquitted. The unrest began shortly thereafter and continued to escalate.

Gabe   Camels, m'lady.

Sydney *reaches for a pack, tosses them on the counter.*

Gabe   Two fifty-nine? Ouch! Sure you're not gouging me?

She just stares at him. He digs in his pocket, tosses money on the counter and is already opening the pack.

Sydney   No smoking.

Gabe   Right. Right. Well, it has been real.

He goes.

Like your boots.

Lights up on **Iz** *planted in front of the TV holding her phone. 4:47PM. The phone rings. She looks at the number. Lets it ring. Finally:*

Iz   Mrs. Gorham, I can't talk right now.

She hangs up. The doorbell rings. Still holding the phone she gets up, not taking her eyes off the screen. Answers. It's **Danny**.

Danny   Hey.

Iz   Hey.

Her eyes go to the TV.

Danny   I could come back, or//

Iz   //No. No. Um, do you want to// come in?

Danny   //I mean, if you're//

Iz   //No, don't be//

Danny   //busy.

Iz   I'm not.

Danny   //just//

Iz   Come in.

Beat. He enters. He eyes the phone.

Mrs. Gorham. She wants to . . . change the locks. In case.

Danny   Is that the trial? //

She gestures. He sits. They watch. After a beat.

Iz   //Unfucking believable. All four.

Danny   I was listening on the way over. You, uh//

Iz   I already cried, so . . .

Danny   You need anything?

Iz I'm fine. I'm . . .

Danny It should've been guilty. I'm sorry. I, uh//

Iz //Don't. Just//

Danny //I was stupid and//

Iz //It's fine. You're fine. Okay? We're fine.

Danny We're not fine.

Iz But that's what you want to hear.

Danny It's not. I//

Iz //No?

Danny I just—it should've been guilty.

Iz . . .

Danny I didn't have all the facts, Iz.

Iz Nope. Just the tape.

Danny I'm trying to say I was wrong, okay? I just . . . I was wrong.

Iz . . .

Danny I, I do see you, Iz.

Iz Except when I tell you. What's real. For me. What's happening to me.

Danny And you punished me for it.

Iz And what do you call the last eleven months?

Danny //

Iz Not even a phone call.

Danny I was giving you your space.

Iz No, that was punishment.

Danny I was//

Iz For telling you the truth.

Danny I'm sorry.

Iz Okay.

Danny I miss you.

Iz //

Danny I'm saying//

Iz //I heard you.

Danny Okay, so//

Iz What do you miss exactly? Don't answer that.

Danny //

Iz The way you'd hold me sometimes. Like I was heavy and light all at once, glass and gold, and your arms were the only thing keeping me tethered to the world. The way you'd brush my cheek with your lips and they were always warm. And then you left. I called. I wrote. I said I hate you. Said I love you, I forgive you. Asked you to forgive me. And you spent the last eleven months pretending I don't exist. Nothing I could ever say will hurt you as much as that. And believe me, I tried. And I thought, how could you hold someone like they're they whole world and then just let go like that. I started to actually doubt my own existence. It's like Schrödinger's cat. A thing is as long as it is observed, except that it is observed and yet it isn't anything. Who knows. Maybe I'm dead. I'm Schrödinger's cat.

Danny . . .

Iz Why are you here?

Pause.

Danny Because I was wrong. Because I miss you and I'm sorry and I love you.

Iz No. People like you aren't happy unless they destroy other people.

Danny People like me.

Iz The only person who matters in the world is you. The only feelings that matter are yours. The only thoughts that are real, that actually matter are yours. And if anyone tells you otherwise, you do everything in your power to destroy them.

Danny So, now I'm a narcissist.

Iz Maybe. Culturally, yes. You're a man. You're white. The whole fucking world revolves around you.

Danny I am here, okay? I'm here.

Iz Why?

Danny Because I give a fuck.

Iz About?

Danny Us! I care about us//

Iz //

Danny Shut up. Just shut up second.

Iz . . .

Danny I love you. I love you and I cannot be near you. Everything for you is a war. I can't touch you. I look at you and all I see are scars, this pain I can't touch. You're white hot with grief and pain and you are fucking radioactive.

Iz Right. You wanted my smile.

Danny I just . . . I want you back. I want you.

Iz I can't just be the parts you like.

Danny I am not asking that.

Iz Yes. You are. It's not me you can't be near. It's my pain. You consume. I used to be so scared you'd swallow me up. And now I realize: you dig and you dig, and you throw away what you don't like. But it is all my life. Right now. Today. Every day. This very minute. My life. And you don't see it. You don't see me. Not all of me.

Danny You're flesh and blood, Iz. You're not just names and dates of atrocities. You're flesh and blood.

Iz Yes, flesh. Yes, blood. You don't live it, you can't see it so it isn't a thing. But it is. This?

Points to her skin.

This is a thing. And it's going to tear this city to pieces.

Danny I don't believe that. I refuse to believe that.

Iz And that is precisely the problem.

Danny Wow. Just . . . Wow. I thought we meant something to each other.

Iz So did I.

Danny Iz//

Iz Goodbye, Danny.

Danny Okay. Okay. Don't end up alone, Iz.

Iz . . .

Danny Just don't be alone.

Iz Thanks for stopping by.

Danny Iz//

Iz //

He starts to go. **Toony** *bursts in.*

Toony The streets is going wild!

Danny Why, what happened?

Toony Whachu mean, "What happened," muthafucka? Not guilty is what happened. What, you been under a rock? The streets is going wild.

Iz *turns up the television.*

Voice of Female Newscaster 1   . . . we have an incident. There is a man trying to be arrested. Officers have rushed one individual. That is what you're looking at . . .

Iz *flips through channels.*

Voice of Male Newscaster 1   . . . LAPD has just told me that they have ordered all police helicopters and all LAPD cruisers out of this area.

Voice of Male Newscaster 2   They're setting buildings on fire. I'm counting one, two, three, four, five, six, seven, eight fires burning out of control. . .

Voice of Male Newscaster 3   Okay. This is it. Terrible, terrible pictures. All this guy did was enter this area. That's his only crime.

Voice of Male Newscaster/Channel 5   That's Santa Monica and Western in Hollywood . . .

Voice of Stan Chambers/Sky Cam 5   The fire's breaking out now in the Hollywood area. Uh, this is one of those commercial buildings along Santa Monica . . .

Iz   Jesus.

Danny   I'd better//

Danny *heads for the door.*

Toony   //Man, I wouldn't if I was you. It's packs of folks out there looking for mothafuckas like you.

Pause.

Iz   I guess you're camping out.

She exits to the bedroom.

II.1

April 30, 1992. In blackout:

Voice of Tom Snyder   . . . this city is reeling tonight after twenty-four hours of naked rioting by hooligans, by thugs, by hoodlums, by looters, by arsonists, and by murderers. Uh, the city is in disarray . . .

Voice of Female Newscaster   . . . reports of looting and arrests being made just outside Beverly Hills . . .

Voice of Stan Chambers/Sky Cam 5   . . . Fire units are on the scene. A lot of people on the street. Let's take a look . . .

Lights up on the roof of Jeong's market. The sky is red with smoke from fires. There is an ever-present rumble in the distance. **Chung-Hee** *sits with his back to the wall in a beanbag chair holding a Glock. Beside him is a radio. BOOM! An explosion somewhere. He peers over the top of the wall. He mutters something, fires. He hunkers down again. The sound of someone climbing the ladder. He aims. The top of a thermos appears followed by* **Heejin.**

Heejin   *Moya, jigeum nal ssolgeoya?* Stupid.

She climbs onto the roof, looks out.

Chung-Hee   You call the fire department?

Heejin   No fire department.

Chung-Hee   You call the police?

Heejin   I call the police. Same as ten times before. No police.

Chung-Hee   . . .

Heejin   . . .

She pours tea into a mug and hands it to him. She settles beside him. They stare straight ahead. Silence. A large BOOM!

Chung-Hee   Car.

Heejin *nods. Silence.* **Chung-Hee** *turns on the radio.*

Voice of Tom Snyder   . . . the police in many cases are not to be seen patrolling our streets and restoring order to our town. Uh, more on that coming up. We intended to program this evening, uh, people related to the Rodney King verdict yesterday, and to the tragic events that have taken place over the past twenty-four hours . . .

He turns off the radio.

Chung-Hee   No police? Go look in Brentwood. Plenty of police.

He peers over the wall. Settles back down.

Sydney?

Heejin   I tell her do her homework.

Chung-Hee   . . .

Heejin   You want her up with you and that thing?

BOOM! **Chung-Hee** *looks over the wall.*

Chung-Hee   Department store.

Heejin   . . .

Chung-Hee   . . .

Heejin   . . .

Chung-Hee   You think I made a mistake. I send him away.

Heejin   . . .

Chung-Hee   No mistake.

Heejin   . . .

Chung-Hee   I did not make a mistake!

Heejin   Tea is getting cold.

He looks at her like she's crazy. They sit there.

Chung-Hee   I work for this. We work. To have a home. This is our home. He has a home. Go there. Not my responsibility.

Another BOOM! **Chung-Hee** *checks below.*

Car.

He turns on the radio.

Voice of Tom Snyder   . . . So far seventeen people are reportedly dead, four hundred and fifty are hurt. There are almost eleven hundred fires burning throughout the Los Angeles area. We are awaiting the presence of some four thousand national guard troops on the streets of Los Angeles and where these troops are is a puzzlement to all of us who live here. We are told they are deployed throughout the city yet in all the coverage that's gone on—and seven television stations have been on the air for the past twenty-four hours with rape, riot, murder and arson—for the past twenty-four hours we have seen hardly any police officers on the street and up until two hours ago no members of the national guard. So where they are I couldn't tell you. In all of this, twenty-four hours of rioting, of looting, of arson on, on a grand scale, by grand I mean enormous because it is now spreading throughout the greater Los Angeles area: the rioters are in Hollywood; they are in Beverly Hills; uh, I have a report that they are in the San Fernando Valley; so far as South Central Los Angeles in concerned, which was the, which was the center of the activity last night, forget it. That area looks like a war zone. Two hundred to two hundred and fifty million dollars in damage that they can count so far. In all of this only four hundred people have been arrested . . .

Chung-Hee *turns off the radio again.*

Chung-Hee Nobody ever mention Korea Town. We are America too.

They sit there. He looks over the wall. Hunkers down again. Silence.

Heejin You think he is with them?

Chung-Hee . . .

Heejin He's a good boy. We are his friends. We are friends.

Sydney *climbs onto to the roof with a book.*

Heejin Sydney, I tell you stay in your room!

Chung-Hee Homework, eh?

Heejin I tell you stay downstairs!

Sydney I got scared.

Heejin You're scared to be in your own room? Stupid.

BOOM! **Sydney** *ducks down.*

Chung-Hee *Bulssanghan aileul naebeolyeo duseyo.* Come.

He gestures her over. She settles beside him. They listen to the sound of fire, angry crowds. BOOM! This one a little too close. **Chung-Hee** *hugs* **Sydney**.

Heejin No time for scared. You think we have time to be scared? You come to America, leave everything, then be scared. Leave everything, everything. Lose everything. Then you be scared.

Chung-Hee *Ije dwaess-eoyo!*

Heejin . . .

They listen to the angry rumble below.

I beg to stay in Korea. I say I don't know what America is. I beg to stay. You don't know what suffering is. You don't know what fear is.

Chung-Hee *pats* **Heejin** *on the shoulder. He turns on the radio. BOOM!*

Voice of Tom Snyder . . . You're a resident of Southern California. You've watched this nonsense with the rest of us and just your own thoughts on this.

Chung-Hee *peers over the wall, gun at the ready.*

Voice of Female Juror I am simply appalled at this act, the destruction, the vandalism, the murdering that's taking place before our eyes. I cannot imagine what these people are thinking about.

Sydney Dad, can we please—?

He shushes her.

Appa!

Voice of Tom Snyder You said earlier today in another interview that I heard that that you believed had the jury voted not to acquit these men had they returned a verdict of guilty, that the same thing would have happened—am I quoting you correctly?

Voice of Female Juror Yes, you are and I truly believe that—

Voice of Tom Snyder Why do you feel that way?

Voice of Female Juror I don't know I just feel that it's an acci—, accident waiting to happen. It seems too closely choreographed to not have been arranged ahead of time.

Voice of Tom Snyder Mmhm.

Voice of Female Juror The actions all over the southern part of the state. All over this country, actually. It just seems to me that it's totally arranged. And it's appalling. What would these people be doing if we didn't have policemen to depend upon?

Chung-Hee *turns off the radio.*

Chung-Hee Sit on the roof and wait.

Pause.

Sydney I talked to Iz. She hasn't been able to find Toony.

Heejin Toony is a good boy. Can take care of himself.

Sydney But he's out there somewhere.

Chung-Hee *Jibeochiwo.*

He turns the radio on again.

Voice of Female Juror . . . if you had the medical reports from the hospital where he was looked at, had you seen the pictures of him made shortly after the incident, you could not see the signs of what appeared to be a bunch of horrible strokes that were given to him. So the only conclusion you can come to is that the, uh, waving batons were not all connecting. Uh, otherwise, he could not have appeared in the condition he was. He had one small bone broken in his right leg, and, uh, the right cheek, uh, up near, around his eye was, uh, had some breaks in it. And that appeared to be, from all the evidence we were presented with and from the, uh, video that we saw, when we slow it down to single frame—the video is very bad but you can still pick out the features, it shows that he fell literally like a tree falling over.

The broadcast continues as **Sydney** *gets to her feet.*

Heejin Sydney!

Sydney How can you stand to listen to this? It's not normal//

Heejin //Many people do worse!

Sydney But what she's saying isn't normal! They're justifying it!

Heejin This America. They say not against the law. Not against the law. I see people do worse!

Sydney But they're blaming us!

Heejin This is why I tell you stay in your room!

Chung-Hee It's alright, Sydney. It's alright. You go.

Sydney I don't want to go//

Chung-Hee //Not our fault. Toony come back. Not our fault.

Sydney . . .

Chung-Hee You go.

Sydney I'm sorry, *Appa*.

Chung-Hee No sorry. You go.

Sydney *starts to go.*

Heejin Sydney.

Sydney *turns to her mom.*

Heejin Going to be okay, okay?

Sydney *wipes her eyes and smiles—what else can she do? It's her mom. She climbs down. Meanwhile:*

Voice of Female Juror . . . and you could see the head bounce down and way up and down again. So that was apparently when that damage was done. Not from the batons of the, uh, officers . . .

Lights up on **Izzy***'s living room.* **Iz** *paces while* **Danny** *listens.*

Iz Toony, pick up. Where are you? Where are you?

Danny *stands. He takes the phone and hangs it up. He tries to hug her. She retracts, sits and watches TV. Lights down.*

II.2

Sydney *paces in her room later. Amid the rumble outside a shower of pebbles on the window.* **Sydney** *peers out, screams as* **Toony** *pops up from below. She opens the window. He scrambles in.*

Sydney Asshole!

She pummels him.

Toony Yo! Yo, yo, yo! Shit! Ow!

Sydney Where the fuck have you been?

Toony Where I been? Have you seen it out there?

Sydney Where did you get those?

Toony Where'd I get what?

She points at his new sneakers.

My sneakers. You worried about my sneakers? I just crawled through a fuckin' back alley.

She stares at him a moment. She hugs him tight. He melts. They stay there.

Mom and Pops okay?

Sydney On the roof.

Toony This some shit. Y'all got someplace you can go? Nancy's?

Sydney Dad won't leave, so.

Toony Maybe we could make it to Izzy's. Ain't but two blocks//That's fifteen minutes

Sydney I can't.

Toony Fifteen minutes! We can make it. I'll protect you.

Sydney How?

He lifts the front of his shirt. Tucked into his waistband is a small pistol.

Toony Like I said.

Sydney You can't even shoot that thing. Where did you get it?

Toony . . .

Sydney . . .

Toony The shit was already broken when I got there.

Sydney I'll bet.

Toony I'm not tryin' to die.

Sydney They don't want you.

Pause.

I've never seen them scared before. Even my mom.

They stare at one another.

Why us?

Toony . . .

Sydney But that's not us! That wasn't us!

Toony Fine. You here. I don't know.

Sydney They hate us just like they hate you.

Toony It ain't the same.

Sydney   How is it not the same?

Toony   It just ain't. Y'all come in here, and//shit

Sydney   //What? Say it.

Toony   I ain't saying shit.

Sydney   Just fucking say it!

Toony   Fine. Y'all come in here, y'all take our shit//

Sydney   Some white guy wants out what are we supposed to do?

Toony   We don't want you here!

Sydney   We?

Toony   Charge a arm and a leg and turn around and hate us too.

Sydney   And my mom? My dad?

Toony   The girl got shot in the back of the head over a soda she was gawn pay for. The lady that shot her got a $500 fine.

Sydney   Soon Ja Du//She has a name.

Toony   //Whatever the fuck her name is//That's how much my life is worth. Latasha had a name too!

Sydney   //And they got robbed before!

Toony   So I got to pay you to get insulted in my own neighborhood? Why you in my hood?

Sydney   We work for what we have. We work hard//

Toony   And we don't? Every time I come in your store I feel like a criminal.

Sydney   Then why do you come back? They came here with nothing.

Toony   And that's still more than we got.

Silence except for the rumbling outside. **Toony** *starts to climb out the window.*

Sydney   I want a good death. Doing something amazing, and I don't know what that is. And this place, it . . . I used to think how I couldn't wait to get away from this fucking place. I used to wish it would burn down to the ground. Because it was just this thing that said I was . . . I don't want to be buried here. I don't care about the store. But it's his. It's his.

Long pause.

Toony   I'll come check on you in a couple days.

Sydney   Bye, Toony.

Toony   It ain't all that. I said I'ma check on you.

Sydney   Why?

Toony I'll see you in a few days.

They stare at one another. He climbs out the window and is gone. **Sydney** *stares at the open window. She moves to her desk and takes out the pendant. Then the sound of glass breaking downstairs. Wrapping the pendant round her wrist, she stares at the bat leaning against her desk.*

II.3

The store. Dimly lit from the fires outside. The sound of glass breaking. A shadow creeps in slowly. The figure begins shaking the contents of a gas can around the store. He fumbles to light a match, tosses it as:

Sydney (*off*) Hello?

The lights pop on. **Gabe** *ducks down as* **Sydney** *enters with the baseball bat.*

Sydney *Eomma? Appa?*

Gabe *steps out of hiding.*

Gabe Sydney, right?

Sydney . . .

Gabe I think somebody may have broken your window. I followed him in here. Fuckin' savages, yeah? You okay?

Sydney What are you doing with that gas can?

Gabe I think they may have dropped it. I mean, it's a good thing we came along, you know? Can you believe this shit? Jesus.

Sydney Get out of my shop.

Gabe Okay. I'm just//

Sydney //Get the fuck out of my shop.

Pause. Suddenly **Gabe** *bolts toward her.*

Sydney *Appa! Appa!*

Gabe *grabs one end of the bat. They struggle.* **Sydney** *falls backward and he finally wrenches it from her and raises it and brings it down. He drops the bat.*

Gabe Hey . . . HEY.

Lights go red, fire from the half-lit match.

Gabe The fuck are you doing here? The fuck are you doing here?

The sound of fire engines in the distance. He backs away and exits the shop. The red light grows.

II.4

The street. **Toony** *stomps in colliding with* **Gabe** *who enters running and stumbles out. The sound of fire engines gets closer.* **Toony** *looks in the direction* **Gabe** *came from. He pulls out his cell phone, dials.*

Toony   Pick up, pick up, pick up.

No answer. He looks in the direction of the store. He runs back, following the sound of the fire trucks.

II.5

Chung-Hee *and* **Heejin** *sit on the curb, dazed, faces smeared with soot and bathed in a red glow as before them their store goes up in flames.* **Toony** *runs in.* **Chung-Hee** *looks at him, blank-faced, looks back at the flames.* **Toony** *backs away. He runs.*

II.6

Izzy*'s living room. Desperate knocking.* **Danny**, *followed by* **Izzy**, *sneaks in from the bedroom carrying a golf club, while she carries a lamp.*

Iz   Toony? Is that you?

She moves past **Danny**, *checks the peephole and unlocks the door.* **Toony** *blows in.*

Toony   I seen the muthafucka//I seen him!

Iz   //Where have you been? You stopped answering your phone.//

Danny   Dude?

Toony   The fuck you still doing here?//What the fuck he still doing here?

Iz   //Where did you get those shoes?

Toony *pulls the gun and aims it at* **Danny**.

Toony   Same place I got this shit.

Danny   Whoa, what the fuck?

Iz   Toony, Jesus!

Toony   The fuck is right. This shit your fault.

Danny   Okay, I//

Iz   Danny, go in the kitchen.

Toony   //Just do whatever the fuck y'all want. We ain't shit.

Danny   The hell is your problem?

Toony You my problem, muthafucka! You my problem!//

Iz Danny, shut up and go in the kitchen!//

Danny //Me? I'm//It's a fucking gun!

Iz //I can see it's a fucking//gun!

Toony //Take! Everywhere I look is y'all taking. Well, now we gawn take. How that feel? Huh? How it feel? We ain't shit!

Iz Not if you do this. You ain't worth shit if you do this, Toony. If you do this to our mom, if you do this to me, I will never forgive you. I swear to God.

Toony Iz, you not hearing me! Syd's dead! She's dead and I seen the muthafucka!

Iz Okay! Okay. We'll fix it, Toony. I promise. We'll fix it.

Stand-off. **Toony** *lowers the gun.* **Iz** *takes it, holds onto him as he sobs.* **Danny** *watches them.*

Danny Fuck this. I don't need this.

Iz Where are you going?

Danny *stomps to the door, opens it. The roar from outside. He slams the door*

Danny Fuck! Fuck this whole fucked-up fucking . . .!

He sinks to the floor. **Iz** *rocks* **Toony** *in her arms.*

Iz Okay. Sh. Okay, we'll fix it. We'll fix it . . .

Voice of Dan Rather . . . Two days after the Rodney King verdict, two days after emotions erupted in the streets there are signs that the city, and our nation, are struggling to reach beyond the rage.

Voice of Rodney King . . . I just want to say, you know, can we, can we all get along? Can we get along?[6]

Danny *crosses, turns off the television. They sit listening to the roar outside. Finally:*

Iz Somebody should go by and see the Jeongs.

II.7

Iz's *place, 10 p.m.* **Toony** *sits up in the middle of the couch wrapped in a blanket listening to the roar, slightly less, but still palpable.* **Iz** *enters with a cup of coffee which she sets in front of him and settles beside him. They listen.*

Iz It's getting further away, I think.

---

6 Much quoted (and much misquoted) line uttered by King in a television appearance during the rioting.

Toony . . .

Iz D'you sleep?

Toony . . .

Iz Mom wants us back in Brentwood. Told her we'd stick it out.

They listen to the roar.

Toony I think she was mad. About the shoes.

He looks down at his feet.

Stupid. I don't even like Cons.

Iz Well, you're an idiot, so.

He barely smiles. Pause.

She was nice.

Rumble above the silence. **Danny** *stomps in from the kitchen holding his keys. He stands there.*

Iz What are you doing?

Danny What am I—I am, I'm fucking pissed.

Iz Oh my God, please don't do this now.

Danny I, I think I have a right//to be.

Iz //I really cannot to do this with you right now.

Danny Uh Hi, sorry. Gun in my face.

Iz I will not do this with you.

Danny Wow. Just . . . Sure.

He stomps to the door.

Iz At least wait until daylight//

He opens the door. Is met by the low rumble. He looks back at them. He goes. After a beat we hear a car start and drive away.

You weren't really going to shoot him?

Toony . . .

Iz Toony//

Toony //

Iz Toony.

Toony He a white boy just like any other.

Iz And you're a black boy just like any other.

Toony Then there ain't nothing to lose.

He is on his feet.

Iz What are you doing?

Toony Where my gun at?

Iz Nigga, I'm about to tie you to that chair.

He steps around her. She beats him to the door, blocks it bodily.

Toony Move, Iz.

Iz Make me.

Toony Iz, move! Move!

She doesn't budge. He glares at her.

What's wrong wichu?

Iz Nothing wrong with me. Something wrong with you.

Toony They took her life!

Iz So what are you going to do, kill everybody?

Toony Fuck you, Iz. Fuck you!

Iz You can't find him!

Toony //

Iz //We'll go to the police, okay?

Toony The police?//

Iz Just to//

Toony //The fuck you talkin' 'bout the police?

Iz I'm talking about you not getting your ass killed or worse.

He steps around. She steps in front of him. They struggle. Finally, he picks her up and deposits her on the couch, then heads for the door.

She's gone, Toony.

He stops.

Iz And if you walk out that door, you won't come back.

Pause.

Toony You gawn be a great lawyer someday, Iz. Always have to have the last fuckin' word.

Iz I'm not going to be a lawyer, Toony.//

Toony Yes, you are. You are, Iz.//

Iz We'll open a school//we'll—a black school. We'll//You asked me to choose//

Toony You are, Iz. You are.

Iz Okay, so then I win.

He smiles at her.

Toony You somebody. I'm proud of you.

Iz Toony //So are you.

Toony //I'm proud to be your brother.

Iz I choose you, Toony! Us. I choose us!

Toony Mom'll be mad, I know//

Iz Don't do this. Don't leave me.//Toony, please, don't leave me. Please.

Toony Bye, Iz.

He's gone.

II.8

Jeong's Market, 11pm. The air rumbles. **Heejin** *sits in the middle of a pile of rubble, cradling* **Chung-Hee***'s gun.* **Toony** *passes the window, enters through what's left of the door.* **Heejin** *stares at him. She extends her arms. He moves to her. Kneels. They hug and weep.*

II.9

Heejin *wanders the shop. She stops.* **Chung-Hee** *and* **Sydney** *appear holding hands a moment, then are gone.* **Gabe** *steps through the broken glass into the store. He freezes when he spies* **Heejin***.*

Gabe Hey! Uh, hey.

She looks up at him. She begins to stack cans.

You, uh, you okay? Okay? English? Okay?

She stacks another couple of cans.

Fuckin' wild, right? Fuckin' wild. Shit.

Toony *enters from the back with a broom.*

Toony Help you?

Gabe She, um, she need, like help, or . . . I was, uh, in the neighborhood. So, like, if you need, like help . . .

Toony *begins to sweep.* **Gabe** *watches* **Heejin** *stack cans.*

Gabe   She alright?

Toony   She'll be alright.

Gabe   I was looking for Sydney.

Toony   Whachu want with Sydney?

Gabe   Just, um. We're friends. Have you seen her?

Heejin *begins to sing. The tune is "Twinkle, Little Star."*

Heejin
Banjjagbanjjag jag-eun byeol
Aleumdabge bichine//

Gabe   //What is that, like, "Twinkle, Twinkle, Little Star"? Hey. Hey!

Toony   Just leave her alone. She'll be alright.

Heejin
Dongjjog haneul-eseodo
Seojjog haneul-eseodo
Banjjagbanjjag jag-eun byeol
Aleumdabge bichine

Gabe   Um, sure. Okay . . .

Toony   You live around here?

Gabe   Not really.

Toony   How you know Syd?

Gabe   Just kind of around. You know? I mean, I didn't really know her. She liked baseball.

Toony   Liked?

Gabe   Likes.

Toony   Well, she ain't here.

Heejin *goes back to stacking cans.* **Toony** *sweeps.*

Gabe   Fucked up coupla days, ya know? I'm not, uh, I'm a light sleeper so, the, the noise. It, uh, it keeps me up.

Gabe *pulls the pendant from his pocket.* **Toony** *freezes.*

Gabe   Wonder if they found the guy who did it?

Toony   Did what?

Gabe   Uh, the fire. Set the fire. It's fucked.

Toony   Yeah.

Toony *stares at the pendant.*

Toony For your girl or//

Gabe Yeah. Yeah. Belonged to my mom.

Pause.

It's hard out here for a brother, you know? You're talking about somebody's life. Some of these people, this is all they got. My dad used to have a shop. Electronics. Bought him out. Paid him shit. I mean, the way they're taking over it's like fuckin' parasites, man. Whole damn country. Guess somebody took it personally.

Toony Yeah.

Gabe Be decent. Leave some for the rest of us, right? I mean, we got here first, right? Shit. Just be decent.

Pause.

I mean, I just, uh, like is she okay, or . . . Just, uh, with everything . . .

Heejin . . .

Gabe Look, you know, it's really rude not to talk. I'm fucking making an effort at conversation. The least you could do is//

Toony //Yo.

Gabe I'm just saying! Shit.

He looks outside.

Look, if you could, uh, just give her a message for me, I just. Tell her I was looking for her. Just, uh . . . Yeah. So. Nice, um, nice chatting with you, you know? Chatty Cathy!

He laughs a little.

Toony You alright?

Gabe *waves, starts to back out of the store.*

Gabe Anyway.

He picks his way through the broken glass and exits. **Toony** *watches a long beat, puts down his broom, moves to* **Heejin** *and crouches. They eye one another. He takes the gun. He goes.* **Heejin** *resumes stacking cans.*

II.10

The alley moments later. **Gabe** *enters. Angry voices. He backs against the wall.* **Toony** *enters, watches him as the angry voices pass.*

Toony Alright?

Gabe Wh—? Yeah. Just, uh, shit.

Toony Not the smartest place to be right now.

Gabe No, shit! You alright, brother? Yo.

He reaches out a hand. Pause. **Toony** *shakes it, then draws* **Chung-Hee**'s *gun.*

What—yo, brother//

Toony //I'm not your brother.

Gabe What the fuck, man?

Toony I'm not your brother.

Gabe Okay. Okay. You're not my brother. What do you want? Look, I don't have any money, I don't//

Gabe *is on his knees with his hands up.*

Toony I don't want your money//

Gabe Dude, not cool!

Toony Oh, you want to be cool?

Toony *shoots.* **Gabe**'s *belly spills blood.*

Gabe What do you want? Just what do you want?

Toony That's what I want.

Gabe What the fuck, bro? What the fuck?

He collapses.

Toony That's for Syd.

Gabe *dies.* **Toony** *stares at the body, the gun.*

Toony Yo.

II.11

Lights up on **Iz**'s *place. The lights flicker on her face as she watches television. Knocking. She rises, moves to the door.* **Toony** *stands there shaking. She goes back to the TV. He enters, stays at the door.*

Iz You found him.

Toony *nods.*

Iz Do you feel better?

He stands there.

I'm sorry.

The phone rings.

They've made us into something . . . else.

The phone continues to ring.

You should go.

She closes her eyes. **Toony** *opens the door.* **Iz** *answers the phone.*

Hello—? I know it's after midnight, Mrs. Gorham . . . He's here, Mrs. Gorham. He's—No. No, there's no strange . . . It's Toony! For the last fucking time, it's . . . You called—? Toony! Toony!

The sound of a helicopter. As a beam of light overtakes the house silhouetting **Toony** *in the doorframe. A voice on a megaphone:*

Voice of a Police Officer   LAPD. Step outside with your hands up.

Iz   Toony! TOONY!

She runs outside as there are gunshots. Lights down.

II.12

May 8, 1992. Jeong's Market, or what's left of it. **Heejin** *sweeps up ash and debris.* **Izzy** *arrives. She stands at the door holding a bouquet.*

Iz   Mrs. Jeong?

Heejin   Isabel.

She gestures about her, a small, listless wave.

Iz   I saw the memorial outside. It's, um . . .

Pause. She lays the bouquet on the counter.

How did he//

Heejin   No daughter. No everything everything. Lie down in bed never get up. Sometimes man die of grief.

Iz   . . .

They float there.

Do you need anything?

Heejin   Unless you can give me back my husband and my daughter I don't need anything.

She turns on the television.

Voice of President George H. W. Bush   . . . And let me say I am truly heartened, uh, by the speed with which the millions of dollars of federal relief have reached, uh, the city. From FEMA grants to small business loans to urgent food aid, and I salute, uh, David Kearns[7] and others who came here to coordinate. Not to dictate, not to try to dominate, but to coordinate with the city and local officials . . .

Heejin *turns off the television.*

Heejin They tell me I can call and they give me a loan. Pay my taxes. Save my money. I lose everything and now I have to get a loan? Give grant to police for overtime. What for?

Voice of President George H. W. Bush So they can stand around some more? Every day I call. Every day they say call again tomorrow. So much American Dream.

She begins to sweep up. **Iz** *watches her a moment. She relieves* **Heejin** *of the broom gently, begins to sweep.* **Heejin** *watches. She sits beside the counter, holding herself steady.*

Heejin Five days no Toony.

Iz He wanted to come. He//

Heejin //Five days.

Iz *sweeps.*

Iz At least the walls are still standing. You could start over.

Heejin No good death. Too many ghosts.

Iz But you can't let them chase you out.

Heejin Nobody chase. I see your America. I go.

Pause.

You should get married. Nice girl should get married.

Iz *laughs a little.*

Iz Yeah, well. Maybe after graduation.

Pause.

Toony's gone. They shot him. He's, uh. Yeah.

Heejin . . .

Iz The neighbor. She thought . . . She worries, so . . .

She finds a charred and melted key chain shaped like the US, places it on the counter.

Heejin Toony was a good boy.

Iz I know. He was. He was good. Just, uh . . .

They stare at one another. **Iz** *sweeps.*

Heejin Why so much? Everything, everything. So much. This America.

---

7 David T. Kearns was appointed by the George H. W. Bush White House as a liaison during the riots.

Iz I don't know.

Pause.

Anyway.

They stare at one another. **Iz** *sweeps.* **Heejin** *finds a second broom and sweeps. Lights fade on the sound.*

END OF PLAY